SE

Agoraphobia and Panic

Agoraphobia and Panic

A Guide to Psychological Treatment

Jeffrey E. Hecker
University of Maine

Geoffrey L. Thorpe
University of Maine

Allyn and Bacon
Boston   London   Toronto   Sydney   Tokyo   Singapore

Copyright © 1992 by Allyn and Bacon
A Division of Simon & Schuster, Inc.
160 Gould Street
Needham Heights, Massachusetts 02194

Library of Congress Cataloging-in-Publication Data

Hecker, Jeffrey E., 1959–
    Agoraphobia and panic : a guide to psychological treatment   /
Jeffrey E. Hecker and Geoffrey L. Thorpe.
        p.   cm.
    Includes bibliographical references and index.
    ISBN 0-205-12906-4
    1. Agoraphobia—Treatment.   2. Panic disorders—Treatment.
I. Thorpe, Geoffrey L.   II. Title
    [DNLM: 1. Agoraphobia—therapy.   2. Anxiety Disorders—therapy.
3. Panic.   WM 178 H449a]
RC552.A44H43   1992
616.85'225—dc20
DNLM/DLC
for Library of Congress   91-4587
                                                                                CIP

Printed in the United States of America

10   9   8   7   6   5   4   3   2   1   95   94   93   92   91

Contents

Preface

The anxiety disorders have been the focus of intense attention from clinical researchers over the past three decades. Investigators working within behavioral and, later, cognitive frameworks have systematically examined various methods of reducing pathological anxiety. Literally thousands of research reports have been produced from this work. In the 1970s, much of this activity focused on agoraphobia. Exposure therapies were tested empirically and found to be helpful in most cases. In the mid-1980s the emphasis shifted to panic disorder, which we now see as a diagnostic category subsuming agoraphobia. Psychological treatments focused on eliminating panic were developed, and the first set of empirical trials has yielded very encouraging results.

The purpose of this book is to describe methods of assessing and treating panic disorder, with or without agoraphobia, that were developed out of this clinical research literature. We have used all of the approaches described here in our own work with panic disorder clients and draw upon this experience in case vignettes. Translating research findings into treatment plans for clients presenting to a primary mental health facility is often challenging and rarely a straightforward endeavor. The clinician must decide which problems to focus on and which interventions make the most sense for a given client. In addition to providing the reader with descriptions of the assessment and treatment strategies that are most effective with panic disorder clients, we try to provide some guidelines for making these difficult clinical decisions.

Although we are both psychologists, we hope we have written a book that will be valuable to mental health clinicians and students of psychotherapy regardless of their training histories. The techniques we describe can be applied by psychotherapists with varied backgrounds, including social work, counseling, psychiatry, psychology, and others.

The reader will note that at different points in the book we use the masculine pronouns (e.g., *he*) when referring to clients and at other times the feminine (e.g., *she*). When we refer to therapists, however, we use "he or she." There is consistency behind our inconsistency. In an effort to avoid language that might be seen as sexist, we have let empirical findings guide us in our choice of pronouns. Because a larger percentage of people with agoraphobia are women than men, we decided to use feminine pronouns when referring to agoraphobic clients. Panic disorder is more evenly distributed in the population, so we decided to use the masculine pronouns when referring to panic disorder clients. We are not aware of any data on the sex distribution of mental health clinicians, so we compromised with the nonsexist, albeit slightly awkward, "he or she" when referring to clinicians.

This work was supported in a number of ways by colleagues, students, and staff at the Psychology Department at the University of Maine. We would like to thank Dr. Gordon Kulberg, department chair, for providing administrative support. Furthermore, we would like to thank Marian Perry, Kathy McAuliffe, and Shelley Rollins for graciously agreeing to type a large portion of the manuscript. We would also like to express our appreciation to Professor Robert G. Meyer, University of Louisville; Michael J. Telch, director, Laboratory for the Study of Anxiety Disorders, The University of Texas at Austin; and John R. Walker, coordinator, Anxiety Disorders Clinic, Department of Psychiatry, Hôpital Général, St. Boniface General Hospital, Winnipeg, Manitoba, whose helpful comments and criticisms of our earlier draft improved the quality of the manuscript.

Finally, our gratitude goes to the many panic disorder and agoraphobic clients with whom we have worked over the past several years. Thank you for the challenges you presented and for the courage and perseverance you demonstrated.

Agoraphobia and Panic

PART ONE ─────────────────────────────

Anxiety Disorders: History, Classification, Epidemiology, and Etiological Theories

The three chapters of Part One set the scene for a treatment manual on panic and agoraphobic syndromes, covering the history of concepts of agoraphobia and panic, by presenting a cross-section of case illustrations from over one hundred years' work on agoraphobia, by describing the current DSM-III-R (*Diagnostic and Statistical Manual of Mental Disorders*, third edition, revised) classification of anxiety disorders and some epidemiological data, and by outlining the theoretical and empirical background to cognitive and behavioral treatment.

Chapter 1, "Agoraphobia, Anxiety, and Panic—Past and Present," tells the story of agoraphobia from its description by Westphal in 1871 to the present day. Presenting case illustrations from each theorist, the chapter progresses from Westphal to Wolpe, Marks, Chambless, Barlow, and other contemporary theorists and researchers. The continuing interplay among classification, treatment outcome, and theory is seen as the story unfolds, and the current emphasis on the panic attack as the central element in what was known as the

1

agoraphobic syndrome is explained. Chapter 2, "Current Concepts of Agoraphobia, Anxiety, and Panic," provides an overview of the major anxiety disorders of the contemporary classification, the DSM-III-R (American Psychiatric Association, 1987). Each disorder is described together with a representative case illustration from our own clinical work. Next, the current panic disorder and agoraphobia syndromes are described, and an extensive case illustration is appended to each of the three descriptions. Finally, an outline of what is known about the epidemiology of these syndromes is presented. Chapter 3, "Theoretical and Empirical Bases for Cognitive-Behavioral Treatment," describes the principal theoretical models of panic disorder and agoraphobia. In the process, the chapter describes conditioning, cognitive, and integrative formulations, together with their central assumptions about phobic avoidance, the causes of panic, and the importance of the client's social environment and personal characteristics.

Agoraphobia, Anxiety, and Panic— Past and Present

The clients who consult clinicians today for the relief of panic attacks, phobias, and other anxiety disorders are inevitably influenced by their cultural environment. In the Western world, at least, they live in industrially developed countries with expanding populations, increasing mobility, progressively greater social interdependence, and an ever-accelerating reliance on technology for the essential tasks of the home and workplace. More and more people live in a world of crowds, automobiles, office buildings, apartment complexes, factories, airports, supermarkets, and shopping malls. The pace of life has quickened since the technologically simpler times of our largely agrarian ancestors. But today's world is not only more complex and fast-paced; it is also more challenging and demanding.

The urban commuter is expected to deal daily with busy streets, crowded cafeterias, and public buildings. The rural resident may need to handle long automobile journeys, extremes of weather, social isolation, and the financial complexities of farming or running a small business. The parent and homemaker must come to terms with the requirements of shopping, health care appointments, and preschool or recreational activities for the children, and encounters in the process parking lots, checkout lines, and waiting rooms. The demands of travel alone require many people to confront limited-access highways, bridges, tunnels, airport lobbies, and air travel in an often cramped cabin with a hundred or so other passengers. The workplace may present elevators, committee meetings, performance evaluations, and noisy shop floor conditions as potential challenges. And everyone in one way or another comes into contact with other people, strangers and friends, individually and in groups, formally and informally.

In any and all of these contexts, anxiety problems that not only cause distress and discomfort but also impair people's functioning are handicapping indeed. Yet, despite the obvious changes in the pace and complexity of life in the last few decades, unwanted anxiety is not an entirely modern phenomenon. Anxiety disorders have been recognized—and have troubled people—for generations, and the patterns of these disorders have remained surprisingly consistent over the years. It is true that formal diagnostic criteria change in response to new findings, and that developments in treatment, discoveries about epidemiology, and new theories of etiology influence one another. Nevertheless, a sense of continuity pervades the writings of the experts over the decades, as can be seen in the following brief review.

1871: WESTPHAL AND AGORAPHOBIA

References to irrational anxiety can be found in the writings of scholars and philosophers from ancient times to the present day. Robert Burton's 1621 *Anatomy of Melancholy* contains vivid descriptions of several patterns of pathological fear, including social anxiety; phobias have been recognized since the time of Hippocrates (Marks, 1987). However, the concept of phobias as specific, irrational fears leading to avoidance behavior first came into focus in the late 1800s. The term *agoraphobia* originated in a classic monograph by the German psychiatrist C. F. O. Westphal in 1871 (Knapp, 1988).

Westphal (1822–1890) practiced in a professional climate of descriptive psychopathology and organically based etiological theories. He chose *agoraphobia* as a "not entirely exhaustive" label for the problems of a clinical series of three men, each of whom feared crossing broad urban squares and empty streets (Westphal, 1871/1988, p. 50). In 1872 S. G. Webber, an American physician, endorsed the label because the Greek *agora* referred to an assembly of people as well as to a marketplace; this allowed the inclusion of crowded rooms as relevant phobic situations (Knapp, 1988, p. 31).

Westphal's three prototypical patients had overlapping fears that collectively included open fields, theaters, churches, concert halls, and a "fear-of-fear" pattern, in addition to their chief problems with streets, public squares, and long unaccompanied walks. During episodes of anxiety in these phobic surroundings, the patients experienced heart palpitations, trembling of the limbs, and sometimes depersonalization. In an amplified description in 1885, Westphal characterized a typical phobic response as "a fear as in dying, with shaking all over, tightening in the chest, pounding of the heart, cold or hot sensations, disorientation, possibly nausea, a feeling of absolute helplessness" (see Knapp, 1988, p. 40).

Westphal was unable to assemble a reliably effective overall treatment plan for agoraphobia. Despite the fact that it foreshadows helpful modern approaches involving systematic graded practice in vivo, Westphal's recommendation of daily real-life exposure to feared situations brought disappointing results. Instead, he urged physicians to use their professional authority to boost patients' confidence in tackling their phobias.

Sigmund Freud (1856–1939) had not developed his psychoanalytic theory of neurosis during Westphal's lifetime. Freud attributed agoraphobia to psychogenic factors and assigned importance to the patient's fear of the recurrence of an anxiety attack in particular situations in which escape is impossible (Knapp, 1988, p. 44). He even made clear reference to the desirability of real-life practice as part of the treatment approach for agoraphobia (Marks, 1972). However, he did not believe it necessary to include phobias in an official classification as a distinct disorder. It was Westphal's pioneering work that eventually led to acceptance of agoraphobia as an anxiety syndrome in current classifications.

CASE ILLUSTRATION

Mr. C

Westphal's first patient with agoraphobia was a 32-year-old man, a commercial traveler, who complained of the sudden onset of fear whenever he tried to walk across an open space. The fears began when Mr. C was 27; he was walking out of the town along an avenue when he had a strange feeling resembling a "hangover." Since then he had avoided solitary walks. His symptoms during a fear episode included heart palpitations and trembling, but he told Westphal that the feeling was "located more in the head than in the area of the heart" (Westphal, 1871/1988, p. 60). Feared situations included walking across huge city squares (Mr. C thought he would never make it across) and walking beside long buildings, but he was most troubled by the idea of being alone in an open place. For that reason, he was most fearful when walking in the city when the shops were closed and the streets deserted. Even the thought of being left alone in the middle of open fields was "unbearable." Mr. C was less anxious when there was the possibility of help nearby, so he could traverse a square if he kept up with a vehicle going across, and he could tolerate walking on the beach provided that there was a row of houses alongside. He had no fear of dining in restaurants, but on his return home he could get there only by walking with someone—sometimes acquainting himself with a "lady of the evening" for this purpose. However, he could not explain his fear of being in churches or theaters despite the presence of other people.

Westphal made detailed observations of Mr. C's physical characteristics and noted a possible indication of neurological problems—occasional visual paresthesias. It was also mentioned that Mr. C had suffered from gonorrhea several times and that his anxieties were worse in the mornings, when he was sober (pp. 62–64). The two other patients described in the 1871 monograph were also men, one of whom suffered from grand mal epileptic seizures; the other had had convulsions in childhood and had a family history of epilepsy.

After a few years of intense professional interest, agoraphobia began to recede into the background as a focus of scholarly attention, with progressively fewer papers published on the topic; Westphal's monograph was cited less and less frequently until it seemed all but forgotten. It is likely that the rapid rise of psychoanalysis, with its psychogenic etiological theories and its preference for a monolithic classification of "neuroses," was responsible for displacing the biologically oriented descriptive psychopathology of Westphal and his colleagues, at least as far as the anxiety syndromes were concerned.

1958: WOLPE AND RECIPROCAL INHIBITION

As a military medical officer in South Africa in the 1940s, Joseph Wolpe dealt with returning combat veterans suffering from war-related anxiety disorders. He grew dissatisfied with the then-dominant psychoanalytic paradigm, for two reasons. First, he encountered published critiques that challenged the universality of Freud's Oedipal theory, and he discovered that the Russians had rejected psychoanalysis in favor of Pavlovian formulations (Wolpe, 1958). Second, he was disappointed by the poor practical results of treatments based on psychoanalytic assumptions, particularly narcoanalysis, in which the patient was aided by intravenous injections of medication to recall and describe disturbing memories of combat (Wolpe, 1981). Recognizing that the ascendancy of psychoanalysis was related not so much to its success as to the absence of a viable alternative, Wolpe set out to develop alternative treatments based on the theories of Pavlov and the American psychologist Clark Hull.

Drawing his procedures from the work of Masserman (1943) on experimental neurosis, Wolpe conducted a series of studies on fear conditioning in cats. He created experimental fears by shocking the cats after a tone was sounded in their cages, a form of classical conditioning. The fear persisted even after the shock mechanism was disconnected. Guided by Hull's motivational theory, Wolpe designed "therapies" to induce the cats to overcome their acquired fears; the central principle was the extinction of conditioned fear responses. Two procedures emerged from this research: gradually bringing the cats into contact with the feared stimuli, and feeding them while doing so. Because feeding evokes neural processes incompatible with fear, and vice versa, Wolpe dubbed the principle "reciprocal inhibition." His application of reciprocal inhibition to clinical settings was a breakthrough that helped establish behavior therapy as the leading alternative to psychoanalytically oriented treatment.

Systematic desensitization is the best known Wolpean technique. Parallel to bringing the cats gradually closer to the feared cages, Wolpe incrementally exposed his phobic clients to the items of an anxiety hierarchy, a graded list of feared situations. Parallel to inhibiting the cats' fear by feeding them, Wolpe attenuated his clients' anxiety during therapy by systematically inducing deep muscle relaxation. The systematic desensitization procedure was implemented slowly and carefully; as the client imagined successive scenes from the hierarchy, the therapist took pains to keep the relaxation uppermost and responded immediately to any signal from the client of rising anxiety. Wolpe tabulated the therapeutic outcome of 210 clients with various neuroses who were treated by reciprocal inhibition principles; 188 were rated as "apparently cured" or "much improved" (Wolpe, 1958, p. 216, Table 3).

Independent of Wolpe's work, clinical researchers at the Institute of Psychiatry/Maudsley Hospital in London were using similar principles but concentrating on real-life exposure to feared stimuli. Meyer (1957) treated agoraphobia successfully in two clients by having them practice walking in crowds, traveling progressively farther from home, and entering claustrophobic surroundings. Interestingly, both clients had initially been seen as having signs of neurological disorders, including blackouts and possible seizure activity.

Despite initial enthusiasm for systematic desensitization as a treatment for agoraphobia, clinicians became discouraged by the results of prospective clinical trials that showed only minimal and short-lived gains from courses of treatment lasting more than a year (Cooper, Gelder, & Marks, 1965; Gelder, Marks, & Wolff, 1967; Marks & Gelder, 1965; Meyer & Gelder, 1963). One impressively large-scale study that did support the effectiveness of systematic desensitization (Gelder, Bancroft, Gath, Johnston, Mathews, & Shaw, 1973) was flawed by a confounding of the technique with real-life practice procedures. Still helpful in the treatment of simple phobias, Wolpe's principal technique has fallen into disuse in application to agoraphobia.

_____ CASE ILLUSTRATION
Ms. K

The client was a 23-year-old woman who had recently been graduated from college. Although she had enjoyed the independence of university life, her life at her parents' home was one of extreme overprotection by her mother. Ms. K's agoraphobic fears began after two accidental falls in the street led her to avoid walking outside. She became housebound and practically bedridden, occasionally making "wall-hugging" journeys from her bedroom to a couch in another room; if she were to sit with her legs down, she would become dizzy and nauseated (Wolpe, 1958, pp. 174–180).

Wolpe made frequent home visits, initially encouraging assertiveness toward the mother and, generally, prompting greater self-sufficiency and independence. At one point Wolpe conditioned a sense of calm to the sound of a metronome, which Ms. K could then use to induce calm when needed. The client had initially resisted Wolpe's plan for relaxation training. Eventually Wolpe used the reciprocal inhibition principle by eliciting a "dominating motor response" while the client imagined falling; the inhibitory response was a flexion of the arm elicited by electric shock. After progressing along an imagined hierarchy of situations involving falling, the client practiced actually falling in a series of carefully contrived exercises. The procedures were effective; Ms. K was able to tolerate staying at the house while her parents were on vacation, and eventually moved to a hotel, from which she could visit Wolpe's office after a walk of several city blocks.

_____ CASE ILLUSTRATION
A 48-Year-Old Married Woman

Wolpe (1970) presented a transcript of an early interview with this client in order to demonstrate the behavioral assessment of agoraphobia. He argued that agoraphobia is a complex disorder in which clients' fears have varying antecedents. Three common patterns are (1) fear of increasing distances from safety, (2) fear of medical catastrophes, and (3) fear of physical isolation and social deprivation in some women whose low self-sufficiency traps them in unhappy marriages that they would rather leave. Systematic desensitization to progressively greater distances from home would be appropriate for a client with the first pattern but would miss the point for someone with the second or third. Wolpe concludes that it is therefore vital to establish the client's particular fear pattern before embarking on a treatment along reciprocal inhibition principles.

The client had a 24-year history of agoraphobia. She had spent the early years of her married life in close proximity to her husband's parents, who were dominant, controlling, and critical. Her first anxiety episode struck when she was pregnant and during a period of intense interpersonal conflict. Wolpe traced the source of this client's fears to a fear of being alone, of being estranged from her husband and relatives. Accordingly, her peace of mind and sense of security were based entirely on the possibly flimsy foundation of her relationship with her husband. Initially, treatment included relaxation and assertiveness training, together with therapy aimed at the marital relationship, with which the husband fully cooperated. Although the marriage clearly improved and the client made obvious practical gains concerning her agoraphobia (she could spend hours at the beautician's among strangers), Wolpe was not content to leave it at that. He considered it essential to help the woman deal with the possibility of leaving the marriage should this become necessary. Failure to address the possibility of an independent life would leave the client, and her anxiety disorder, vulnerable to any resurgence of marital stress.

1978: MARKS AND BEHAVIORAL PSYCHOTHERAPY

In 1978 Isaac Marks published *Living with Fear* as a practical version for the general reader of his extensive work on behavioral treatment of anxiety disorders. In the same year he gave the Salmon Committee Lectures to the New York Academy of Medicine on the same topic; an expansion of the lectures into book form was available three years later (Marks, 1981b). Like Wolpe, Marks is an experimentally oriented psychiatrist who has conducted original research on clinical anxiety; unlike Wolpe, however, Marks has been reluctant to accept conditioning and learning mechanisms as proven causal agents in the etiology of anxiety disorders. Marks is best known for his long series of clinical experiments on the use of flooding and related methods to treat phobias and obsessive-compulsive disorder.

Joseph Wolpe had advocated systematic desensitization and other reciprocal inhibition procedures because he believed that both gradual approach and inhibition of anxiety were necessary procedural elements in treatment programs for phobic individuals. Marks and his associates came to disagree with that view when they recorded poor practical results from systematic desensitization applied to agoraphobia. Influenced by the work of Baum (1970) on extinguishing fear in laboratory animals, Marks experimented with flooding, a procedure in which the client is confronted for prolonged periods with feared stimuli at high intensity.

Marks, Boulougouris, and Marset (1971) treated 16 clients with various phobias by systematic desensitization and flooding in fantasy. The experimental design—a crossover study—allowed each participant to receive six sessions of each treatment. In the flooding sessions clients were asked to imagine frightening phobia-relevant scenes without benefit of relaxation training or of graded anxiety hierarchies. The results generally favored flooding, especially for the agoraphobic clients. Marks later attributed the superiority of flooding in this study to the real-life confrontation of feared surroundings that followed the experimental treatment procedures (Marks, 1981b, p. 53). A series of studies on the various procedural parameters of flooding led to the conclusion that confrontive, real-life exposure is the most efficient and effective technique; *exposure in vivo* is now the accepted term for this procedure. Although exposure treatment allows extinction mechanisms to operate, Marks is cautious about identifying the vital therapeutic process. Arguing that several processes could be at work, including habituation or simply "getting used to it," Marks prefers to avoid the language of conditioning and refers, instead, to "evoking stimuli" (those that trigger anxiety) and "evoked responses" (fear and avoidance of the stimuli). The general principle of effective treatment is to persuade the client to confront feared stimuli until the evoked anxiety responses disappear (Greist, Marks, Berlin, Gournay, & Noshirvani, 1980).

_____ CASE ILLUSTRATION

Agoraphobia—Average Difficulty

The client, a 40-year-old woman, had a 15-year history of agoraphobia and, at the start of therapy, could not leave home alone. In the first treatment session of one and a half hours, the therapist accompanied her as she practiced crossing a road near the clinic. The client recognized that she felt considerably less anxious even after a single session. Subsequent sessions involved confronting situations progressively further from the clinic, with the therapist gradually withdrawing his support. The client was urged to practice similar ventures from home between her clinic appointments. Only eight sessions were needed to bring her to the point at which she could shop alone without anxiety; improvement continued steadily over the six months following the termination of therapy (Marks, 1981b, p. 52).

1980: DSM-III, ANXIETY DISORDERS, AND INTEGRATIVE THEORIES

The upsurge of interest in clinical anxiety that followed Wolpe's pioneering work on behavior therapy in 1958 culminated in Marks's work on the practical parameters of exposure treatment in the 1970s and early 1980s. In his 1969 book, *Fears and Phobias,* Marks had described agoraphobia in some detail, rediscovering Westphal in the process, but the then-current classification made few discriminations among disorders now recognized as distinct. In the second edition of the *Diagnostic and Statistical Manual of Mental Disorders* (DSM-II) (American Psychiatric Association, 1968), the disorders discussed in this book were classified somewhat vaguely under the headings of "Anxiety Neurosis" and "Phobic Neurosis." No distinctions were made between agoraphobia and simple phobia, or between syndromes with and without panic attacks. But 1980 saw a revolution in classification with the publication of the third edition of the *Diagnostic and Statistical Manual of Mental Disorders* (DSM-III) (American Psychiatric Association, 1980). For the first time in an official classification, "Agoraphobia" was recognized as a distinct category among the phobias, and "Panic Disorder" appeared as an anxiety disorder. The relationship between panic attacks and agoraphobia was affirmed with the inclusion of the subcategory "Agoraphobia with Panic Attacks."

Several developments had converged to give panic attacks prominence in clinicians' conception of agoraphobia. Alan Goldstein and Dianne Chambless had provided a reanalysis of agoraphobia in 1978 by describing "complex agoraphobia" as a syndrome that includes fear of fear, or fear of environmentally cued panic attacks, as a central phobic element. Other elements in the reconceptualized agoraphobic syndrome included the initial onset of panic attacks in the context of interpersonal conflict, the client's tendency to misunderstand the source of anxiety episodes and other emotional states, and the low levels of autonomy and self-sufficiency seen in the typical agoraphobic client (Goldstein & Chambless, 1978). This reformulation was clearly a logical development from Wolpe's ideas on agoraphobia and from Goldstein's earlier work (Goldstein, 1970).

Another relevant development, this time from a pharmacological perspective, was the work of Donald Klein on the treatment of different kinds of anxiety within agoraphobia (Klein, 1981). His clinical research had allowed a "pharmacological dissection" of the agoraphobic syndrome in which it was seen that anticipatory anxiety about entering feared situations responds to the minor tranquilizers or benzodiazepines, whereas panic attacks respond to the tricyclic compounds and the monoamine oxidase inhibitors hitherto used exclusively in the treatment of depression. Klein's studies of systematic desensitization and pharmacotherapy for agoraphobia had produced disappointing findings for the former treatment, which he attributed to the resensitization produced in the real world between clinic visits when the client experienced a spontaneous panic attack (Klein, Zitrin, & Woerner, 1977). From Klein's perspective, recognition of the therapeutic value of antidepressant medication in blunting or offsetting panic attacks left open a limited role for exposure-based therapy in treating clients' anticipatory anxiety concerning avoided situations. Recent studies have shown that medication and exposure methods can each be effective in isolation for agoraphobia, and that the effects of tricyclics may not be specifically "panicogenic" (Barlow, 1988, p. 446). Nevertheless, Klein's work has influenced the classification of anxiety in the DSM-III and its successor.

The early 1980s saw the appearance of integrative models of agoraphobia and panic disorder that stemmed largely from the Goldstein and Chambless (1978) reanalysis. Clarke and Wardman (1985), a therapist–client team, describe from their unique vantage points the broader context of agoraphobia, which is commonly embedded in family tensions and is often complicated by the client's difficulties with assertiveness. In her analysis, Fodor (1978) had argued that agoraphobia itself represents an exaggeration of a typical female sex-role stereotype, that of the passive, dependent, helpless woman who stays in the house while men go out to dominate the world. A formulation of agoraphobia that places great emphasis on its social context was put forward by Hafner (1977, 1982), who draws from systems theory concepts to describe abnormal marital relationship patterns that create and maintain agoraphobia. Mathews, Gelder, and Johnston (1981) presented a holistic theory of the etiology of agoraphobia based on epidemiological findings and on their extensive research on treatment. Their theory encompasses possible inherited anxiety traits, background stress, a pattern of generalized anxiety, and the development of avoidance behavior after the client has come to dread having a panic attack in particular surroundings. These authors agree with other theorists in acknowledging the potential importance of clients' tendencies toward dependency on other people and toward ascribing fear reactions to the immediate surroundings rather than to generalized stress. All of these formulations lead to the recommendation that clinicians offer holistic, multimodal treatment plans to address all aspects of their clients' problems, rather than aiming treatment solely at the situational avoidance element.

─── CASE ILLUSTRATION

Ms. AB

One of Hafner's (1982) clients, Ms. AB was a 38-year-old woman who had first experienced agoraphobic problems over twenty years earlier, at about the time she met her husband-to-be. The onset of panic attacks had led her to give up her job for six months. Treatment by group exposure in vivo had produced rapid gains, but a few months later problems in her husband came to the fore when he attempted suicide. It turned out that the husband had responded to her initial therapeutic progress by accusing her of infidelity and demanding that she account for her movements when away from him. She had partially relapsed into agoraphobia, apparently to avoid further criticism and stop "rocking the boat." Despite these marital complications, Ms. AB persevered with her efforts to overcome her agoraphobia and largely succeeded in doing so; however, marital dissatisfaction persisted. Hafner attributed her uneven progress to the husband's feeling threatened by her newfound independence, and it emerged that the husband himself had longstanding issues with dependency, insecurity, and hostility. In cases like this, which Hafner argues are more common than is usually supposed, comprehensive treatment involves addressing the problems of both partners.

1987: DSM-III-R, PANIC DISORDER, AND COGNITIVE-BEHAVIORAL THERAPY

The 1987 revision of the DSM (DSM-III-R) (American Psychiatric Association, 1987) revised the classification of anxiety disorders yet again to place the typical agoraphobic syndrome as a subcategory of "Panic Disorder": "Panic Disorder with Agoraphobia." This reclassification follows from the view that it is the onset of panic attacks that explains clients' progressive avoidance of specific situations associated with panic. Consistent with this formulation of agoraphobia, the later 1980s saw a redirection of theorists' interests toward eliminating panic attacks themselves instead of addressing them indirectly through attacking avoidance of situations.

Brehony and Geller (1981) had attributed the onset of panic attacks in an agoraphobic client to generalized anxiety, high autonomic arousal, and low stress tolerance. Once begun, the cycle of panic attacks perpetuates itself through anticipatory fear mechanisms. Avoidance of typical agoraphobic situations follows, and the client then suffers loss of self-esteem and reduced self-confidence as a direct result of the agoraphobic symptoms. Brehony and Geller anticipated recent etiological theories by arguing that agoraphobics fear novelty, largely because they are uncertain what attribution to make for bodily sensations produced by emotional activation. Interpreting these sensations as fear creates worrisome thoughts, which engender further anxiety, thus creating a cycle of rapidly increasing anxiety that culminates in a panic attack. (Other accounts that deal with panic disorder in general, not just agoraphobia, have also concentrated on such fear-of-fear cycles; see Jacob & Rapport, 1984; Stampler, 1982.)

Recent developments in theory and practice center upon eliminating panic attacks, whether or not the panic disorder client also has the agoraphobic avoidance pattern. Barlow (1988) believes that there are strong indications that panic itself may be eliminated in close to 100 percent of cases, an unprecedented development (p. 447). Acknowledging that panic attacks are sometimes eliminated in agoraphobic clients through exposure treatment, and that medication also has an impressive record in this area, Barlow maintains that the strongest findings derive from the therapeutic principle of exposing clients to the relevant feared stimuli: the actual bodily sensations experienced during panic attacks. The procedures for achieving this exposure vary— voluntary hyperventilation, physical exercise, ingestion of drugs that elicit panic sensations, and carbon dioxide inhalation have all been used—but they all involve a form of flooding to the bodily sensations of fear. Exposure to these internal cues may work for the same reasons that exposure in vivo works (extinction, habituation, learning to cope with the feared stimuli, and the like); according to the fear-of-fear view, however, reducing a client's fear of the bodily signs of panic is a particularly effective way of breaking out of the vicious circle.

The notion of fear of fear and the vicious circle of anxiety sensations and anxious attributions has also led to an interest in the other element in the pattern: the client's anxiety-provoking thoughts about the bodily sensations. Referring to individual variations in response to medications that can produce panic, Clark (1986) argues that it is the client's interpretation of the resulting sensations that produces panic. Even if the bodily sensations of fear persisted, they would not be followed by increasing anxiety or the development of a panic attack if the client could abandon the anxious cognitions about the sensations. These cognitions commonly take the form of attributing the bodily sensations of emotion to the presence of a dire physical disease. The client's "catastrophic misinterpretations" of panic sensations as signals of imminent medical disaster can themselves be made the target of treatment, the appropriate method being cognitive therapy in this case. Beck (1985) describes a model similar to Clark's and has developed a treatment manual for applying his cognitive therapy approach to anxiety disorders. Recent research findings described in conference presentations by Barlow, Beck, and Clark indicate that cognitive therapy can be as effective as exposure to internal cues in abolishing panic attacks.

_____ CASE ILLUSTRATION
Client with Panic Attacks

Clark and Beck (1988) give a detailed outline of cognitive therapy for panic disorder and include clinical vignettes. Generally, clients are taught to identify and change the negative thoughts that accompany their anxiety problems. This can be a difficult undertaking because clients often need to learn to isolate the relevant automatic thoughts—those that appear without deliberate logical reasoning but which contain the unhelpful assumptions that are linked to anxiety. Because clients often respond to questions about thoughts with statements about feeling states, therapists ask, "What was going through your mind?" rather than, "What were you thinking?" This can elicit relevant imagery as well as verbalisms. For example, a client described having had a panic attack when she was watching television and knitting in her living room. Initially she regarded the attack as having arisen "out of the blue," but the therapist was able to identify the antecedents by a series of exercises and questions, as follows. The client was asked to relax, close her eyes, and imagine the scene of the panic attack; when she had formed a vivid image, she was asked to describe what was going through her mind. She recognized that she was not attending to the television but was thinking about her mother's former psychological difficulties. In response to the therapist's inquiry, the client described her mood as a little tense, but as she proceeded to describe the details of the panic attack, she identified an image of being accosted by a man in a white coat and her husband, who were about to take her to a psychiatric hospital in which she would be incarcerated indefinitely. It was this image that the client was able to cite as the precursor of her panic attack.

In cases like this, therapists would proceed by pointing out the link between thoughts or images and feelings, and then presenting a rationale and explanation of normal anxiety mechanisms, usually resulting in some welcome reassurance for the client. Cognitive therapy proper involves developing a nonchallenging partnership with the client in which he or she is gently asked questions about the negative automatic thoughts that have been identified. The client noted here could be asked to estimate the likelihood that people will develop their parents' mental disorders; whether, if the likelihood is high, that would inevitably mean involuntary hospitalization; whether, even that being the case, the length of stay would be indeterminate; and so forth. Applying such methods to the client's thoughts about panic sensations themselves has been particularly effective (the client's automatic thoughts about being gravely ill during an attack are identified; the client's logical bases for such thoughts are gently explored; the client evaluates the objective evidence supporting the thoughts; and so forth).

The cognitive theories of Beck and Clark emphasize thoughts and images of which the client is aware or can easily become aware. Recently developed conceptions of panic have implicated nonconscious cognitive processes in panic disorder (McNally, 1990). The role of information-processing biases in the development and maintenance of anxiety and other emotional disorders is receiving increasing attention (Williams, Watts, MacLeod, & Mathews, 1988). This approach to psychopathology is based in experimental cognitive psychology.

Using research paradigms developed in cognitive psychology laboratories, experimental psychopathologists have shown biases in automatic cognitive processes that are peculiar to clients with panic disorder. It has been shown, for example, that when agoraphobics and nonclinical comparison subjects are asked to read neutral passages and passages that describe situations relevant to agoraphobia (e.g., a woman entering a crowded shopping mall), both groups recall a comparable number of phrases from the neutral passage. Agoraphobics, however, recall significantly more phrases from the phobic scenes (Nunn, Stevenson, & Whalen, 1984). It has been suggested on the basis of research such as this that panic disorder clients exhibit memory biases that result in their storing and retrieving threatening information more easily than others. Using other paradigms drawn from cognitive psychology, it has been shown that panic disorder clients have greater difficulty ignoring threatening information (Hope, Rapee, Heimberg, & Dombeck, 1990) and recognize threatening information more easily (Clark et al., 1988) than other groups of people.

Exploration of information-processing biases in individuals with panic disorder will undoubtedly contribute significantly to our understanding of the problem. Although the implications of these biases for therapeutic work with clients have not been worked out fully as yet, the 1990s will likely see considerable development in this area.

CONCLUDING REMARKS

Westphal recognized agoraphobia as a coherent syndrome that included severe anxiety episodes connected with, and leading to avoidance of, streets, squares, public buildings, open places, crowded places, and closed-in places. His clients were troubled by fear, avoidance, and disturbing thoughts when in contact with such surroundings. In all of these respects, Westphal's clients had a pattern of problems similar to that of the agoraphobic clients of today. The chief advances in our understanding of panic disorder and agoraphobia in recent years have centered on the development of effective treatment procedures. Westphal had suggested graded exposure in vivo to his clients, but he found it unsatisfactory. He did not pursue procedures like cognitive therapy or exposure to internal fear cues. Wolpe, who derived treatments from conditioning concepts, also avoided cognitive therapy; but his account of successful treatments based on reciprocal inhibition may be reinterpreted as resting simply on graded exposure to feared situations and on assertiveness training to help the client deal with troublesome interpersonal relationships. Marks provided a strong empirical basis for procedures based on exposure to situations, but avoided endorsing any particular theory of problem causation. The most recent integrative theories have called attention to maladaptive thinking patterns and adverse social contexts in addition to possible conditioning factors in the etiology of agoraphobia and panic. The most recent treatment approaches follow the exposure principle, but the client confronts actual fear sensations rather than feared external environments. Applications of cognitive therapy to the negative automatic thoughts of panic disorder clients have also proved successful and can be seen as another way (supplementary to exposure to internal cues) of breaking a vicious cycle in which sensations of emotional activation and thoughts of alarming illness reciprocally amplify each other.

In the chapters that follow we shall describe the contemporary anxiety disorders, summarize what is known about them, and indicate suitable treatment programs for panic and agoraphobia syndromes.

CHAPTER 2

Current Concepts of Agoraphobia, Anxiety, and Panic

The problems of Westphal's agoraphobic clients in the 1870s were probably very similar to those of our own clients in the 1990s, but the official classifications and formal descriptions of anxiety disorders have changed a great deal in the last dozen decades. Emil Kraepelin (1856–1926), one of Westphal's best known contemporaries, pioneered the classification of mental disorders in his extensive writings; he concentrated particularly on syndromes thought to be related to an organic disease process. For example, in his *Lectures on Clinical Psychiatry,* Kraepelin (1901/1914) presented 32 chapters, each devoted to a particular disorder or diagnostic grouping. Interestingly enough, the first case illustration in the chapter on anxiety described a 31-year-old man, a teacher, whose problems were strongly reminiscent of Westphal's case descriptions—the client feared gatherings of people, wide squares, and streets; traveling by train or boat; and crossing bridges; and eventually "the apprehension of apprehension itself caused palpitations and oppression on all sorts of occasions" (Kraepelin, 1901/1914, p. 271). Despite this intriguing allusion to agoraphobia, Kraepelin did not refer to Westphal or use his diagnostic label; the chapter on anxiety took up only 10 of the book's 350 pages; and anxiety disorders, cited under the chapter heading of "Irrepressible Ideas and Irresistible Fears," were included somewhat dismissively among the various forms of "morbid personality."

The classification of anxiety fared little better at the hands of the psychoanalysts, who tended to use the global term *neurosis* for most psychogenic disorders. Neurosis referred to a variety of disorders in which anxiety either appeared as a prominent symptom or was assumed to underlie the clinical features of the disorder. The classic cases of "hysteria" reported by the early psychoanalysts (Breuer & Freud, 1895), together with the phobias of "Little Hans" and others (Freud, 1909/1955), were all examples of neurosis. The term was used widely by clinicians of various orientations for decades until, with the publication of the DSM-III in 1980, *neurosis* was replaced by other terms in the formal nomenclature of the American Psychiatric Association. Agoraphobia, panic disorder, and other disorders in which anxiety is a conspicuous feature are known as "Anxiety Disorders" in the DSM-III-R (American Psychiatric Association, 1987).

THE DSM-III-R ANXIETY DISORDERS

Panic Disorder

Panic disorder is characterized by frequent episodes of panic, an upsurge of intense anxiety in which the client experiences various bodily sensations usually associated with fear, together with extremely alarming apprehensions of death, loss of control, or imminent mental illness. By definition, the panic attacks are not maintained by a recognized physical disorder. The episodes are often unsignaled and unpredicted, and can occur potentially at any time and in any situation, including during sleep. Typically clients come to fear the panic attacks, especially dreading the onset of panic at a time or place in which it would be particularly distressing, embarrassing, or inconvenient.

In *panic disorder with agoraphobia,* the client restricts her mobility to some degree or requires the support of a trusted companion when away from home or a place of safety. Essentially the client fears or avoids the typical agoraphobic situations—travel away from home, crowded public places, public transportation, sometimes confined environments—because of the possibility of a panic attack. The client's chief concern is about being unable to escape or obtain assistance in the event of a panic attack.

In *panic disorder without history of agoraphobia,* the client has frequent panic attacks, meeting the criteria for panic disorder, but has not developed a pattern of agoraphobic avoidance.

Agoraphobia without History of Panic Disorder

This disorder—we will call it "agoraphobia" for convenience—is a phobia of the usual array of agoraphobic stimuli and environments, but without panic attacks. The client fears becoming helpless or handicapped in some way in a situation away from help or a sense of safety; some of the features of panic attacks may be present, but not enough to warrant the Panic Disorder label.

The three syndromes noted so far (panic disorder with agoraphobia, panic disorder without history of agoraphobia, and agoraphobia without history of panic disorder) will receive most of our attention in this book because they have presented notorious treatment challenges for therapists, they are prevalent and unusually distressing and handicapping to clients, and professional knowledge about these disorders has increased dramatically even within the last decade. We shall return to them in greater detail later in this chapter.

Social Phobia

In social phobia the client's chief fear is of being appraised, evaluated, and scrutinized by other people; the sense of being the center of attention in a group would be particularly distressing. Situations that could lead to distress or avoidance include social gatherings, job interviews, eating in public, or even using public rest rooms. Writing out a check under the gaze of other people, as in a supermarket or a bank, is a notorious problem to many socially phobic individuals. Particularly challenging for most social phobics (and, indeed, for many people without anxiety disorders) would be a public performance of some kind, such as presenting a formal speech before a large audience.

Unlike the panic and agoraphobic patterns, social phobia is not a distinct syndrome; a client may have difficulties with some or all of the situations listed here or, alternatively, may be troubled in only one of them. Clinicians have often been puzzled to encounter socially phobic clients with a seemingly inconsistent pattern of fears. For example, a 30-year-old male college graduate interviewed recently would dread answering the telephone or taking part in a small-group discussion, but was untroubled by endorsing a check at a bank, attending an important job interview, or being married in a long ceremony before a huge congregation. Apparently arbitrary patterns of social anxiety like this are seen commonly in clinical practice, and this is recognized in the DSM-III-R.

Social phobia often includes a fear-of-fear element in which the client is distressed by the idea that other people can detect his or her increasing anxiety. This idea itself can, of course, amplify the anxiety. Once entered, a vicious circle like this can maintain and exacerbate an anxiety episode that otherwise presumably would have been self-limiting. Particularly susceptible to the fear-of-fear cycle are those whose chief anxiety reaction is readily apparent to other people, such as blushing, perspiring, or trembling.

<hr>

CASE ILLUSTRATION

Don

The client was a 26-year-old man who had been laid off from his job at a paper mill some months before. When employed, he had had few problems interacting with his workmates under normal circumstances, but he had encountered significant difficulties when attending mandatory safety meetings. Not only did the meetings necessitate sitting for an hour or so in a classroom format, but the instructor would typically call on someone at random to make a comment or suggestion. In Don's view, he was able to go to these meetings at all only by making a superhuman effort to do so. Every minute seemed an eternity as he waited for the instructor to call on him.

Don's problems were not resolved by his involuntary absence from work. He and his fiancée had been engaged since high school, and the chief impediment to the marriage was his extreme dread of the prospect of enduring the ceremony. Furthermore, Don's unemployment compensation had been arranged under a new scheme that required employment retraining. His income was therefore contingent on his participation in the training program, which involved class attendance, group discussion, and oral presentations. Don ascribed the origins of his phobia to an incident in childhood in which he was made to give a class presentation in school. Initially undaunted by the prospect of speaking formally before an audience, he had become tongue-tied over a difficult word and his classmates had consequently ridiculed him. His social anxiety had been developing and spreading ever since.

Don's treatment chiefly took the form of graded real-life practice. His therapist moved the treatment sessions to a small classroom with a chalkboard, and Don began to make brief presentations in front of an imaginary class. After one or two sessions of this kind, the therapist brought in her clinical supervisor (with Don's prior approval) and the lectures proceeded with an audience of two. Eventually, Don learned to talk before a small group of clinic staff members, and to interact with them in group discussions.

<hr>

Simple Phobia

The category *simple phobia* includes any specific, unreasonable fear not subsumed under agoraphobia or social phobia. Common examples are phobias of small animals, reptiles, or insects; of blood, injury, and illness; and of heights, darkness, and confinement in small, enclosed places (claustrophobia). According to the DSM-III-R, confronting the feared situation practically always elicits an anxiety reaction—feeling panicky, perspiring, finding it hard to breathe, noticing the heart racing, and so forth. The anxiety reaction usually varies directly with increasing proximity to a phobic stimulus, or with increasing similarity of a stimulus to the original object of fear. Avoidance of phobic stimuli is typical, but sometimes the client will make heroic efforts to confront the situation despite strong anxiety. People with simple phobias recognize that their fears are at least exaggerated if not entirely groundless.

―――――――――――――――――――――――――――――― CASE ILLUSTRATION
Simple Phobia of Dogs

The client was a married woman in her thirties who was treated by one of the authors (GLT) in the late 1960s in England. She had been unable to ascribe the origin of her phobia to any particular adverse experience; it seemed to her that she had always feared dogs. The larger and less familiar the dog, the greater the fear. The client showed a typical avoidance pattern in which she limited her activities and movements to areas free of dogs. She had carefully mapped out her neighborhood so as to identify the safe, dog-free routes, and this cognitive map was continually updated. Sometimes, sympathetic neighbors would call their dogs into their houses when they saw the client approaching along the street. A significant early barrier to the client's treatment (but one that was later used to therapeutic advantage) was the frequent appearance of a small, but unusually loud and active, dog in the long driveway leading to the outpatient clinic in which the treatment sessions were held. The client was ultimately successfully treated by a sequence of systematic desensitization and graded real-life practice.

―――――――――――――――――――――――――――――― CASE ILLUSTRATION
Claustrophobia

The client was a middle-aged man who feared and avoided situations in which he felt confined, trapped, or shut in. Despite his love of hunting, he refused to stay overnight on a hunting trip because that would involve sleeping in a bunk bed at a hunting lodge, where he would feel hemmed in by the close proximity of either the upper bunk or the ceiling, depending on which bunk he slept in. He was also handicapped by his inability to travel by air on business trips, his fear being not so much of aviation itself (he was not particularly troubled by the prospect of the plane crashing) as simply a dread of the prolonged confinement in close quarters involved in air travel.

The client could vividly recall the onset of the phobia. While traveling in Egypt, he had taken the opportunity to visit and enter one of the pyramids. This involved walking with a crouched posture and in single file along a low, narrow, poorly lit passageway that seemed to become more oppressive with each step. The client began to think of the thousands of tons of stone above his head. Because there were people in front of and behind him, he could not escape easily and was effectively trapped for the duration of the excursion. His anxiety mounted rapidly. His inclination was to cry out and beg to be let out, but the prospect of doing this only added to his discomfort. After what seemed an interminable incarceration in the pyramid, his relief at again being free to move about in the fresh air and sunshine was beyond description. From that point, however, his fear of confined places gradually developed and spread.

The client was treated somewhat successfully during a study to evaluate the contribution of different cognitive therapy procedures added to a program of self-initiated graded practice.

Obsessive-Compulsive Disorder

Obsessive-compulsive disorder is marked by *obsessions* (intrusive and troublesome thoughts or images that the client attempts to resist—for example, thoughts about being contaminated by unseen filth) and/or *compulsions* (urges to repeat ritualistic behavior patterns apparently designed to offset anxiety—for example, touching something a given number of times, or washing the hands in elaborate and protracted cleansing rituals). Typically, as in the case of phobias, the person realizes that the obsessions or compulsions are exaggerated and senseless. The DSM-III-R criteria require that the disorder be associated with impairment in the client's work or social life, significant subjective distress, or the allocation of excessive time periods to the obsessional thinking or compulsive behavior patterns.

_____ CASE ILLUSTRATION
Obsessive-Compulsive Disorder

The client, a man in his fifties, had had obsessive-compulsive concerns for years, and their precise origins were unknown to him. At the time he sought therapy from one of us (GLT), he had already improved somewhat from an earlier pattern of extreme involvement in ritualistic behavior, which had pervaded practically all aspects of his life. He attributed his partial improvement to *clomipramine,* a prescribed medication from a class of drugs, the tricyclic compounds, commonly used to treat depression.

The client recalled that, at its worst, his disorder had led him to undertake checking rituals that bordered on the bizarre. These rituals seemed entirely unnecessary and unrelated to any of his actual work responsibilities as an administrator. For example, he once minutely examined each square inch of a parking lot so as to locate and remove any particles of broken glass that might have been present. If someone's car had suffered a flat tire as a result of broken glass, then (the client reasoned) there could be an accident on the highway in which the driver and others could be killed. If such a thing happened, the tragedy would be his, the client's, fault for not having checked properly for glass.

Similarly, the client was often troubled when driving his car by the idea that perhaps he had seen, out of the corner of his eye, a nail lying on the side of the highway about ten miles back. His response to such a thought was to turn his car around at the next intersection, drive back to an exit more than ten miles away, resume his original direction of travel, and search earnestly for the putative nail.

The client's chief concerns at the time he began therapy included prolonged washing and showering rituals, inability to wear even new clothing if it had been "contaminated" in some way by unseen filth, and extreme worry over the possibly adverse consequences of important decisions he had to make in the course of his administrative duties. Treatment—still continuing—has taken the form of exposure with response prevention, in which the client touches obviously "contaminated" objects, such as the sole of the therapist's shoe, and then confronts the anxiety aroused by this while resisting the impulse to perform a cleansing ritual.

Posttraumatic Stress Disorder

In posttraumatic stress disorder (PTSD) the client's anxieties have their origin in a genuinely distressing event that is beyond the bounds of everyday human experience. In the aftermath of such an experience—military combat, a natural disaster, a sexual assault, or a serious automobile accident, for example—the client has persistent anxiety symptoms that may include voluntary isolation from other people; vivid, unbidden memories of the traumatic event; and avoidance of stimuli reminiscent of the original stressor. In PTSD the

original trauma is reexperienced repeatedly in nightmares, flash-
backs, or waking fantasies. In unusual cases the client may enter a
dissociative state in which he or she appears to be literally reliving the
event (behaving as if in the original situation). The PTSD client avoids
stimuli connected with the trauma, or even reduces his or her involvement with the world in general, sometimes withdrawing into an entirely reclusive existence and seldom appearing in public. Finally, the
client has an array of anxiety symptoms that may include sleep disturbance, increased startle response, increased general muscle tension, and hypervigilance. The symptoms of the disorder may appear
immediately or soon after the original traumatic event or, alternatively, may first arise months or even years afterward.

_____ CASE ILLUSTRATION

Posttraumatic Stress Disorder

The client was a single woman in her twenties who had sought help at a
residential facility for alcohol and drug abuse treatment. As she progressed
through the rehabilitation program, it emerged that she had anxiety issues
that required treatment in their own right. In therapy groups, the client
gradually talked more and more about her horrendous history of victimization
in childhood by sexual abuse. In the aftermath of the years of abuse that she
was unable to prevent or escape, the client had developed a typical PTSD
syndrome. She had recurrent bad dreams about the abuse and was often
awake in the middle of the night, seeking the company of the staff members
on the night shift. In the daytime her attention often seemed to wander away
from the task at hand; she was experiencing unwanted but persistent images
of the trauma. She would leave a room at any mention of child abuse or if this
topic was dealt with in any way on a television program she was watching.
The occasional group meetings that included males as well as females were
highly challenging for the client because she normally distanced herself from
men as much as possible. Staff members and other clients noticed that she
was almost constantly fidgeting, shredding tissues, crushing Styrofoam coffee cups, or tapping with her fingers. She once dropped a plate she had
been drying when the telephone in the communal kitchen rang unexpectedly.
The sound of a door slamming could be relied on to provoke a startle
response in the client.

The treatment challenge in PTSD is to reduce the client's current distress and impairment while recognizing that this anxiety disorder, unlike the
others, is not based on irrational assumptions. Accordingly, it is a delicate
matter to help the client come to terms with the stimuli that are needlessly
avoided currently but that indeed *were* associated with genuine trauma

initially. This client, for example, gradually learned to tolerate dealing with men in work and some social situations, while maintaining a realistic degree of caution in avoiding placing herself in another potentially harmful situation.

Generalized Anxiety Disorder

The generalized anxiety disorder pattern is a syndrome of persistent anxiety and worry about more than one general life issue, showing little fluctuation from situation to situation. The anxiety and worry are excessive and unnecessary, and, by definition, the pattern has been prolonged for at least six months. The typical symptoms fall into three groups: tension (for example, restlessness, muscle tension, trembling), autonomic arousal (for example, accelerated heart rate, dizziness, "lump in the throat"), and hypervigilance (for example, having difficulty concentrating, feeling on edge, startling easily).

—————————————————————————— CASE ILLUSTRATION
Generalized Anxiety Disorder

The client was a graduate student in her late thirties who worked part time in her scientific discipline to help pay for her education. Operating under a great deal of objective stress and high performance demands, she showed a marked pattern of overconcern about her level of achievement and the presumed dire consequences of failure. Although she was able to maintain some social activity apart from her job and her studies, her friends noticed that she never seemed to relax or forget her problems and was always preoccupied with the possibility of making mistakes or failing to deal properly with one of the tasks for which she was responsible. The client did not have a simple or a social phobia as such, but she worried about her academic progress in general and about tests and formal presentations in particular. Objectively, she consistently produced satisfactory or excellent work.

She was equally worried, and equally unnecessarily, about working inefficiently and inaccurately at her paid job, and this concern was quite unrelated to the possible evaluation of other people. Her worries included anxiety about decisions she had made (including the decision to return to student status after having worked in the field for years), concern for the well-being of her pet animals, and perpetual apprehension about the health of her objectively healthy relatives. Treatment has largely taken the form of cognitive therapy procedures aimed at helping the client to distinguish realistic from exaggerated concerns.

THE PANIC DISORDER AND AGORAPHOBIC SYNDROMES

Panic disorder, with or without agoraphobia, begins when the client experiences the first panic attack. The attack involves the sudden onset of a variety of physiological and psychological components of fear. The attacks appear to be distinct from high levels of generalized anxiety and are experienced as different by clients (Barlow, Vermilyea, Blanchard, Vermilyea, DiNardo, & Cerny, 1985; Cohen, Barlow, & Blanchard, 1985). Somatic symptoms involve autonomic nervous system arousal, with shortness of breath, palpitations, dizziness, and trembling predominant (Stampler, 1982). Thoughts that the individual may be dying or becoming mentally ill are common, as is a concern over losing behavioral control (Burns & Thorpe, 1977a, 1977b; Chambless, Caputo, Bright, & Gallagher, 1984). Clients will often report that during an attack they experience depersonalization, a feeling of dreamlike detachment, and a subjective change in their sense of themselves. A related phenomenon, derealization, is also frequently experienced during a panic attack. It refers to perceiving the environment as altered and to a sense of unreality about the surroundings. The DSM-III-R criteria for a panic attack are listed in Table 2.1.

TABLE 2.1   DSM-III-R Diagnostic Criteria for Panic Attack

At least four of the following symptoms developed during at least one of the attacks:

1. Shortness of breath (dyspnea) or smothering sensations
2. Dizziness, unsteady feelings, or faintness
3. Palpitations or accelerated heart rate (tachycardia)
4. Trembling or shaking
5. Sweating
6. Choking
7. Nausea or abdominal distress
8. Depersonalization or derealization
9. Numbness or tingling sensations (paresthesias)
10. Flushes (hot flashes) or chills
11. Chest pain or discomfort
12. Fear of dying
13. Fear of going crazy or of doing something uncontrolled

Source: Reprinted with permission from the *Diagnostic and Statistical Manual of Mental Disorders, Third Edition, Revised.* Copyright 1987 American Psychiatric Association.

Note: Attacks involving four or more symptoms are panic attacks; attacks involving fewer than four symptoms are limited-symptom attacks.

Clients often report that their first panic attack was experienced during a stressful period in their lives. Significant life changes such as a new job, marriage, moving, interpersonal conflict, and the death of a loved one have all been associated with initial panic attacks with some frequency (Klosko, Rotunda, & Barlow, 1987; Ottaviani & Beck, 1987). Initial panic attacks may also occur during or immediately following an experience with illicit psychoactive drugs (Hollon, 1981). The following is a description of the initial panic attack experienced by one of our clients who subsequently developed panic disorder with agoraphobia. This particular client had taken on the responsibility of caring for her elderly father shortly before the first panic attack. In this description she goes on to talk about some of the physical symptoms she experiences during most panic attacks.

> My father and I had a little bit of an argument, nothing too serious, the night before. Things got calmed down and everything was fine . . . We was sitting at the table eating our breakfast when this just really strange feeling came over me like nothing I had ever had before. So I says, well maybe I need some air . . . I went outside and it got worse, so then I thought I was having a stroke . . . It gradually got worse and worse and finally they contacted my husband . . . and he took me to the hospital. They did a complete checkup. They said, "You're not having a stroke, you're having an anxiety attack" . . . It's really very hard to explain. It's like something takes over my body. I can't fight it . . . I get lightheaded and kind of dizzy . . . and it's like palpitations. The heart goes very rapid . . . I shake. I just start to shake . . . sometimes my whole body just goes numb.

Panic disorder clients may or may not develop varying degrees of avoidance behavior after experiencing one or more unexpected panic attacks (Thyer & Himle, 1985; Uhde, Roy-Byrne, Vittone, Boulenger, & Post, 1985). A proportion will go on to develop the full cluster of problems associated with the agoraphobic syndrome. Most agoraphobics fear traveling away from home or from some other place that is considered safe. Many can travel more freely when with someone they trust, such as a spouse or a parent. Fears of crowds or situations in which clients might find themselves confined, such as a bus or an elevator, are also common, and these situations are usually avoided. Typically agoraphobics will describe fears of waiting in line such as in a grocery store, sitting in a movie theater, and attending religious services. Having a definite appointment, for example with the hairdresser, is often very anxiety-provoking and is anticipated with dread. Agoraphobics are frequently worried that they will lose control in a public place. Fears of having a panic attack are evident in almost all agoraphobics. They tend to be vigilant for any sign of anxiety that might signal an attack. The situations most frequently feared, and usually avoided, by agoraphobics share two common themes: Escape would be difficult should the client experience an attack, and assistance might not be available should the client become incapacitated.

_____ CASE ILLUSTRATION

Panic Disorder with Agoraphobia: Louise

Louise was 59 years old when she was first seen in our clinic. She had been married for 39 years and had six adult children. Louise had never worked outside of the home. She reported that the happiest time in her life was when she was raising her children. Louise's husband worked as an engineer specializing in bridge construction. Throughout their marriage Louise's husband was frequently away from home for weeks at a time living at a work site. Louise reported that she felt that her husband was not very understanding of her or her problems. In her own words: "I'll say something. Try to express my opinion and it seems that there is always something. I mean he'll have some wise remark to say about it." Louise reported that she has always had problems asserting herself. She said that she frequently acts in ways that she thinks other people want her to act rather than being herself.

Louise first began to experience mental health problems about 25 years ago. At that time she was hospitalized for about a month with severe depression. Louise's recollection of the episode was that she had felt overwhelmed by other people telling her how to live her life and raise her family. She stated that she felt she had to please her mother, her husband, and other members of her family and that the task was too much for her. Louise was released from the hospital and maintained on antidepressant medication for approximately one year. Since that time, however, she has experienced intermittent episodes of depression.

Louise had her first panic attack about seven years ago. At that time she was caring for her elderly father in her home. The initial attack (described earlier in her own words) lasted about 90 minutes. It was experienced as a sudden onset of dizziness, lightheadedness, rapid heart rate, and shaking, which Louise interpreted as symptoms of a stroke. She was taken to a local hospital, examined, and released. Louise did not experience another attack for approximately six months. The second attack occurred during a severe snowstorm. Louise recalled that she had been worrying about her daughter, who was traveling in the storm, when she was overcome by panic. After this incident the panic attacks increased in frequency and no longer appeared to be associated with any particular problem or stressor. Despite the fact that

Louise had been told that the attacks she experienced were due to anxiety, she continued to believe that she had a life-threatening illness whenever she had an attack. She reported that she had herself taken to the emergency room on an average of once a month. Over the next few years Louise began to avoid a variety of situations. She stopped going out to public places such as restaurants and shops. Eventually, she rarely traveled from home unless accompanied by a trusted companion such as one of her children. Even when accompanied by another adult, she still avoided certain situations such as elevators and public rest rooms. By the time she came to our clinic, she was spending nearly every day at home alone.

In the seven years since the onset of her panic attacks and her entry into our program, Louise had been involved in a variety of forms of treatment. She had been seen for insight-oriented psychotherapy for over a year and had been prescribed benzodiazepines, which she continued to take despite the fact that she felt they were ineffective. Most recently she had participated in a support group for agoraphobic women at the local community mental health center. The leader of this group referred her to our program.

Although some proportion of people who develop panic disorder go on to become agoraphobic, some clients never develop the avoidance behaviors associated with this syndrome. At this time we do not know what percentage of individuals with panic disorder will develop agoraphobia and what percentage will not. Nor can we identify the important variables that distinguish these two groups. Some recent findings suggest that certain personality styles may be related to the extent to which the individual is incapacitated by panic attacks. We will discuss these variables later in this chapter.

Panic disorder clients tend to present with a similar clinical picture. Typically, panic clients are preoccupied with thoughts that they are morbidly ill, in danger of sudden death, or likely to lose control of their minds. It is not uncommon for these clients to present themselves repeatedly to their local hospital emergency rooms reporting that they believe they have had a stroke or a heart attack.

CASE ILLUSTRATION

Panic Disorder: Barbara

Barbara was 24 years old when she was referred to our clinic by her family physician. In the letter sent to accompany the referral, the physician stated that Barbara had been evaluated by a succession of doctors to rule out a physical basis for the problems she was experiencing. In the past year Barbara had undergone an extensive cardiac evaluation including multiple cardiograms, Holter monitoring, and chest X-ray. She also had had a complete neurological evaluation, which included a CT scan, and a full gastrointestinal series. Without exception, the tests revealed no physical disorder. During our initial interview Barbara reported that she had been to the emergency room approximately ten times in the past six months.

Barbara was the oldest child in a family of three. She was still living with her parents when she was referred to our program. Barbara described her mother, with whom she is very close, as an extremely nervous woman. She stated that her mother is the only person who understands her and the only one who believes her physical complaints. Barbara has two younger siblings, one of whom suffers from cerebral palsy and a seizure disorder. The other was also diagnosed as having a seizure disorder, but after a recent reevaluation the medication was discontinued. Barbara has a high school education and has been working as a secretary since graduation. Between the ages of 18 and 22, Barbara used a variety of illicit drugs, including marijuana, cocaine, and amphetamines, recreationally.

Barbara's problems began about two years prior to her referral to our program. She stated that she woke one Saturday morning feeling dizzy and nauseated. As she roused herself, Barbara noted that her heart was pounding and her hands were trembling. Feeling overwhelmed by a sense of impending doom, she began to fear that she was going to die. She was taken to the emergency room by her mother, but no physical cause for her symptoms could be found. Barbara had used cocaine the night before this first panic attack, a fact she concealed from her mother and from the emergency room personnel. Barbara's next attack occurred while she was using marijuana. This attack lasted about 15 minutes and was marked by an extremely rapid heart rate. Barbara recalled that she was afraid she was going to have a heart attack. Frightened by these two experiences, Barbara stopped using all illicit substances. However, she became increasingly concerned about her physical and mental health. She developed the habit of checking her pulse to see how quickly her heart was beating. She was preoccupied with the thought that she had done some permanent damage to herself through experimenting with illicit substances. Despite the fact that she had stopped using drugs, Barbara continued to experience frequent panic attacks. These attacks usually arose without warning and at nearly any time of the day or night, including while she slept. At their worst the attacks occurred daily.

Barbara was treated by her family physician with tricyclic antidepressants, but they proved ineffective. A subsequent change of medication to alprazolam (Xanax) reduced the frequency of her attacks. At the time of our initial interview, Barbara was experiencing panic attacks approximately once a week. Her medication was prescribed to be taken at specific times each day, but she could also take an additional pill if she felt a panic attack coming on. She stated that the medication helped reduce the intensity of the attacks. Despite the panic attacks, Barbara was not handicapped by situational fears. She continued to work and was not significantly impaired socially. Barbara had, however, quit exercising because she felt panicky whenever she became short of breath. Prior to the onset of panic attacks, she had enjoyed aerobic exercise classes.

The recent reorganization of the diagnostic manual emphasizes the relationship between panic disorder and agoraphobia. There are, however, individuals who demonstrate the avoidance behavior of agoraphobia but who have never experienced the debilitating panic attacks seen in panic disorder.

CASE ILLUSTRATION

Agoraphobia without History of Panic Disorder: Arabella

An unmarried mill worker in her forties, Arabella lived with her sister near the town center. Her home was only a short bus ride away from the mill. Arabella did not own or drive a car; she usually traveled on foot, on her bicycle, or by bus. Having been referred by her family physician to a research program on agoraphobia treatment, Arabella revealed to her new therapist that she struggled daily to maintain her mobility despite high levels of anxiety when away from home. Instead of having distinct panic attacks, she simply felt more and more anxious with increasing distances from home. Her most prominent anxiety symptom was profuse perspiration. When accompanied by her sister, Arabella felt able to go practically anywhere, although this would still be at the expense of some discomfort. When alone away from home, she would struggle hard against the temptation to escape to the safety of home. Despite high anxiety levels, Arabella was usually able to do many of the things that she would have done if she had not had agoraphobia (going to work, shopping locally, and visiting friends in the immediate neighborhood), but there were some distinct areas of avoidance. She could not bring herself to sit in a theater or auditorium under any circumstances, and travel alone beyond a radius of a mile or so was impossible.

Arabella described herself as a "born worrier" who could always find something anxiety-provoking in any situation. She was embarrassed by her tendency to perspire a lot, and was troubled by the specific fear that she might become nauseated and possibly vomit while in a public place. She participated in a 16-session treatment research program. The procedures used included systematic desensitization, graded practice, and a form of cognitive therapy.

At a follow-up interview eight years after treatment, Arabella continued to report some agoraphobic difficulties, but she had made considerable progress from her pretreatment status. Unaccompanied by her sister, she used public transportation to attend the follow-up interview at a relocated clinic some miles from her home. On her arrival she expressed relief to find that she would be interviewed alone—she had had the fantasy of a large number of people gathered together in an auditorium, each one expected to address the audience formally! She told her former therapist that she had made definite progress in unaccompanied travel.

The most significant challenge Arabella had encountered in the years since treatment had ended was a television appearance. She and her sister were interviewed in their home by a network television crew producing a documentary on working conditions in the industry in which Arabella and her sister were employed. She had been dismayed at the number of people—technicians, camera operators, and interviewers—who managed to cram themselves into her tiny living room for the filming. The most difficult part was not the interview itself but the realization, as soon as the battery of high-intensity camera lighting was switched on, that she was perspiring under their heat as she had never perspired before!

CHARACTERISTICS OF AGORAPHOBIC AND PANIC DISORDER CLIENTS

Panic disorder and agoraphobia are among the most disturbing and handicapping problems that clients bring to the attention of mental health clinicians. Estimates of the prevalence of anxiety disorders in general seem to increase with each new study; indications from a recent door-to-door survey are that at least 5 percent of the general population have anxiety disorders, and approximately 25 percent of these people seek treatment (Weissman, 1985). Depending on the location and on the respondents' ethnicity, estimates for agoraphobia alone range from 3 to 6 percent. This represents a striking increase in prevalence estimates from the 6 or 7 per thousand suggested by Agras, Sylvester, and Oliveau in 1969.

Not only prevalence estimates but also diagnostic classifications have been revised in the last twenty years or so, as we indicated in Chapter 1. Because the relationship between agoraphobia and panic disorder has only recently been identified and formalized in the diagnostic manual, much of what we know about both disorders is based on studies using the language of earlier classifications. As a result, much of the literature refers to "agoraphobia" when dealing with what we now recognize as panic disorder and agoraphobic syndromes. The following discussion of client characteristics is drawn from this literature, except where otherwise indicated.

Age at Onset

The peak age for onset of agoraphobia is young adult life. A large-scale survey of English citizens with agoraphobia carried out by Burns and Thorpe (1977b) indicated a mean age of 28 at the onset of symptoms. Other authors have reported two peak ages, the first at about 20 years and the second at approximately 30 to 35 years old (Bowen & Kahout, 1979; Marks, 1971). Panic disorder without agoraphobia also appears to begin at around the age of 29 years (Klosko et al., 1987). Our case of Louise, though representative of most agoraphobics in many respects, is atypical because of the late onset of panic attacks. Experiencing one's first panic attack at age 52 is apparently quite rare.

Sex Ratio

Approximately three-quarters of agoraphobic clients are women (Thorpe & Burns, 1983). Panic disorder clients who do not demonstrate extensive avoidance behavior appear to be more evenly represented in the sexes (Myers et al., 1984; Thyer, Parrish, Curtis, Nesse, & Cameron, 1985). As we have indicated earlier, in light of the disproportionate number of women in agoraphobic samples, it has been suggested that the development of the disorder may be related to sex-role stereotyping (Fodor, 1978). This view will be discussed in more detail.

Childhood Problems

Although it has been suggested that the incidence of childhood problems in agoraphobic samples is high (for example, Marks & Gelder, 1965), most survey studies do not support this view. The prevalence of such problems as nightmares, nocturnal enuresis, thumb sucking, and stammering in agoraphobic samples is strikingly similar to that revealed by a survey of normal children (Lapouse & Monk, 1959).

Separation anxiety in childhood has been implicated as a predisposing factor for agoraphobia in the DSM-III-R. Klein (1981) has argued that agoraphobia may be due in part to a lower threshold for activation of what is basically a normal separation anxiety response. This response, according to Klein, is an innate biological mechanism that is important in controlling attachment behavior. Anxiety associated with separation from a parent, usually the mother, is commonly observed in early stages of development in humans and other species. This may in fact be adaptive in that it signals a need for protective attachment. The panic and dependent behavior seen in some people with agoraphobia may be construed as the separation anxiety response. In this context, however, it is a pathological pattern because it is no longer developmentally appropriate. Klein (1981) argues that agoraphobics have a lower threshold for the activation of this response, presumably because of a variety of factors including endocrine imbalance, actual separation experiences, and constitutional variables.

Support for the relationship between separation anxiety in childhood and adult agoraphobia is found in case studies and descriptive reports (Thyer, Nesse, Cameron, & Curtis, 1985). However, studies that have compared agoraphobic clients to suitably matched control samples do not consistently support this. Buglass, Clarke, Henderson, Kreitman, and Presley (1977) assessed 30 agoraphobic and 30 general-practice patients on measures of positive, negative, and ambivalent feelings toward parents and found no differences between the two groups. Thyer, Nesse, et al. (1985) found no differences between agoraphobics and simple phobics in their responses to 14 questions dealing with separation trauma in childhood. In a similar study with panic disorder and simple phobic clients, no clinically relevant differences were found on the same 14 questions (Thyer, Nesse, Curtis, & Cameron, 1986). Berg, Marks, McGuire, and Lipsedge (1974) surveyed 786 women in an agoraphobia correspondence club regarding past school phobia, a problem thought to be related to separation anxiety. Twenty-two percent of the sample reported at least a tendency toward school phobia, which is not dissimilar to the percentage of nonphobic controls reporting school phobia problems. School phobia did, however, predict an earlier onset of agoraphobia and more severe psychiatric status in the sample. Casat (1988) has recently reviewed the literature evaluating the possible relationship between childhood anxiety disorder and adult panic disorder and agoraphobia. On the basis of his review, Casat concludes that although many of the studies on the relationship between childhood separation anxiety and adult agoraphobia and panic disorder are seriously flawed, they do suggest a possible link in a subset of clients. The relationship appears to be stronger in women with agoraphobia than in men.

Biological Variables

Evidence has accumulated that implicates genetic factors in the development of agoraphobia and panic disorder. Family studies, for example, find an increased risk for anxiety disorders among family members of anxious clients (Margraf, Ehlers, & Roth, 1986). That genetic factors influence panic attacks appears clear (Lader, 1991). In a study of panic disorder probands, Crowe, Noyes, Pauls, and Slymen (1983) found an incidence of over 20 percent in first-degree relatives when marginal cases are included. This is in contrast to less than 3 percent in the relatives of healthy controls. Twin studies generally yield consistent data. The concordance rates among monozygotic twins tend to be higher than among dizygotic twins in various studies (Lader, 1991). However, not all studies have found this difference (see Margraf et al., 1986, for a discussion of inconsistent findings). Even in the studies finding higher concordance rates in monozygotic twins, these rates are always far below 100 percent. In most studies, in fact, discordant monozygotic twins are found more frequently than concordant pairs, which highlights the importance of nongenetic factors in the development of panic disorder.

Panic attacks can be induced with some reliability in panic disorder clients using a variety of pharmacological agents and laboratory procedures. The various methods of inducing panic attacks include sodium lactate infusion (Liebowitz, Gorman, Fyer, Dillon, Levitt, & Klein, 1986), yohimbine ingestion (Charney, Heninger, & Breier, 1984), high doses of caffeine (Lader, 1991), carbon dioxide inhalation (Griez & van den Hout, 1986), and hyperventilation (Salkovskis, Warwick, Clark, & Wessels, 1986). Each of these methods tends to produce an experience akin to a panic attack in panic disorder clients but not in most non–panic disorder individuals. This has been taken by some as evidence that panic disorder is a biologically based phenomenon in which psychological factors play a minimal role (for example, Klein, 1981; Sheehan, 1984). Lactate-induced panic, for example, has been interpreted as a biological marker for panic disorder. This view, however, is a narrow one in that it ignores the serious methodological problems in the studies produced to date (Margraf et al., 1986) as well as the role cognitive factors may play during these biologically based procedures (Clark, 1986). An alternative account of the induction of panic attack in the laboratory will be presented in Chapter 3.

Personality Variables

Agoraphobic clients are frequently described in clinical reports as passive, dependent individuals who have difficulty expressing their thoughts and feelings (Thorpe & Burns, 1983). Empirical evidence is consistent with this description in that agoraphobics tend to score low on measures of assertiveness (Chambless, Hunter, & Jackson, 1982; Fisher & Wilson, 1985; Thorpe, Freedman, & Lazar, 1985) when compared with adult normative data and with college student responses.

Fodor (1978) has suggested that different developmental experiences for men and women in our culture may account for the predominance of women in agoraphobic samples. Women, according to this view, are raised to be passive and dependent and therefore are more likely to be avoidant in the face of frightening situations. A recent correlational study has lent some support to this view. Chambless and Mason (1986) found that agoraphobic subjects' scores on a scale of masculinity were inversely correlated with phobic avoidance and other measures of anxiety (that is, fear of negative evaluation, social avoidance, frequency of panic attacks), regardless of the client's sex. These results suggest that the development of agoraphobia may be due to cultural factors similar to those suggested by Fodor. The distribution of the sexes in panic disorder and panic disorder with agoraphobia samples can also be seen as consistent with the view that sex-role characteristics may be important in the development of avoidance. As we have seen, approximately three-quarters of most samples of agoraphobics are women, whereas the distribution of men and women with panic disorder without agoraphobia is approximately equal. Lower levels of traits typically associated with masculinity (that is, active, assertive), therefore, may be instrumental in the development of extensive avoidance behavior.

In addition to dependency and low assertiveness, agoraphobic clients have also been described as hypochondriacal. Buglass et al. (1977) classified over half of a sample of agoraphobics as hypochondriacal, with the most frequent concern being over whether or not they had a fatal illness. Similarly, recent studies have indicated that panic disorder clients entertain thoughts of illness and death more often than others (reviewed by Clark, 1986). Hibbert (1984), for example, found that nonphobic clients with a history of panic attacks were more likely than clients without a history of panic attacks to report that they are concerned by an anticipation of illness, death, or loss of control.

Interpersonal Relationships

Clinical reports have frequently referred to problems in the marriages of agoraphobic clients. Hand and Lamontagne (1976), for example, reported that 14 of 21 clients in an agoraphobic sample involved in their treatment research program had marital problems. Some authors have, in fact, conceptualized agoraphobic avoidance as a means of coping in an unsatisfactory marriage (for example, Goldstein & Chambless, 1978; Milton & Hafner, 1979). According to this view, which is based primarily on clinical observations, the agoraphobic is involved in an unsatisfactory marriage but lacks the sense of self-sufficiency necessary in order to leave the relationship. The development of agoraphobia helps the client avoid dealing with the conflict over leaving. This conception of the problem will be discussed in greater detail in Chapter 3.

Empirical findings concerning the marital relationships of agoraphobics do not support the view that, as a group, agoraphobics are involved in distressed marriages. Burns and Thorpe (1977a, 1977b) did not find anything unusual about the marriages of agoraphobics who responded to their large-scale survey. Approximately one in five respondents, however, reported that the agoraphobia was putting a considerable strain on their marriages. Buglass et al. (1977) compared 30 married agoraphobic women to a matched control group from a general psychiatric practice and found no differences on measures of marital interaction or domestic organization. Similarly, no differences in marital satisfaction between a group of 17 agoraphobics and 11 paid volunteer control subjects were found by Fisher and Wilson (1985). Thus, although the marital conflict described in many cases of agoraphobia may have been significant in those cases, the marriages of agoraphobics in general appear to be no more distressed than those of comparison groups.

CONCLUDING REMARKS

As this introductory survey shows, panic disorder and agoraphobic syndromes are multifaceted, so that researchers have addressed not only the anxiety elements but also a range of issues including personality, marital, and social phenomena. This stands in contrast to the literature on simple phobias, for example, in which anxiety itself has been a far more prominent issue. The greater complexity of panic disorder and agoraphobia demands a more holistic approach to assessment and treatment, as we shall indicate in the chapters that follow.

CHAPTER 3

Theoretical and Empirical Bases for Cognitive-Behavioral Treatment

The behavioral movement in psychiatry and psychology was initiated by clinicians who were dissatisfied with the conceptual and empirical shortcomings of psychoanalysis. These pioneers of behavior therapy turned to experimental psychology as an alternative source of ideas from which to develop new treatments. In devising behavioral techniques to relieve clients of situational anxieties, Joseph Wolpe (1958, 1973) and others instigated a major new approach to mental health care in general. New procedures like systematic desensitization and flooding appealed to clinicians and researchers alike, not only because of the fresh conceptual perspective they offered, but also because of their empirically demonstrable success.

The first techniques of the early behavior therapists were aimed specifically at the situational anxiety disorders. In the initial reports of Wolpe (1958), rapid and dramatic success was often attributed to systematic desensitization as applied to simple phobias. The success of the technique appeared to be consistent with the learning theory model from which it was drawn.

Cognitive-behavioral approaches developed out of the early successes of interventions based on a learning theory model of psychopathology. Conditioning theory has been particularly valuable in developing treatments for agoraphobia, especially when increased mobility is the goal. As our understanding of the panic disorder and agoraphobic syndromes has developed, however, it has become clear that more complex models, which integrate cognitive and psychosocial factors, are necessary. In this chapter we will present the models that have been most useful in developing the cognitive-behavioral approaches. Empirical support for the cognitive-behavioral interventions will also be presented.

CONDITIONING MODEL OF AGORAPHOBIA

In a classical conditioning model of phobias, phobic stimuli gain their anxiety-inducing properties through association with stimuli that naturally produce fear, or with stimuli that have already been conditioned to produce fear (that is, in second-order conditioning). In the case of agoraphobia, an individual presumably fears crowds or confinement because these situations have been associated with a frightening or traumatic experience in the past. In order to account for the avoidance component of phobias, operant conditioning principles need to be invoked. According to Mowrer's (1947) two-factor theory, conditioned fear can motivate escape and avoidance. In the more recent terminology of operant learning, avoidance is said to be learned and maintained through negative reinforcement. Escape from, or avoidance of, phobic situations is followed by a reduction in the classically conditioned fear. In this way, the escape response is strengthened. The development of avoidance behavior precludes the extinction of conditioned fear, because the necessary exposure to the conditioned stimuli never occurs or is of insufficient duration. In the case of agoraphobia, because the client avoids the shopping mall, for example, her fear of this otherwise "neutral" stimulus fails to extinguish.

Despite the appeal of two-factor theory for behavior therapists, evaluation of the model with respect to available empirical evidence has found it lacking (Franks & Wilson, 1978). The theory has been criticized on several grounds, including the following:

1. Laboratory studies with human subjects have generally failed to establish lasting conditioned fears (Hallam & Rachman, 1976).
2. Many people who are exposed to intensely frightening conditions in the presence of a variety of potential conditioned stimuli fail to develop phobias of these stimuli (Rachman, 1978).
3. In clinical samples it is often difficult to find any traumatic experience that might have produced the conditioned fear reaction (Marks, 1969).
4. Given that the component of a phobia that is most difficult to change is the subjective distress associated with entering the phobic situation, the relevance of avoidance conditioning might be called into question (Mineka, 1985).

Although conditioning theory may not provide a satisfactory account of all phobic disorders, recent changes in our conception of agoraphobia provide cause for reevaluation of the conditioning model for this disorder. As we have seen, in the DSM-III-R panic disorder is given predominance over agoraphobia. Agoraphobic avoidance appears to develop after the client has experienced panic attacks in most cases (Thyer & Himle, 1985). In other words, the client learns to avoid crowded places and the like for fear of having a panic attack there. The panic attack is described by most clients in such terrifying terms that it could very well qualify as an unconditioned stimulus–unconditioned response combination in itself. When the experience is conceptualized in this way, it seems plausible to view the situations in which panics occur as conditioned stimuli. Fear of these situations develops as a conditioned response.

To take this analysis even further, we can consider the typical pattern in which the onset of mild anxiety is rapidly followed by the development of a full-blown panic attack. In this pattern, the sensations of mild anxiety routinely precede the full panic attack. A conditioning view would lead us to predict that symptoms of mild anxiety might serve as conditioned stimuli, with escalating anxiety as the conditioned response. In this way, we can view the panic attack as the end product of a vicious circle involving "fear of fear" (Evans, 1972). (It is difficult to follow this line of reasoning very far without paying attention to the client's expectations; this cognitive view will be amplified in later sections.)

Marks (1981a) has pointed out that it can be confusing to pursue a conditioning explanation of a client's phobia; it can be difficult, for example, to determine the precise nature of the conditioned stimulus for the agoraphobic client (is it the shopping mall, or the fear sensations themselves?). Despite these difficulties, a clear advantage of the conditioning model is that it has proved valuable in designing useful interventions. When agoraphobia is conceptualized in conditioning terms, an effective approach to treatment becomes obvious. Extinction of the conditioned fear response should occur if the client repeatedly confronts the feared situation in the absence of some unconditioned fear stimulus. Treatments based on the principle of repeated or continuous exposure to phobic objects or situations have been shown to be very powerful in the treatment of most clinically significant fears, including agoraphobia, particularly when avoidance is the primary treatment target (Barlow & Wolfe, 1981; Emmelkamp, 1982a, 1982b; Marks, 1981b; Mavissakalian & Barlow, 1981; Thorpe & Burns, 1983). The success of exposure treatments does not, of course, prove the conditioning view of etiology, since one cannot support a theory simply by showing that treatments derived from it are effective (Marks,

1981a). Nonetheless, the conditioning model can help the clinician in designing and implementing treatment strategies.

EXPOSURE-BASED TREATMENT OF AGORAPHOBIA

The first widely used exposure-based treatment of phobias was systematic desensitization (Wolpe, 1958), which involves graded presentation of phobic scenes in imagination while the client is deeply relaxed. Early clinical reports of the use of systematic desensitization in the treatment of agoraphobia suggested that this approach could be helpful in reducing clients' fear. As we have seen, however, positive effects were not reliably found, and comparison treatments were often ill defined. It is now generally accepted among behavioral researchers that systematic desensitization, by itself, is of little value in the treatment of agoraphobia (for example, Emmelkamp, 1982a; Thorpe & Burns, 1983). When systematic desensitization has been applied with success, positive changes have most likely been due to exposure in vivo encouraged by the therapists.

Real-life, or in vivo, exposure methods are generally considered to be the treatment of choice for agoraphobics. Collapsing across the variety of forms that live exposure treatment can take (for example, graded practice, participant modeling, prolonged or brief duration), empirical studies indicate that approximately 60 to 70 percent of people with agoraphobia who complete a trial of exposure treatment will show clinically significant improvement (Barlow & Wolfe, 1981). When compared to imaginal exposure treatments, in vivo methods usually result in greater fear reduction (Emmelkamp & Wessels, 1975; Stern & Marks, 1973; Watson, Mullet, & Pillay, 1973), although at least one study found no difference between these two approaches (Chambless, Foa, Groves, & Goldstein, 1982). James (1986) has recently examined the literature comparing imaginal and in vivo flooding techniques and concluded that the widely held view that in vivo techniques are superior to imaginal ones may be premature because the available studies have serious limitations. Distinction between imaginal and in vivo flooding techniques might be arbitrary in that identical therapeutic processes may very well be operative in each (Hecker & Thorpe, 1987).

Exposure-based treatment of agoraphobia is problem-oriented in that the primary goal of treatment is improved mobility and reduction in situation-specific fear. Despite the success of exposure therapies, it has been argued that such "symptom removal" leaves untouched personality or interpersonal problems in many agoraphobics. Phobia removal, therefore, will likely lead to problems in other areas of the client's life or to relapse into phobic behavior over the long run (for example, Milton & Hafner, 1979). But assessment of agoraphobics years after behavioral treatment does not support this notion. Munby and Johnston (1980) reinterviewed 63 of 66 agoraphobics treated in clinical studies five to nine years earlier. They did not find evidence for either relapse into phobic patterns or the development of new problems. Clients in this study did, however, return to pretreatment levels of general anxiety and depression. Burns, Thorpe, and Cavallaro (1986) evaluated 20 agoraphobics eight years after behavioral treatment using interview, self-report, and behavioral measurements. On the behavioral test and self-report measures, clients had maintained improvements apparent at one year follow-up.

INTEGRATIVE MODELS OF AGORAPHOBIA

In our brief historical outline in Chapter 1, we introduced some integrative models of agoraphobia and panic disorder with agoraphobia that sought to encompass the varied clinical features of these syndromes. The models that have been most important for cognitive-behavioral approaches have emphasized classical conditioning, operant conditioning, social learning, and cognitive factors in the development and maintenance of agoraphobia. The various models share some common features, which will be discussed here with respect to factors that may predispose an individual to agoraphobia, the experience of a panic attack, and the development and maintenance of avoidance.

Predisposing Factors

A variety of predisposing factors have been suggested by clinicians and researchers experienced with agoraphobic clients. As indicated earlier, clients with agoraphobia tend to be low in assertiveness and lack a sense of self-sufficiency (Chambless, Hunter, & Jackson, 1982; Thorpe et al., 1985). They are also commonly seen as dependent (Mathews et al., 1981). Developmental experiences are presumably involved in the creation of these traits. Mathews and colleagues, for example, suggested that parental over- or underprotection of the preagoraphobic child may lead to dependency as an adult. These personal style factors set the stage for agoraphobia in that the individual experiences anxiety when in novel situations or when separated from someone who could rescue her should she find herself unable to cope.

Agoraphobia tends to develop when an individual is experiencing elevated levels of background stress. Goldstein and Chambless (1978) and others have focused attention on interpersonal relationships as the source of this stress. These authors have suggested that an agoraphobic may feel trapped in an unsatisfactory marriage but may lack the sense of independence necessary to leave the situation. Fishman (1980) suggested, more generally, that an agoraphobic may be dissatisfied with her life situation but, as in the Goldstein and Chambless view, may feel unable to instigate changes in her life. Genetic factors may also be involved in the high levels of background anxiety experienced by most agoraphobics. Mathews et al. (1981) suggested a possible genetic predisposition toward "anxiety neurosis," or more contemporarily generalized anxiety, in people who develop agoraphobia. This constitutional diathesis, coupled with increased background stress, may produce the generalized anxiety state that sets the stage for the initial panic attack.

A third factor cited by several writers as potentially instrumental in the development of agoraphobia is a tendency to make attributional errors with regard to emotional states. Mathews et al. (1981), for example, have suggested that agoraphobics tend to attribute acute anxiety to external stimuli. The client who experiences an increase in anxiety when alone in a crowded shopping mall, for example, may attribute the feelings to the mall. Goldstein and Chambless (1978) suggested a similar type of attributional error. They argued that agoraphobics ignore the true causes of emotional distress, instead explaining the feelings as having come "out of the blue." This tendency to fail to recognize the true source of emotions may have its origins in early childhood experiences in which the expression of negative emotions was punished. Recognition of anger, for example, may be anxiety-provoking because it has been associated with punishment in the past. According to Goldstein and Chambless, the agoraphobic who is trapped in an unsatisfactory marriage feels anger toward her spouse but is incapable of expressing this feeling. Instead she feels anxious, which she attributes to some external agent or for which she is unable to identify a cause.

A third angle on the attributional problems of agoraphobics was offered by Brehoney and Geller (1981), who suggest that agoraphobics fail to make distinctions among various arousing states. Instead, they experience all arousal as aversive and indicative of impending anxiety or panic. They note that the tendency of agoraphobics to experience anxiety in novel situations may be due to a failure to distinguish excitement from anxiety.

Panic Attacks

Low levels of assertiveness and self-sufficiency, a high degree of background stress, and perhaps a tendency to misattribute the causes of emotional reactions may set the stage for the development of agoraphobia. The onset of the syndrome itself, however, is marked by the experience of extreme anxiety—the panic attack. It has been suggested that the panic attack may be the product of chronic high levels of anxiety resulting from the predisposing factors that have been described. Mathews et al. (1981) write, "This attack is . . . the joint product of increased general anxiety and exposure to arousing environmental stimuli, which together provokes an upward spiral of autonomic responses" (p. 48). In a similar analysis, Goldstein and Chambless (1978) suggest that the panic attack is likely to occur when the interpersonal conflict, presumed to be the cause of generalized anxiety, persists. The first attack usually coincides with a significant stressor such as illness or the death of a loved one. The panic attack itself likely reinforces the agoraphobic client's view that she is helpless and needs someone to take care of her. Thus she continues to feel trapped in the interpersonal relationship. The situations most feared by agoraphobics and most often associated with panic attacks are those in which escape is impeded by either physical or social barriers (Brehony & Geller, 1981). Goldstein and Chambless offer the intriguing suggestion that these situations may serve to remind the agoraphobic that she is trapped in her life situation and may therefore produce anxiety through a process of "semantic generalization."

Cognitive processes also appear to be important in the onset and maintenance of panic attacks. Interpretation of physical symptoms of mild anxiety as signals of an impending heart attack, death, or insanity likely lead to increased anxiety, which itself may support the client's catastrophic interpretation. This cycle of thoughts and feelings may propel the client into a panic attack. A more detailed description of the cognitive analysis of panic attacks will be presented later in this chapter.

Avoidance

Avoidance of crowds, shopping malls, grocery stores, theaters, and the like appears to develop after the agoraphobic has experienced one or more panic attacks (Thyer & Himle, 1985). Several factors have been implicated in the development and maintenance of agoraphobic restrictions. As was mentioned earlier in our discussion of the classical conditioning model, escape from the situation in which the agoraphobic experiences anxiety is likely strengthened by the decrease in fear associated with leaving. Escape behavior, therefore, may be learned through negative reinforcement (Brehoney & Geller, 1981).

Once an agoraphobic starts to avoid difficult situations, other factors appear to become operative in maintaining avoidance. *Fear of fear* refers to the anxiety experienced by agoraphobics in anticipation of the consequences of feeling afraid (Goldstein & Chambless, 1978). Loss of control of bodily functions, fainting, mental illness, heart attacks, and even death are concerns expressed by agoraphobics about the consequences of allowing themselves to feel frightened. Because the consequences of fear are so great, situations that are associated with feeling frightened are avoided. When an agoraphobic knows that she will be taking a trip, for example, the anxiety experienced in anticipation of the journey is often greater than during the actual event (Marks, 1969).

Once the avoidance pattern is well established, agoraphobic clients may come to view themselves, and may be viewed by others, as "sick" or in need of special treatment. The spouse, children, or parents frequently assume many of the agoraphobic individual's responsibilities. Consequently, avoidance becomes more acceptable to the client and those around her. Adoption of the sick role, therefore, can be another factor that restricts the agoraphobic.

In those agoraphobic clients whose marital relationships are stressed, it has been suggested that avoidance may serve to maintain the marriage (Goldstein & Chambless, 1978; Milton & Hafner, 1979). Two factors may be operative in these cases. First, for the agoraphobic, leaving the marriage may not be a realistic option, because the idea of independent living is untenable. Second, the spouse may feel compelled to stay in the marriage in order to help and support the client. Although the research literature does not support the notion that these factors operate in all agoraphobics, there is evidence that they may be important in some cases (see Thorpe & Hecker, 1991, for a review of the salient literature).

Summary of Integrative Models

The integrative models of agoraphobia that have been presented in recent years share some common features. Predisposing factors important to these models include a lack of assertion skills, a poor sense of self-sufficiency, high levels of background stress, and a tendency to make attributional errors about the causes of anxiety. The experience of one or more panic attacks is also an important factor in the development of the disorder. The panic attack may reinforce the client's view of herself as incapable of self-care and hence dependent on someone else. Avoidance appears to develop after the onset of panic attacks. Fear of the consequences of fear and adoption of a sick role are factors that may serve to maintain agoraphobic avoidance. Once a pattern of avoidance is established, relationship factors may undermine the efforts of some clients to achieve increased mobility.

Treatments Based on Integrative Models

The integrative models of agoraphobia have led clinicians and researchers to investigate alternative approaches to treatment. These treatments have in common the assumption that if the factors that predispose an individual to develop the syndrome, or are implicated in the maintenance of the disorder, can be ameliorated, then additional improvements may be obtained, with relapse less likely. At least three approaches to treatment have been inspired by the integrative models. Assertiveness training may help agoraphobics learn to express themselves more effectively and to develop a stronger sense of self-sufficiency. Cognitive therapy has been used to address the attributional errors frequently seen in these clients. Finally, marital therapy has been employed in an effort to change the relationship factors that may be instrumental in the development and maintenance of the disorder.

Assertiveness Training

As we have seen, the available research suggests that people with agoraphobia are characteristically underassertive. This deficit in assertiveness has been assigned a prominent role in at least one model of agoraphobia (Goldstein & Chambless, 1978). According to this view, agoraphobic anxiety develops during interpersonal conflict in which the agoraphobic has not asserted herself. Because she lacks the skills necessary to resolve the interpersonal conflict, the agoraphobic finds herself trapped in the interpersonal struggle. On the basis of this idea, it has been suggested that assertiveness training may be useful in ameliorating agoraphobic anxiety and avoidance.

Early studies of behavior therapy for agoraphobia sometimes included assertiveness training, but it was used in combination with systematic desensitization and hence was not the chief focus of interest (Gelder & Marks, 1966). The first empirical investigation specifically to address assertiveness training with agoraphobics was conducted by Emmelkamp, van der Hout, and de Vries (1983). They compared three treatments in a between-group investigation. The treatments were: assertiveness training; prolonged in vivo exposure; and the combination of assertiveness training with in vivo exposure. All three treatments led to significant improvements on measures of phobic anxiety and avoidance, but there were also significant between-group differences. A clear advantage for in vivo exposure, alone or in combination with assertiveness training, over assertiveness training alone was found on measures of phobic severity. Assertiveness training and the combined treatment led to significant improvement on measures of assertiveness, which in vivo exposure alone did not. A criticism of this study is that it employed an assertiveness training procedure that focused on teaching clients assertion skills. An alternative method of assertiveness training focuses on changing the negative self-statements that underlie low assertiveness. It has been argued that effective assertiveness training should include cognitive restructuring techniques to address these negative beliefs (Cavallaro, 1987; Schwartz & Gottman, 1976).

In a partial replication of the Emmelkamp et al. (1983) study, Thorpe, Freedman, and Lazar (1985) compared in vivo exposure to an assertiveness training package that included both cognitive and skill development techniques. Their results were similar to those of Emmelkamp and his associates: In vivo exposure was a more effective treatment of avoidance and phobic anxiety, and assertiveness training was more effective in ameliorating assertion deficits.

In a third study of assertiveness training and agoraphobia, Cavallaro (1987) compared two approaches to assertiveness training, one based on the skills deficit model of assertiveness and the other based on a cognitive model. Although she found few treatment differences, assertiveness training did lead to significant improvement on measures of phobic anxiety and avoidance as well as on assertion.

In summary, comparison studies of assertiveness training and in vivo exposure treatments show a clear advantage for in vivo exposure when anxiety and avoidance are the primary targets of treatment. In vivo exposure has minimal effects on assertiveness. Across studies, however, assertiveness training has led to improvements on measures of agoraphobia. The results suggest that, though not a primary treatment for agoraphobia, assertiveness training may be a useful adjunct to in vivo exposure methods.

Cognitive Therapy

Cognitive distortions have been implicated in the development and maintenance of agoraphobia. Several types of errors in information processing have been suggested. Agoraphobic clients have been described as misattributing the true cause of their anxiety, failing to distinguish among various states of arousal, attributing anxiety inaccurately to external stimuli, and catastrophically misinterpreting body sensations. Cognitive restructuring procedures would appear to be a useful approach to treatment given these cognitive errors. Of the several available studies on the efficacy of cognitive approaches, we shall focus in this section on those that have targeted agoraphobic avoidance and anticipatory anxiety. Studies of cognitive therapy for panic attacks and panic disorders will be addressed in a later section.

In comparison studies of cognitive restructuring and in vivo exposure, exposure methods have generally been found to be more effective. Emmelkamp, Kuipers, and Eggeraat (1978) compared prolonged in vivo exposure with a cognitive restructuring treatment package that employed various cognitive techniques. In vivo exposure was clearly superior. However, several problems with this study limit the findings. First, a crossover technique was employed in which both procedures were implemented over a two-week period. Cognitive procedures may take time to have their effects because clients need to assimilate a new style of thinking. The crossover design did not allow for the examination of potential long-term effects. In a subsequent study with a between-group design, Emmelkamp and Mersch (1982) did in fact find evidence for delayed effects of cognitive restructuring. In this study, in vivo exposure was again superior to cognitive restructuring at posttest. The differences disappeared at one-month follow-up, however, as a result of continued improvement for the subjects treated with cognitive restructuring and a slight deterioration for the in vivo condition.

A second criticism of the Emmelkamp et al. (1978) study is that cognitive restructuring consisted of a combination of cognitive techniques including relabeling of anxious feelings, discussion of irrational beliefs, and self-instructional training. Differential effects for different cognitive procedures were therefore confounded. Thorpe, Hecker, Cavallaro, and Kulberg (1987) examined the effects of different cognitive restructuring techniques in the treatment of clinical phobias. Half the clients treated in this study were agoraphobic. A procedure that focused on helping clients gain *insight* into irrational beliefs was compared with one that emphasized *rehearsal* of positive self-statements. Although few strong treatment differences emerged, those that did gave the edge to the *insight* approach. The results did indicate, in any event, that cognitive restructuring led to significant improvements in phobic avoidance and anxiety. Furthermore, as in the Emmelkamp and Mersch (1982) study, continued improvement occurred over the one-month follow-up period subsequent to each intervention.

Cognitive restructuring techniques therefore show promise as an adjunct to exposure methods in the treatment of agoraphobic avoidance and anticipatory fear. Although direct comparisons give the edge to in vivo exposure methods at the conclusion of therapy, follow-up studies suggest continued improvement for clients treated with cognitive procedures.

Marital Therapy

The integrative models of agoraphobia have focused attention on the interpersonal context in which the disorder develops and is maintained. The marital relationship has been a particular concern for some clinicians and researchers. It has been suggested that the spouses of agoraphobic clients may pressure clients to "return to more dependent behavior once the client begins to function more autonomously" (Goldstein & Chambless, 1978, p. 57). Thus, treatment failure and relapse may be due to relationship factors in at least some agoraphobics. Hafner (1977, 1979) has reported that some clients treated with intensive, brief in vivo exposure therapy improved less, and were more likely to relapse, if their marriages were problematic. In some cases, for example, the clients' husbands became very jealous when their agoraphobic wives improved. These women relapsed in their agoraphobic symptoms. Milton and Hafner (1979) and Bland and Hallam (1981) found that clients with unsatisfactory marriages improved less and were more likely to relapse than were agoraphobics from satisfactory marriages. This finding, however, has not been consistently replicated. Other investigators have found no relationship between marital satisfaction and response to exposure treatment (Emmelkamp, 1980; Himaldi, Cerny, Barlow, Cohen, & O'Brien, 1986).

Similar inconsistencies are found when the related question of whether marriages of agoraphobics are affected by exposure treatment is examined. In most studies, inconsistent, and oftentimes opposite, relationships between agoraphobia improvement and marital satisfaction are found across different clients. In some clients, improvement in agoraphobic symptoms is accompanied by a deterioration in marital adjustment, whereas in others the opposite relationship is found (Barlow, Mavissakalian, & Hay, 1981; Milton & Hafner, 1979). In one study, for example, out of the six clients treated, two showed improvement in agoraphobia with concomitant deterioration in marital satisfaction, whereas four showed parallel improvement in agoraphobia and marital adjustment (Barlow et al., 1981).

Given the fact that, in at least some cases, marital factors and treatment response interact, it would seem important to examine the effect of including spouses in treatment. Barlow, O'Brien, and Last (1984) found an advantage for including spouses in group treatment of agoraphobia when cognitive restructuring and self-initiated exposure were employed. Mathews, Teasdale, Munby, Johnston, and Shaw (1977) showed that a home-based treatment program that used spouses as therapists was beneficial in treating agoraphobic complaints. Recent research has shown that couples communication training following exposure treatment led to greater improvement than did exposure plus couples relaxation training (Arnow, Taylor, Agras, & Telch, 1985). Communication training focused on helping couples to identify and change styles of interacting that might interfere with agoraphobics' efforts to overcome their phobic avoidance.

Although it is clearly not a general phenomenon, some marriages are negatively affected when an agoraphobic spouse makes improvement. Furthermore, for some clients, relationship factors may undermine therapeutic gains. Given these findings, clinicians need to examine the interpersonal relationships of agoraphobic clients closely before launching into a behavioral treatment. Marital therapy may be an appropriate addition to prolonged in vivo exposure in some cases.

COGNITIVE MODEL OF PANIC DISORDER

To return to an important recent development that we introduced in Chapter 1, cognitive models of panic disorder have recently been proposed by Beck (1988) and Clark (1986, 1988). Though developed independently, these models are strikingly similar and will be presented together. The cognitive model provides the theoretical basis for the cognitive-behavioral treatment of panic disorder presented in Chapter 5.

The crux of the cognitive model of panic disorder is the idea that a panic attack results from catastrophic misinterpretation of what are essentially normal body sensations. The sensations are usually ones that make up a nonpathological anxiety response. Increased heart rate, sweating, and rapid breathing are examples of sensations associated with anxiety that are misinterpreted by panic disorder clients. Instead of viewing these feelings as relatively harmless, the panic disorder client interprets them as signals of impending disaster. Heart palpitations, for example, are perceived as signs of an incipient heart attack. Similarly, dizziness may be taken as evidence for a stroke, and concentration impairment as a signal that the client is about to lose his mind. Because the belief that some physical or psychological disaster is about to befall the client is itself anxiety-producing, the sensations of anxiety are exacerbated, which is taken as further evidence for the dreaded outcome (Clark, 1986). Thus, a mutually escalating cycle of thoughts and sensations is established, which results in the panic attack. Figure 3.1 illustrates the cyclical relationship between bodily sensations and cognitions central to the cognitive model of panic attacks. Once the panic cycle is established, a variety of physical sensations can serve as triggers. In our clinical work, for example, we have seen a client in whom panic attacks were triggered by perceived distortions in body schema (for example, perception of the cheeks feeling swollen), another for whom simply thinking about breathing tended to induce panic, and another whose panics began when she noticed a sensation of warmth in her face.

Beck (1988) describes five essential characteristics of panic disorder from the cognitive standpoint. First, the individual who is likely to experience a panic attack is one who is keenly sensitive to bodily sensations that do not seem to be normal. Second, the client is most likely to focus attention on these sensations if a nonthreatening explanation cannot be found and if a catastrophic interpretation could potentially account for them. Catastrophic interpretations seem to fall into three general classes of disaster: biological (death), mental (insanity), or behavioral (loss of control). Third, the client's attention is riveted to the potentially dangerous sensation, which serves to exacerbate autonomic arousal. Fourth, the cycle illustrated in Figure 3.1 is created by the reciprocally intensifying relationship between cata-

FIGURE 3.1 Panic cycle of thoughts and feelings.

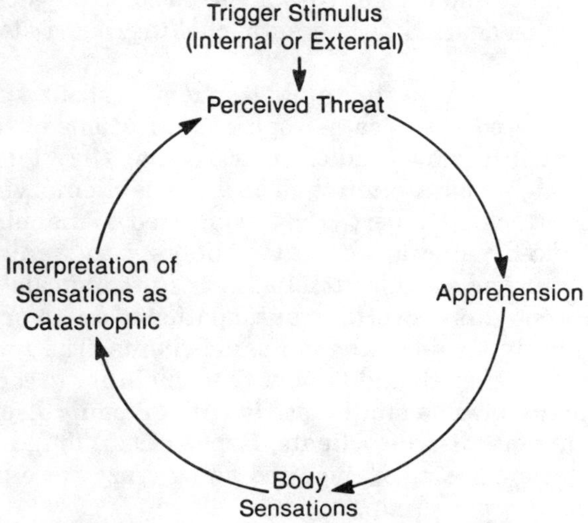

Source: From Clark, D. (1986). A cognitive approach to panic. *Behaviour Research and Therapy, 24,* 361–370, Figure 1, p. 463. Copyright 1986 Pergamon Press. Reprinted by permission.

strophic interpretations and anxious sensations. Fifth, there is a loss of capacity to evaluate physical symptoms realistically.

The cognitive models developed by Beck and Clark were based for the most part on clinical experience with anxious clients. Beck (1988) is careful to point out that the model is descriptive and does not necessarily imply a primarily biological or psychological causation. Although empirical support for the model is limited, relevant research findings are beginning to emerge.

Empirical Support for the Cognitive Model

One method of examining the accuracy of the cognitive model would be to study clients' phenomenological descriptions of panic attacks. Clients frequently report that the first thing they notice during a panic episode is some physical sensation (Hibbert, 1984; Ley, 1985). This is, of course, consistent with the cognitive model. Clients' descriptions of cognitions associated with panic are also consistent with the model. Ottaviani and Beck (1987) examined the thoughts and images experienced during the early stage of panic episodes in 30 clients who met DSM-III criteria for panic disorder. In every case, panic attacks were preceded by thoughts and images that involved some physical or psychological catastrophe: death, loss of breath, choking, heart attack, or going crazy.

Panic disorder clients appear to think frequently about bodily sensations and about the potential catastrophic implications of these sensations. Two recent interview studies indicate that they tend to have these types of thoughts more often than do anxious clients who do not experience panic attacks. Hibbert (1984) compared 17 nonphobic patients who experienced panic attacks to 8 clients who were also nonphobic but had never had a panic attack. The results indicate that the panic clients had thoughts concerning anticipation of death or loss of control more frequently than did the nonpanic clients. The groups did not differ in how often they thought about their inability to cope or about social embarrassment. In a similar study with 38 panic disorder and 48 generalized anxiety disorder clients, Rapee (1985) found that thoughts of heart attack, fainting, dying, and going crazy were more common in the panic disorder group.

A third line of inquiry that has lent some support to the cognitive model of panic disorder comes from laboratory studies in which panic attacks have been induced in panic disorder clients. As we have seen in Chapter 2, a variety of pharmacological agents can be used to induce panic attacks in the laboratory. Probably the most frequently used method is sodium lactate infusion. Between 60 and 90 percent of panic disorder clients will experience an attack when given an infusion of sodium lactate (Clark, 1988). In contrast, only 0 to 20 percent of normals and anxious clients who have never experienced a panic attack will have one under these conditions. This differential response to sodium lactate has been seen by some as support for a purely biological explanation for panic disorder (Carr & Sheehan, 1984; Klein, 1981). There are, however, other reasonable explanations for these results. Lactate infusions produce a variety of physiological and biochemical changes, many of which can be perceived by the client (Liebowitz et al., 1985). Thus, it is possible that panic disorder clients detect these changes and catastrophically misinterpret them, as suggested in the cognitive model. Furthermore, inconsistencies in experimental instructions may account for the different responses to lactate infusion experienced by the panic and nonpanic patients. For example, in one study panic disorder clients were told they "might experience a panic attack" prior to receiving the infusion, whereas control subjects were told they might experience "an attack with symptoms analogous to those of public speaking" (Appleby, Klein, Sachar,

& Levitt, 1981). Different instructions may have set the stage for different responses in the two groups. The influence of preinfusion instructions was studied by van der Molen, van den Hout, Vroemen, Lousberg, and Griez (1986). In a double-blind, placebo-controlled, crossover study, they found that subjects were more likely to panic if they were told that a sodium lactate infusion would produce anxiety than if they were told it would produce a state of pleasant excitement. When subjects were given an infusion of glucose, the effect of the instructions was not evident. Expecting a panic attack appears to influence how clients interpret sensations produced by sodium lactate infusion. When they expect to panic, clients are more likely to interpret physiological sensations as indicative of an attack.

Treatment Studies

Treatment of panic disorder, according to the cognitive model, would need to break the cycle between physiological sensations and catastrophic thoughts in order to be effective. One approach to this problem would be to identify catastrophic misinterpretations and to test their validity through discussion and behavioral experiments (Clark, 1988). A second approach might be to have the clients learn, by repeatedly experiencing the physical sensations associated with a panic attack, that the dreaded consequences of these sensations do not, in fact, occur. Both approaches have been tested in recent treatment studies.

In an early study that predated the explication of the cognitive model by Beck and Clark, cognitive-behavioral treatment of three panic disorder clients was described by Waddell, Barlow, and O'Brien (1984). Treatment consisted of cognitive therapy followed by a combination of cognitive therapy and relaxation training in a multiple-baseline across-subjects design. Cognitive therapy involved identifying maladaptive beliefs and examining them objectively, focusing on illogical thought patterns frequently associated with anxiety, and practicing the use of coping self-statements. Progressive muscle relaxation procedures were added to cognitive treatment during the final phase of the intervention. There was a marked decrease in frequency and duration of panic attacks following the introduction of cognitive therapy for each client. Improvements were maintained throughout the combined procedure.

David Clark and Paul Salkovskis have tested a treatment procedure that derives directly from the cognitive model as described by Clark (1986, 1988) but emphasizes the role of hyperventilation in panic disorder. Treatment consisted of three phases: voluntary hyperventilation, description of the effects of overbreathing and reattribution of the sensations produced by hyperventilation, and training in respiratory control techniques. Clark, Salkovskis, and Chalkley (1985) found that this intervention led to a significant reduction in the frequency of panic attacks. Their subjects were chosen because their panic attacks appeared to involve breathing irregularities. In a subsequent study, a marked decrease in panic attacks following intervention was again found (Salkovskis, Jones, & Clark, 1986). In the second study, there was also evidence suggesting that clients' improvement was related to the perceived similarity between sensations produced through hyperventilation and those experienced during a panic attack, with the clients who perceived the closest relationship improving the most. This finding is consistent with the cognitive model. Clients who perceived hyperventilation and panic as similar had an opportunity to change the attributions they made about the sensations that were typical of their panic attacks.

Utilizing a procedure similar to that employed in the Clark and Salkovskis studies, Griez and van den Hout (1986) found that repeated CO_2 (carbon dioxide) inhalation was an effective treatment for panic disorder. These researchers conceptualized panic disorder as a fear of interoceptive sensations. Following an exposure therapy paradigm, they had subjects inhale CO_2, which produces autonomic symptoms similar to those of a panic attack. CO_2 inhalation led to a 50 percent reduction in panic attacks. Although Griez and van den Hout did not give subjects explicit reattributional instructions regarding the sensations produced by CO_2 inhalation, their subjects did have the experience of these sensations as nondangerous. Thus it is possible, and perhaps likely, that clients formed their own new attributions regarding the dangerousness of their sensations.

The first report of a large-scale controlled study investigating cognitive therapy in the treatment of panic disorder has recently appeared. Barlow, Craske, Cerny, and Klosko (1989) treated over 40 panic disorder clients in one of three conditions: exposure to panic sensations and cognitive therapy; relaxation therapy developed specifically for panic disorder (modeled after Ost, 1988); and a combination of exposure to panic sensations, cognitive therapy, and relaxation therapy. These treatments were compared to a waiting-list control condition. The results indicated that clients in all three treatment conditions improved more than the control group on a variety of measures. Of those clients who completed the study, over 85 percent of those who were treated in conditions which included cognitive therapy were panic-free at posttreatment. Only the conditions that included cognitive therapy yielded results superior to the waiting-list control on this measure.

The few studies that have examined cognitive approaches to the treatment of panic disorder have been encouraging not only in terms of the reduction in panic attacks they seem to produce, but also in that the results are consistent with the cognitive model.

Summary of Cognitive Model

According to the cognitive model, panic attacks result from catastrophic misinterpretations of essentially normal bodily sensations. The anxiety created by these misinterpretations produces further evidence for the expected catastrophe, which in turn results in exacerbated anxiety. Once this cyclical relationship is established, panic disorder clients live in fear of continued attacks. Support for the cognitive model is found from at least three sources. First, when the conscious cognitive processes of panic clients are examined, they indicate a vigilance for potentially dangerous sensations and concerns about death or loss of control. Second, manipulation of expectations prior to introduction of pharmacological agents that tend to produce attacks in panic patients produce findings consistent with the cognitive model. When patients are led to believe that they will likely have a panic attack, they tend to do so. Nonpanic expectations make a panic attack less likely. Finally, preliminary studies of treatments that have developed from the cognitive model have yielded encouraging results. Interventions that involve some combination of inducing panic sensations and reattributing these sensations as nondangerous have led to significant reductions in the frequency and intensity of panic attacks.

CONCLUDING REMARKS

Although it is difficult to confirm theories of the etiology of panic and agoraphobia syndromes, behavioral and cognitive formulations of these disorders have led to several viable treatments. When handicapping avoidance is present, systematic programs of exposure to relevant settings have proved remarkably successful. When panic attacks cannot be linked to specific surroundings, treatment emphasizing reattribution and cognitive restructuring has shown encouraging results. Comprehensive clinical management often requires additional interventions to address various individual differences. These include marital distress, assertiveness difficulties, and unhelpful attributional styles.

PART TWO ───────────────────

Clinical Management of Panic Disorder and Agoraphobia

───────────────────

The procedures for cognitive behavioral treatment of panic disorder and agoraphobia are described in Part Two. These approaches follow from the models of panic disorder with and without agoraphobia outlined in Chapter 3. The assessment and treatment procedures are those that are most strongly supported by clinical research findings. Where empirical findings are not available, guidelines for clinical decision making are discussed.

Chapter 4, "Diagnosis and Assessment," describes the initial stage of clinical management. Guidelines for making differential diagnoses and common problems in the diagnostic process are discussed. Procedures for behavioral assessment of panic disorder and agoraphobic clients, including self-monitoring, questionnaire measures, and behavioral assessment, are presented. In Chapter 5, "Panic: Psychological Approaches to Treatment," the steps in cognitive-behavioral treatment of panic attacks are described in detail. Examples of verbatim treatment rationales and excerpts from sessions are also included. Chapter 6, "Exposure-Based Treatment of

Agoraphobic Avoidance," provides an overview of the parameters of in vivo exposure therapy. Imaginal exposure procedures are also presented, along with suggestions for situations in which the clinician might consider using imagery procedures. Case examples and relevant research findings are discussed. Chapter 7, "Adjuncts to Cognitive-Behavioral Treatment of Panic Disorder and Agoraphobia," looks beyond panic attacks and phobic avoidance to related problems that clients bring with them to treatment. Marital difficulties, assertiveness deficits, personality disorders, alcohol abuse, and depression are discussed, and the clinician is provided with some guidelines for developing treatment plans for clients presenting with complex problems. Case examples are used to illustrate how treatment of the anxiety disorder and related problems can be integrated. Part Two closes with Chapter 8, "The Course of Treatment," in which three detailed case illustrations are described and the unique issues presented by each are discussed.

CHAPTER 4

Diagnosis and Assessment

The assessment of panic disorder and agoraphobia is a multistage process. The first step is to establish the diagnosis. The second is to examine the degree and specificity of the disability so that appropriate treatment targets can be established. The third step is to identify and evaluate related problems. Finally, continued evaluation throughout the course of treatment is necessary to examine progress and identify potential stumbling blocks to effective therapy.

DIAGNOSTIC PROCEDURES

Panic disorder clients are referred to mental health facilities through a variety of channels. In the case of agoraphobia, friends or relatives who have learned of the disorder through the popular press or personal experience will often encourage a client to seek mental health services. Panic disorder clients with less severe agoraphobic avoidance are more frequently referred by physicians to whom they have presented themselves complaining of the physiological symptoms of panic or fearing that they may have had a heart attack. Regardless of the source of the referral, it is important that mental health clinicians be aware of physiological disorders that can produce anxiety and panic. Some of the physiological disorders that produce features characteristic of anxiety include hyperthyroidism, Cushing's syndrome, hypoparathyroidism, pheochromocytoma, mitral valve prolapse, temporal lobe epilepsy, hypoglycemia, and caffeine intoxication (McCue & McCue, 1984). Before a diagnosis of panic disorder is confirmed, it is important to know whether a client has had a thorough physical evaluation to test for the presence of these or other disorders. Some of these disorders can be managed effectively with medical procedures, and this should precede a cognitive-behavioral intervention. Some of the physical disorders that are associated with panic attacks are described in Appendix A.

Identification of a physical cause for panic symptoms does not, in and of itself, preclude either the diagnosis of panic disorder or the use of a cognitive-behavioral intervention. Physical conditions may coexist with panic disorder (Barlow, 1988). In deciding whether or not to treat the panic disorder in its own right, the crucial test is whether or not the client continues to panic once the physical disorder has been diagnosed, explained to the client, and treated. For example, one of our clients was referred for treatment by a cardiologist. Mitral valve prolapse had been diagnosed, and the symptoms of this condition had been explained to the client. The physician had reassured him that the occasional chest pain he experienced was not dangerous. Nonetheless, the client continued to experience panic attacks and to avoid a variety of important activities such as driving. At intake, he met diagnostic criteria for panic disorder with agoraphobia. Despite the existence of the physical condition, in vivo exposure therapy proved to be highly successful.

The presence of a physical disorder that produces panic or panic-like symptoms does not nullify the value of the cognitive model of panic disorder described in Chapter 3. Recall that the essential feature of the cognitive model is the supposition that a panic attack results from the catastrophic misinterpretation of bodily sensations. Furthermore, two important characteristics of panic disorder clients are a keen sensitivity to body sensations and the failure to find a nonthreatening explanation of these sensations (Beck, 1988). If a client has a physical disorder such as hypoglycemia, frequent alterations in body sensation would occur, and a sensitivity for these changes might develop. If a client is unaware that she is hypoglycemic, she may interpret the relatively nondangerous sensations associated with the problem as indicative of some far graver problem, such as a stroke or developing insanity. This interpretation would likely exacerbate the symptoms, and the cycle of thoughts and feelings discussed in Chapter 3 may develop (see Figure 3.1). When the diagnosis of hypoglycemia is made and treatment initiated, the client will have a nonthreatening explanation for the physical sensations she experiences during a hypoglycemic episode. If the client doubts the explanation, however, or if she assumes that she should no longer experience the symptoms because the physical disorder has been treated, she may continue to think in catastrophic terms. In the latter case, we would expect the panics to continue, and cognitive-behavioral treatment would be in order.

DIAGNOSIS

When a client presents for help, the clinician is dependent primarily on the client's description of the problem in the initial stages of the diagnostic process. We have heard a variety of descriptions of presenting problems that, after extensive evaluation, resulted in the diagnosis of panic disorder or agoraphobia. "Nerves," "spells," and "episodes" are typical of the kinds of descriptors clients apply to panic attacks and generalized anxiety. The clinician's task is to determine whether the problem fits one of the diagnostic categories available in our current system. In reviewing some of our clients' records in preparation for this chapter, we realized that uncomplicated cases of panic disorder with or without agoraphobia are found more often in the textbook than in real life. Most clients present with a variety of issues and often describe their own conception of the problem. Marital discord, parent–child conflict, and alcohol abuse are the types of problems that frequently accompany anxiety disorders. Mood disorders, usually major depressive episode or dysthymia, can also coexist with anxiety disorders. The presence of one of these problems, however, does not preclude the diagnosis of panic disorder (American Psychiatric Association, 1987).

As mentioned earlier, in most panic disorder clients the initial panic attack occurs during a stressful life period. Frequently, therefore, the client will see the attack as having been caused by the stressful life event. For example, a client who experiences her first attack shortly after the death of a loved one may interpret the panic attack as a signal that she has never resolved her feelings about the deceased and may present this as the essential problem for which she needs help. The clinician needs to be careful to strike a balance between helping the client with the problem she has presented without misleading her into expecting that an exhaustive discussion of the deceased will reduce the frequency or intensity of the panic attacks. Although the client may develop some insights through supportive psychotherapy, empirical evidence suggests that a more direct approach is necessary to address the anxiety disorder.

In making the diagnosis of panic disorder, the clinician must first establish that the client has experienced a panic attack. In order to achieve this goal, it is probably best to start by allowing the client to describe an attack in his own words. Open-ended questions, such as, "Tell me about these spells that you mentioned," are a good way to start because they provide the client with ample scope within which to describe the experience. Specific questions can follow to clarify and expand upon the client's description. Starting with direct specific questions can be misleading in that a compliant client may give you what he thinks you want to hear. Some clinicians prefer to interject questions about irrelevant symptoms in order to detect an acquiescent response bias. Clients who respond positively to the question, "Do you find that you blink a lot?" may have adopted such a response style. Once the client has had an opportunity to describe a panic attack, the clinician can proceed to determine whether or not the experience meets the criteria for a panic attack. It is best to ask about each of the symptoms of an attack specifically. The symptoms of an attack are listed in section C of the diagnostic criteria in DSM-III-R and in Table 2.1 of Chapter 2. The current diagnostic system defines an attack as involving at least 4 of 13 possible symptoms. The presence of fewer than four symptoms is described as a "limited-symptom attack." Panic disorder clients typically report 10 or more of the 13 possible symptoms (Barlow et al., 1985).

Establishing that a client has in fact experienced a panic attack does not in and of itself determine that he has panic disorder. In questionnaire survey studies of "normal" samples, the proportion who report experiencing at least one panic attack in the past year is around 35 percent (Norton, Dorward, & Cox, 1986; Norton, Harrison, Hauch, & Rhodes, 1985). Furthermore, panic attacks are relatively common in other disorders (Barlow, 1988). One study, for example, found that 80 percent of a group of patients with major depression reported experiencing panic (Breir, Charney, & Heninger, 1984). The clinician's next task is to determine if the panic attack is triggered by any particular object or situation. For example, a client who reports panic attacks that occur only when he is lecturing to his class is more likely suffering from a form of social phobia. The panic disorder client must have had at least one experience of panic that is unexpected.

Once the clinician has determined that the client has experienced one or more panic attacks that were unexpected, the next step in the diagnostic interview is to determine the frequency of the attacks. The DSM-III-R criteria for panic disorder specify four or more attacks in the past month. It is possible to be diagnosed with panic disorder when the frequency of attacks is less than four in the past month if the client reports a persistent fear of having an attack. In these cases the disability is caused not so much by the attacks themselves as by the client's preoccupation with the possibility of having another attack.

The presence of agoraphobic avoidance needs to be inquired about directly. Usually by this point in an interview the clinician will have an idea of whether there are situations that the client avoids for fear of having a panic attack. Nonetheless, it is important to ask directly about situations that are avoided. Again, it is best to start with a relatively open-ended question, such as, "Are there any situations that typically cause you to feel panicky or which you simply avoid?" In listening to the client's description of avoided situations, the clinician needs to determine whether the client avoids the situation out of fear that escape might be difficult or help unavailable, or whether there are unrelated reasons that the client avoids these situations.

We are reminded of a client seen by one of our graduate students. The student-clinician reported that the client avoided driving and was dependent on her neighbor to take her places. Therefore, the student-clinician decided that driving should be the first target for intervention. Unfortunately, she failed to ask whether or not the client in fact had a driver's license or access to a car, which she did not. In this case it turned out that the client did not avoid driving for reasons of anxiety. In fact, she had never learned how to drive.

It is usually worthwhile to ask the client about some specific situations that are usually avoided by agoraphobics. Examples of such situations include going to the grocery store or the shopping mall, going to a movie theater, traveling on a bus or a plane, riding in or driving a car, and being alone. Many agoraphobics are also troubled by claustrophobic surroundings such as elevators or congested traffic at a stop light, and the clinician may wish to ask directly about such situations. Asking the client what it is about the situation that causes fear can provide valuable diagnostic information for determining differential diagnoses between, for example, social phobia and agoraphobia.

Another factor that a clinician needs to keep in mind when determining the extent of avoidance is the client's utilization of safety signals (Rachman, 1984). Certain persons, places, or objects are sometimes considered "safe" by agoraphobics; in the presence of one of these, the client is significantly less restricted. A safety signal can be a particular person, often a spouse or a relative, or it may be access to some safe place such as a car. People are more likely to serve as safety signals if they know about the client's problem. Agoraphobic clients are sometimes capable of almost unrestricted movement if they are with a safe person. Anxiety medication is also a very common safety signal used by people with agoraphobia. Traveling a great distance from home or entering a crowded place may be possible if the agoraphobic knows that she has her medication. Alcohol, too, can serve as a safety signal.

A client seen in one of our research studies felt he could not make the 40-minute drive to our clinic unless he had a six-pack of beer in the trunk of the car. In the six months that he worked with us, he reported that he never stopped to have a drink. Nevertheless, he could not imagine making the drive without easy access to the alcohol. At times, inanimate objects take on the properties of safety signals. Purses, bracelets, cigarettes, and flashlights have all functioned as safety signals for agoraphobics (Barlow, 1988). Failure to identify safety signals can yield a false impression of the client's degree of disability. Furthermore, weaning a client from her safety signals may become a worthwhile treatment goal.

Differential Diagnoses among the Anxiety Disorders

Panic disorder is not the only anxiety disorder in which clients experience panic attacks (Barlow, 1988). People who meet diagnostic criteria for simple and social phobia can also experience panic, as do clients with obsessive-compulsive disorder and generalized anxiety disorder. It is also possible that the same individual may meet diagnostic criteria for panic disorder as well as those for one or more of the other anxiety disorders. An accurate diagnostic formulation is crucial in treatment planning. The treatments described in Chapters 5 and 6 have demonstrated efficacy in the treatment of panic disorder. Variations of these treatments have been developed for the other anxiety disorders (see Appendix C). Differential diagnoses among the anxiety disorders are often not as straightforward as one might suspect. A thorough familiarity with the diagnostic criteria for each anxiety disorder is a necessary first step in making differential diagnoses (see Chapter 1 for an overview of the anxiety disorders). Simple and social phobia can be distinguished from panic disorder by the generality of situations in which the client experiences panic attacks. The intense emotional reaction experienced by phobic clients in the presence of feared stimuli can be equivalent to a panic attack.

It has been suggested, in fact, that clients with phobias may avoid phobic stimuli, not so much out of fear of the stimuli themselves but, rather, because they fear experiencing a panic attack (Barlow, 1988). There is some empirical support for this notion (McNally & Steketee, 1985).

In differentiating panic disorder from simple phobias, the clinician needs to determine whether the client experiences "unexpected" attacks or whether the attacks are reliably and exclusively associated with the phobic stimulus. In simple phobia the client recognizes that his or her fear is unreasonable and excessive given the actual danger presented by the phobic object or situation.

Distinguishing panic disorder with agoraphobia from other anxiety disorders, particularly social phobia and obsessive-compulsive disorder, can be particularly challenging in some cases. In each of these disorders there is often extreme avoidance of a variety of situations. Agoraphobic clients and socially phobic as well as obsessive-compulsive clients may avoid the same situations, but they do so for different reasons. In social phobia, avoidance is motivated by fear of being scrutinized or negatively evaluated by others. For example, socially phobic clients might avoid eating in restaurants because they fear humiliating themselves while eating. Agoraphobic clients who avoid eating in restaurants might do so out of a fear that, should they panic, escape would be blocked by a crowd or by the confinement of the setting. Knowledge of the demographics of agoraphobia and social phobia can also assist the clinician in making the differential diagnosis. Social phobia tends to start at an earlier age (that is, in adolescence) and is more common in males, whereas agoraphobia occurs more frequently in women and usually begins later in life (Agras et al., 1969).

In obsessive-compulsive disorder, individuals may also avoid the types of situations commonly avoided by people with agoraphobia, but they do so for different reasons. Typically, obsessive-compulsive clients fear that they may encounter a trigger for their intrusive thoughts and compulsive rituals. Lipschitz (1988), for example, described the case of a 28-year-old man who would not leave his home. At this level of description, it might appear that the man was agoraphobic. However, the client's reasons for staying home stemmed from an obsessive-compulsive problem. He feared encountering a funeral procession or passing a funeral parlor because he knew that either circumstance would trigger a fear that a family member would die. The young man would then feel compelled to cross himself 100 times while repeating a prayer. The appropriate diagnosis in this case was obsessive-compulsive disorder rather than agoraphobia.

Generalized anxiety disorder and panic disorder often coexist in the same individual. One study, for example, found that in a group of clients with panic disorder, all had shown signs of generalized anxiety disorder for 2 to 10 years prior to the first panic attack (Cloninger, Martin, Clayton, & Guze, 1981). Differentiation of the two disorders is usually based on the extent to which worry, the central feature of generalized anxiety disorder (see Chapter 2), is a broader problem. If the client reports worrying about a wider variety of issues, then a diagnosis of generalized anxiety disorder is appropriate, given the presence of the other accompanying features.

Structured Interview

Structured interviews designed to yield the information necessary to make diagnostic decisions have been developed in recent years. The Anxiety Disorders Interview Schedule—Revised (ADIS-R) (DiNardo et al., 1985) was designed to accompany the DSM-III-R. The interview was developed for clinical research purposes and is quite extensive. It provides not only the information necessary to make differential diagnoses among the DSM-III-R anxiety disorder categories, but also a history of the problem, cognitive factors in anxiety, and detailed ratings of the severity of symptoms. Furthermore, since depression and anxiety often coexist, the ADIS-R examines depressive symptoms in some detail. Finally, the interview contains sections that screen for addictive and psychotic disorders. Data from an earlier version of the interview schedule, which was tied to DSM-III, indicate that the instrument allows for the reliable diagnosis of most anxiety disorders (Barlow, 1987).

The ADIS-R is currently in use at clinical research centers throughout the world. Its value in every clinical setting, however, is somewhat limited by the length of administration—two hours or more in some cases. Administration of the full interview is not appropriate in every clinical setting (Barlow, 1988). Nonetheless, familiarity with this instrument can help the clinician understand the diagnostic organization of the DSM-III-R anxiety disorders. Furthermore, utilizing appropriate subsections from the schedule can be helpful in gathering diagnostic information while also providing a detailed clinical picture.

DIAGNOSTIC PROBLEMS

Arriving at the diagnosis of panic disorder with or without agoraphobia is rarely a straightforward task. Diagnostic interview schedules such as the ADIS-R are helpful because following the schedule ensures that the clinician will gather the breadth and depth of information necessary to arrive at a diagnosis. Nevertheless, the diagnostician in clinical practice is often presented with issues that can complicate the diagnostic procedure. Because some of these problems occur relatively frequently, we will discuss them in some detail.

The Self-Diagnosed Client: "I'm an Agoraphobic"

In the late 1970s and throughout the 1980s, the anxiety disorders received increasing amounts of attention in the popular media. Publications ranging from the *National Enquirer* to *Newsweek* have carried stories on agoraphobia and panic disorder. One consequence of this increase in media interest is that clients arrive at mental health facilities already firmly convinced of their diagnosis. In some situations this can be very valuable. Agoraphobics who might have otherwise remained house-bound for years, unsure of the cause of their restriction, may seek help once they learn that their problem has a name and can be treated. A complication that self-diagnosis presents, however, is that clients (like clinicians) are not always reliable diagnosticians. A client who may actually have one of the physical problems described in Appendix A, for example, may prematurely seek psychological intervention. The clinician needs to guard against accepting without reservation a client's description of her diagnosis.

The way in which a clinician gathers and interprets information can be colored by a client's description of herself as agoraphobic. The influence of "preconceived notions" on clinical judgment has been described by Arkes (1981). People tend to recall information that is consistent with their preconceived notion about which behaviors (and traits) tend to go together. It has been found that a person's "implicit personality theory" influences his or her recall of another person's behavior (Bruner & Tagiuri, 1954). In one study, for example, recalling the behavior of a child who was described as aggressive tended to trigger the inference that the child was also "cold" and "self-centered," traits commonly seen as coinciding with the trait of aggression. Consequently, more behaviors consistent with the traits of coldness and self-centeredness were recalled. Applying this finding to the diagnostic process, a clinician who knows that certain behaviors tend to be part of the agoraphobic syndrome may ask specifically about these behaviors while ignoring others that may suggest an alternative diagnostic formulation. Furthermore, our knowledge that, for example, agoraphobics tend to avoid closed places can influence our recall of the information a given client actually presented. We may remember that the client told us she avoided closed places because it fits with our preconception of agoraphobic clients, rather than because she reported this. This tendency to recall symptoms not presented but consistent with a diagnosis has in fact been found (Arkes & Harkness, 1980). In addition, under certain circumstances symptoms that were actually presented but were inconsistent with the diagnosis were not remembered.

The danger of being influenced by a client's self-diagnosis are obvious. We run the risk of designing treatment plans that do not address the client's real problem. Consequently, we may inadvertently withhold a treatment that might be more appropriate.

The Medicated Client

Oftentimes clients present to nonmedical clinicians for treatment of panic disorder while they are being treated pharmacologically for the same problem. This presents several issues with regard to treatment, which are discussed in Appendix B. Diagnostically, the medicated client also presents some special problems. Symptoms of the clinical syndrome may be attenuated by the medication. Furthermore, as we discussed earlier, medication itself may serve as a safety signal for the client. Diagnosis of a medicated client may by necessity depend on the records of the prescribing physician. When a medicated client presents for treatment, it is always a good idea to work closely with the physician who prescribed the medication.

DIAGNOSIS: RELATED DISORDERS

Individuals with panic disorder also present with a variety of other mental health issues. Often they will meet diagnostic criteria for one or more other psychiatric disorder. Sometimes they present with other anxiety disorders, but often nonanxiety disorders occur along with panic disorder. Some types of disorder co-occur with panic disorder with some frequency, and we will discuss these here. In order to develop the appropriate diagnostic formulation using the *Diagnostic and Statistical Manual,* however, the clinician must first understand the general organization of the DSM-III-R.

The DSM-III-R utilizes certain rules of hierarchy for assigning multiple diagnoses (American Psychiatric Association, 1987). The rules are not as extensive as those used in the previous edition of the manual. In the DSM-III, for example, if an affective disorder such as major depression was diagnosed, than an additional diagnosis of panic disorder would not have been given even if the client met diagnostic criteria, if the panic attacks occurred only during an episode of major depression. This decision rule was based on the notion that major depression was a "more pervasive" disorder and, therefore, higher in the hierarchy than panic disorder. Clinical research and experience have led to the elimination of most of the DSM-III hierarchy rules in the DSM-III-R. Major depression and panic disorder would both be diagnosed when a client meets diagnostic criteria for each disorder using DSM-III-R. There are, however, some general rules that have been carried over to the DSM-III-R.

The first general hierarchy rule in DSM-III-R is that "nonorganic" diagnoses should not be given when an "organic mental disorder" can account for the client's symptoms. This rule would be applicable in the case of panic disorder if the panic attacks can be accounted for by an organic anxiety syndrome. These syndromes can have a variety of biological bases, but typically involve an endocrine disorder or use of a psychoactive substance (for example, caffeine or cocaine). Several of the physiologically based problems described in Appendix A can cause an organic anxiety syndrome. As we have seen, a diagnosis of panic disorder may still be appropriate if the physical problem has been successfully treated and the client continues to experience panic attacks.

The second general hierarchy rule deals with the pervasiveness of different disorders. A less pervasive disorder is not given as the diagnosis if its defining symptoms are symptoms of a more pervasive disorder. An example from the anxiety disorders might be the co-occurrence of obsessive-compulsive disorder and simple phobia in the same client. A diagnosis of simple phobia of dirt would not be appropriate for a client with obsessive-compulsive disorder whose problem focuses around a fear of contamination (Lipschitz, 1988). More than one diagnosis should be given, however, when characteristics of one disorder are not subsumed within the defining characteristics of another.

Depression

Depression is a common concomitant of panic disorder with and without agoraphobia. A recent review of the clinical research literature found that when clients present with a diagnosis of panic disorder or agoraphobia, estimates of the percentage who also have some type of depression vary from 45 percent to 92 percent. Averaging across studies, 67 percent of patients presenting with panic disorder are also depressed (Clark, 1989). Examining the problem from another angle, when clients present with a diagnosis of major depression, 8 percent to 39 percent will also have panic disorder or panic disorder with agoraphobia (Clark, 1989). The frequency with which panic disorder and depression occur together makes it crucial for clinicians to assess for depression when evaluating anxious clients.

The most obvious feature of depression is a mood state that is marked by sadness. There is usually a loss of motivation and a lack of interest in most activities, including activities that the client usually finds pleasurable. Disturbances in sleep patterns and appetite are also associated with depression. Depressed individuals often lose weight without dieting. Sleep disturbances can involve either insomnia (that is, difficulty falling asleep, frequent wakening, or early morning wakening) or hypersomnia (excessive sleeping). Depressed people typically report difficulty in concentrating, feelings of worthlessness, and thoughts about death or suicide. A major depressive episode is defined by the presence of all or most of these symptoms for a period of at least two weeks.

Mood disorders are organized in the DSM-III-R into two general types, bipolar disorders and depressive disorders. The bipolar disorders are marked by one or more manic episodes, discrete periods of abnormally elevated or expansive mood. These episodes usually begin suddenly and can last from days to months. Bipolar disorders are much rarer than depressive disorders, and the clinical research does not indicate any particular link with panic disorder.

When panic disorder and a mood disorder occur together in the same person, the latter is usually a type of depressive disorder. The types of depressive disorders are major depression and dysthymia. Major depression involves one (single-episode) or more (recurrent) major depressive episodes as defined previously. In most studies, major depression is the type of depressive disorder that is found to coincide with panic disorder (Clark, 1989). Dysthymia, a disorder that is marked by a chronically depressed mood, has been seen in a large number of clients with panic disorder with agoraphobia in at least one study (Sheehan & Sheehan, 1982). Clients with this disorder report feeling sad or depressed on most days. The associated symptoms of depression, such as appetite and sleep disturbances, low energy, poor concentration, and feelings of hopelessness, are also present in dysthymia but are not as pronounced as in a major depressive episode.

Personality Disorders

Behaviorally oriented clinicians and researchers have traditionally paid little attention to personality disorders when studying and treating psychopathology. This disregard of "characterological" problems was likely due to two factors. First, the whole notion of personality traits has been eschewed by behavioral thinkers in favor of increased attention to variables that maintain observed behavior. Although one could accept the idea of personality disorders without accepting a trait view of personality, a second problem for empirically minded clinicians and researchers has been the poor diagnostic reliability of the personality disorders.

There has, however, been a recent emergence of interest in personality disorders and their possible role in the etiology and maintenance of anxiety disorders among cognitive-behavioral clinical researchers (for example, Chambless & Renneberg, 1988, cited in Brooks, Baltazar, & Munjack, 1989). This interest has likely been spurred on by improvements in the diagnostic system and the development of structured interviews, which have dramatically improved the diagnostic reliability of the personality disorders (Pfohl, Stangl, & Zimmerman, 1984). Furthermore, although the cognitive-behavioral therapies have demonstrated efficacy with most anxiety disorders, some clients fail to benefit, and many of those who improve continue to have difficulties. An examination of personality disorders may help us to understand clients who are difficult to treat and may lead to improved intervention.

A personality disorder is defined by a set of personality traits that are "inflexible" and "maladaptive" (American Psychiatric Association, 1987). Personality traits are characteristic ways of thinking, acting, and relating to oneself and others. Personality disorders are unique among the mental disorders in that they refer to behaviors or traits that have been characteristic of the individual since adolescence and throughout adult life. One never has an "episode" of personality disorder. By definition, the problems associated with the disorder are characteristic of the individual.

The personality disorders are organized into three clusters in the DSM-III-R. Cluster A (paranoid, schizoid, and schizotypal) personality disorders are characterized by odd or eccentric behavior. Cluster B (antisocial, borderline, narcissistic, and histrionic) personality disorders are marked by erratic, emotional, and excessively dramatic behavior. Finally, cluster C (avoidant, dependent, obsessive-compulsive and passive-aggressive) disorders have social anxiety and general fearfulness as common characteristics.

The question of just how frequently personality disorders and panic disorder coexist has only recently been empirically studied, and the data do not paint a clear picture at this time (see Brooks et al., 1989, for a review). Differences in diagnostic procedures appear to be at the heart of the confusion. When questionnaire measures of personality disorder are used, the prevalence of personality disorders among panic disorder clients would appear to be quite high. In one study, over 90 percent of agoraphobic subjects were found to have at least one personality disorder (Chambless & Renneberg, 1988, cited in Brooks et al., 1989). This is almost certainly an example of overdiagnosis, which was likely due to misinterpretation of questionnaire items or to response bias. Studies using structured interviews generally yield lower estimates of diagnostic overlap. Dependent and avoidant personality disorders appear to occur most frequently with panic disorder. One of these two personality disorders is seen in about 20 percent of panic disorder clients (Brooks et al., 1989).

Avoidant personality disorder is marked by extreme social withdrawal. The person with this disorder has a strong desire to be loved and accepted by others but avoids relationships out of a fear of rejection or humiliation. Typically, an individual with avoidant personality disorder has no close friends and is not willing to get involved with other people unless assured that he or she will be accepted.

The central features of dependent personality disorder are low self-esteem and dependence on others. People with this problem are submissive in relationships and allow other people to make important decisions for them. A strong fear of abandonment is presumed to underlie the submissive and dependent behavior.

We recommend that clinicians proceed with caution when considering a personality disorder diagnosis in a client presenting primarily with signs of panic disorder. There are still many questions that need to be answered about the relationship between anxiety and personality disorders. At this time, it is not clear whether the maladaptive personality traits seen in some agoraphobic clients represent distinct and autonomous phenomena or whether they are artifacts of the disorder (Brooks et al., 1989). Although we will discuss treatment of personality disorders in Chapter 7, the empirical support for therapy with these disorders is not strong. Furthermore, we have noted beneficial changes in unhelpful personality characteristics coincident with improvements in phobic avoidance in some clients.

When the characteristics of a personality disorder present themselves, clinicians should consider using a structured clinical interview to assist in diagnosis. The Structured Clinical Interview for the DSM-III-R(Axis II) (SCID-II) (Spitzer & Williams, 1984) can be used for this purpose. Although published reliability and validity data are sparse at this time, preliminary reports have been encouraging (Brooks et al., 1989) and this measure has the advantage of utilizing DSM-III-R criteria. When using the structured interview, clinicians need to caution clients to describe themselves at times when they are not experiencing panic. Without this caution, clients may endorse problems as characteristic of themselves (for example, depersonalization) that in fact occur only during panic attacks. This can lead to overdiagnosis of personality disorder.

Alcohol Abuse

The use of alcohol by some anxious clients to alleviate anticipatory anxiety and panic has long been recognized by clinicians. Westphal (Knapp, 1988, p. 74) noted that his agoraphobic patients used alcohol for this purpose, as "the pleasurable stimulation of alcohol makes it easier to overcome the painful condition." A possible consequence of the use of alcohol as an anxiolytic is the escalation of use to the point of alcohol abuse and even dependence. Although this is an established part of clinical lore, there has only recently emerged a body of empirical research examining the relationship between anxiety disorders and alcohol abuse.

Most of the research on the relationship between alcohol and anxiety disorders has focused on phobic disorders, including agoraphobia. Studies examining the prevalence of phobic disorders in samples of alcohol-dependent patients have found phobic problems to be quite common in this population. Mullaney and Trippett (1979) found that one-third of a sample of inpatient alcoholics were severely agoraphobic or socially phobic. Another third of these patients were described as "borderline" phobic. Somewhat lower rates of agoraphobia and social phobia among individuals involved in inpatient treatment for alcohol problems were reported by Smail, Stockwell, Canter, and Hodgson

(1984) who found 18 percent of their inpatient sample severely, and 35 percent mildly, phobic. Chambless, Cherney, Caputo, and Rheinstein (1987), using rigorous diagnostic interviews, found that 40 percent of a sample of 75 inpatient alcoholics received a lifetime diagnosis of one or more anxiety disorders. Interestingly, most of Chambless and colleagues' subjects with anxiety disorders and alcoholism did not perceive their anxiety disorder to be related to the development of alcohol abuse, even though most indicated that the anxiety disorder preceded abusive alcohol use. Finally, 33 percent of a sample of 48 inpatient alcoholics met criteria for phobias, including 13 percent who were agoraphobic, in a study by Bowen, Cipywnyk, D'Arcy, and Keegan (1984). Twenty-one percent of their sample met criteria for panic disorder, and 22 percent had generalized anxiety disorder.

Although these studies suggest that anxiety disorders, including panic disorder and agoraphobia, are commonly seen in inpatient alcoholic populations, not all studies have found such high rates of co-occurrence. Schuckit, Irwin, and Brown (1990) carefully interviewed 171 alcoholic male veterans undergoing inpatient treatment. They found that, although reports of anxiety symptoms were very high (98 percent reporting one or more symptoms of anxiety), these symptoms were associated with episodes of heavy drinking or withdrawal. They concluded that rates of anxiety disorders independent of heavy drinking or withdrawal occurred at a rate comparable to that expected in the general population. Alcohol-abusing populations do appear to experience panic attacks more frequently than the general population (Cox, Norton, Dorward, & Fergusson, 1989). But most of these attacks have occurred during periods of heavy drinking, during detoxification, or shortly after detoxification.

A relatively high co-occurrence of anxiety disorders and alcohol problems is found when agoraphobic clients are evaluated for alcohol abuse. Bibb and Chambless (1986) found that between 10 percent and 20 percent of a sample of agoraphobics were alcoholic. Exact prevalence rates for alcoholism in the agoraphobia sample depended on the criteria for identifying alcohol abuse or dependence. Reports of using alcohol to cope with phobic symptoms are common in people with agoraphobia (Bibb & Chambless, 1986; Smail et al., 1984). Men appear to use alcohol for its anxiolytic properties more often than women do, and alcoholism is seen more frequently in males with agoraphobia (Bibb & Chambless, 1986). A family history positive for alcoholism has also been observed in agoraphobic clients (Munjack & Moss, 1981).

The nature of the relationship between alcohol consumption problems and anxiety disorders is not clear at this time. The idea that alcohol abuse develops as a secondary complication of phobic anxiety has received equivocal support. Whereas some research has found phobic symptoms preceding the development of alcoholism (Mullaney & Trippett, 1979), others have not found a consistent order of problem onset (Bibb & Chambless, 1986). Most investigators agree that the interaction between alcohol problems and phobic anxiety is not a simple one.

The coexistence of alcohol abuse and panic disorder can complicate treatment. Clinicians are advised to screen for alcohol-related problems as a routine part of evaluating anxious clients. Inquiry usually progresses from questions about use, to abuse, and finally to dependence. "How frequently do you drink?" is a standard initial question. Evaluation of quantity of alcohol consumed and of the situations where drinking takes place follows. Next, the clinician should assess whether alcohol is used to cope with anxiety or to prepare to face feared situations. Sample questions might be, "Do you ever drink to alleviate anxiety?" or "Have you ever used alcohol to prepare to face a difficult situation?"

Alcohol abuse refers to a maladaptive pattern of alcohol use. The clinician can assess for alcohol abuse by asking whether the client has ever experienced legal or medical problems secondary to alcohol use. Social problems such as strained relationships with family or friends or a loss of job due to alcohol use also provide clues about abuse. Alcohol dependence involves the use of increasing amounts of alcohol in order to obtain the desired effect and the presence of signs of withdrawal associated with cessation of alcohol use. The quantity of alcohol consumed may suggest dependence. Smail et al. (1984), for example, found that one of their male agoraphobic subjects drank an average of 180 grams of alcohol per day (approximately 10 pints of beer or its equivalent). This man was found to be alcohol-dependent. Repeated failed efforts at ceasing alcohol use can also suggest dependence.

BEHAVIORAL ASSESSMENT

What Is Behavioral Assessment?

Behavioral *therapy* differs from traditional therapy in theory, technique, practice, and aims. Consequently, behavior therapy has required an equally distinctive approach to clinical assessment.

Behavioral assessment is an inseparable component of behavior therapy that has developed and changed in parallel with advances in therapeutic techniques (Barrios, 1988).

The chief aims of behavioral assessment are to identify clients' problems, to identify the factors that maintain them, to select appropriate treatment interventions, and to evaluate treatment effectiveness (Barrios, 1988). Assessment is conducted chiefly in order to facilitate treatment.

Behavior therapists assume that human behavior, normal and abnormal, is influenced by particular factors in the current environment and by certain client variables. To consider environmental factors, first, behavioral assessment has attended to people's behavior in specific situations, with the aim of investigating whether the problem is seen in a broad or narrow set of circumstances. This is in contrast to making the initial assumption that people will display similar behavior in different contexts. Consistent with their interest in learning principles like stimulus control and reinforcement, behavior therapists focus on the factors that precede, accompany, and follow a client's problem behavior. A client's responses to a given test situation are taken as samples of what the person *does*, rather than as signs of characteristics the person *has* (Nelson, 1983).

Consider two anxious clients who usually avoid shopping malls. One client learns to leave rapidly when doing so takes her away from claustrophobic surroundings and a stuffy atmosphere. The other learns to escape when doing so takes him away from the scrutiny of other people. Different reinforcement patterns are presumably operating in these two individuals. The next issue in assessment is for the clinician to find out how specific or general each escape pattern is. The client who fears feeling boxed in may also avoid elevators and driving through tunnels, for example. Alternatively, she may only avoid shopping centers. The second client may also avoid going to weddings or job interviews. Instead of assuming that both clients possess general phobic characteristics, the behavior therapist will delineate which situations are feared and avoided, and which are not, by each client.

To consider personal factors in behavioral assessment, imagine two clients who are distressed by recurrent panic attacks. One may report consistently feeling worse, or having more frequent attacks, when she develops the idea that there is nothing she can do to cope with the situation adequately. The other may recognize that he can endure panic attacks without losing control completely, yet may feel worse when tormented by the idea that he will make his children fearful for life unless he overcomes his problem successfully.

Behavior therapists assess a broad spectrum of issues and circumstances in the client, not only those that relate to the specific presented problem. A client who feels unable to cope with the general demands of life without the support of a devoted and capable wife may be extremely fearful of risking divorce by displeasing her. If she derives satisfaction in the relationship from helping her husband cope and from having him dependent on her, then he may fear getting better because that could mean that she would leave him. By contrast, a client who does not have a significant other will probably have different preoccupations and may approach treatment with a less ambivalent attitude.

Repeated evaluation is an important characteristic of behavioral assessment. Rather than administering a battery of tests only once, before treatment begins, behavior therapists often repeat specific evaluations of problem behavior so as to gauge the progress of treatment. Usually, several behaviors are sampled. A formerly agoraphobic client who, following treatment, can travel by public transport and remain in shopping malls for hours without discomfort may have overcome the original problem entirely, especially if she has not had a panic attack for weeks. Alternatively, however, if she still doubts her ability to withstand a panic attack should one arise, treatment is incomplete and assessment is required to determine when this aspect of her original problem has been resolved.

Self-Monitoring

Self-monitoring, which involves having the client record behaviors, thoughts, and feelings on a regular basis, is an integral component of behavioral assessment. Research has shown that frequent self-monitoring by clients of overt behavioral, cognitive, and emotional events yields far more reliable information about client functioning than does periodic recall (Barlow, 1988). Self-monitoring plays a role both in the initial assessment of panic disorder and agoraphobia and throughout treatment.

Panic Disorder

The goals of self-monitoring in a cognitive-behavioral treatment of panic disorder are to gather accurate information about the frequency, duration, and intensity of panic attacks, to identify situations and thoughts associated with panic attacks, and to monitor daily fluctuations of general anxiety. Prospective self-monitoring of panic attacks is essential for accurate diagnosis. Retrospective reports of panic frequency have been found to be fraught with exaggerations and distortions (Turner, Beidel, & Jacob, 1988).

Table 4.1 contains the self-monitoring form we use in our clinic. The form is completed daily throughout the duration of assessment and treatment. Completing the daily rating of panic attacks can help the client to start to understand his panic attacks better. The panic attacks, which are often perceived by clients as having arisen spontaneously, begin to become associated with some identifiable cues. This recognition can be therapeutic in itself in that clients can gain an increase in their sense of control over the panics when they are seen as predictable.

Agoraphobia

The initial step in developing self-monitoring instruments for use in assessment and treatment of agoraphobia is the development of a

TABLE 4.1   Daily Record of General Anxiety and Panic

Client # _____   Today's Date _____

Daily Self-Rating   Day of the Week _____

General anxiety (0 = no anxiety, 8 = extreme anxiety):

Morning	0	1	2	3	4	5	6	7	8
Afternoon	0	1	2	3	4	5	6	7	8
Evening	0	1	2	3	4	5	6	7	8
Bedtime	0	1	2	3	4	5	6	7	8

Panic attacks:

Each time you have an anxiety episode or attack when you would rate the level of anxiety at 4 or above on the 0–8 scale, please write down the following:

Time It Started	Time It Ended	Highest Level (0–8)	Where You Were	What You Were Thinking About

Episode #1: _____

Episode #2: _____

Any other comments about your anxiety today:

hierarchy of challenging situations. Development of the hierarchy is a collaborative effort between therapist and client. The goal is to come up with 8 to 10 situations that either tend to be associated with anxiety or are completely avoided by the client. Establishing the hierarchy really marks the beginning of therapy. The process of establishing the hierarchy sets the tone for cognitive-behavioral intervention. It is the first opportunity for the therapist and client to collaborate on the problem. Identifying the specific situations serves the dual functions of setting the immediate goals for therapy and demonstrating for the client that cognitive-behavioral therapy is problem-oriented.

The hierarchy of anxiety-provoking situations serves several roles in therapy. Clients rate the items in the hierarchy for the amount of fear they would experience in the situation, the likelihood that they would avoid the situation, and their confidence in their own ability to cope with the situation. Figure 4.1 contains the hierarchy rating sheet

FIGURE 4.1 Example hierarchy ratings of client ratings of fear, avoidance, and confidence.

Client # _____

Date ___6/11___

Please rate each of the situations listed below for <u>fear</u>, <u>avoidance</u>, and <u>confidence</u>.

<u>Fear</u>: How much fear would you feel in the situation?

0	1	2	3	4	5	6	7	8
No fear		Slight fear		Definite fear		Marked fear		Extreme fear

<u>Avoidance</u>: How much would you avoid the situation?

0	1	2	3	4	5	6	7	8
Would not avoid it		Slightly avoid it		Definitely avoid it		Markedly avoid it		Always avoid it

<u>Confidence</u>: How confident do you feel in your ability to handle the situation?

0	1	2	3	4	5	6	7	8
Not at all confident				Definitely confident				Perfectly confident

FIGURE 4.1 (*Continued*)

1. Driving to supermarket alone

Fear	0	1	2	③	4	5	6	7	8
Avoidance	0	①	2	3	4	5	6	7	8
Confidence	0	1	2	3	4	⑤	6	7	8

2. Walking to beautician during the day

Fear	0	1	2	③	4	5	6	7	8
Avoidance	⓪	1	2	3	4	5	6	7	8
Confidence	0	1	2	3	④	5	6	7	8

3. Working in the office alone

Fear	0	1	2	3	④	5	6	7	8
Avoidance	0	①	2	3	4	5	6	7	8
Confidence	0	1	2	3	④	5	6	7	8

4. Going to the mall alone in the daytime

Fear	0	1	2	3	④	5	6	7	8
Avoidance	0	1	2	3	4	⑤	6	7	8
Confidence	0	1	②	3	4	5	6	7	8

5. Going to lunch at the mall in the daytime

Fear	0	1	2	3	4	5	⑥	7	8
Avoidance	0	1	2	3	4	⑤	6	7	8
Confidence	0	1	2	③	4	5	6	7	8

6. Going to the mall alone at night

Fear	0	1	2	3	4	5	6	7	(8)
Avoidance	0	1	2	3	4	5	6	7	(8)
Confidence	0	(1)	2	3	4	5	6	7	8

7. Going to visit a friend in Portland

Fear	0	1	2	3	4	5	6	7	(8)
Avoidance	0	1	2	3	4	5	6	(7)	8
Confidence	(0)	1	2	3	4	5	6	7	8

8. Going out and coming back to empty house at night

Fear	0	1	2	3	4	5	6	7	(8)
Avoidance	0	1	2	3	4	5	6	(7)	8
Confidence	(0)	1	2	3	4	5	6	7	8

for one of our clients. The second role for the hierarchy items is to provide the immediate treatment targets for exposure therapy (see Chapter 6). Finally, the hierarchy items provide the basis for individualized behavioral tests, which we will discuss.

Self-monitoring for agoraphobics also usually involves a daily log or diary of activities. The daily diary (see Table 4.2) provides a record of the amount of time the agoraphobic spends outside of the home. This form provides information about the types of situations the client is able to enter and the level of anxiety associated with these encounters. In addition, it provides ratings of anxiety for each venture out of the home as well as a global measure of anxiety for the entire day. Finally, the diary provides some information on whether or not the client ventures out alone or with a "safe person." When self-exposure homework is used as part of the intervention, the daily diary provides a check on homework compliance.

TABLE 4.2 Daily Diary

Date	Activity	Time Out	Time In	Alone	Anxiety Rating Trip	Day

0 = No anxiety
2 = Mild anxiety
4 = Definite anxiety
6 = Severe anxiety
8 = As anxious as I have ever been (panic)

BEHAVIORAL TESTS

Individualized behavioral tests utilize the items from the hierarchy of challenging situations to provide data on a client's mobility and progress in therapy. The actual behavioral test can be conducted in a number of ways. Usually it will be necessary for the evaluator to travel to the client's home for the test. Several items from the hierarchy are chosen depending on the feasibility of completing them within a reasonable time period (for example, one to two hours). The client is asked to attempt the items chosen. For each item, there are three possible outcomes: (1) The client successfully completes the item; (2) the client attempts the item but cannot complete it (escaped); or (3) the client refuses to attempt the item (avoided).

It is usually a good idea for the evaluator not to accompany the client on the behavioral test, in order to avoid two potential confounds. First, the evaluator may serve as a safety signal for the client, in which case range of mobility may be overestimated. Second, the presence of the therapist may place implicit demands on the client to complete the item. In the evaluator's absence, the reliability of the client's self-report may be suspect. In collecting behavioral test data for a follow-up study of treated agoraphobics (Burns, Thorpe, & Cavallaro, 1986), it was recalled that during the original study one client was actually discovered hiding in the bushes during the timed behavioral walk. Clinical researchers have been creative in devising checks on the reliability of the client's report. Clients have been asked, for example, to pick up credit card applications from various stores in the shopping mall that is part of the behavioral test (Cavallaro, 1987). Other researchers have had clients use portable tape recorders to describe certain landmarks encountered in the behavioral test (Vermilyea, Boice, & Barlow, 1984).

An important part of the behavioral test is the evaluation of the subjective experience of anxiety during the test. This can be accomplished through the use of a portable tape recorder or a simple rating form. The degree to which a client allows herself to experience anxiety during the behavioral test can help us to understand the nature of escape and avoidance for that client. Some clients demonstrate Herculean courage in attempting difficult steps in the behavioral test. On the other hand, there are clients for whom the minimal amount of anxiety is a signal to escape the situation.

An alternative approach to the behavioral test is one developed by Thorpe et al. (1987). We constructed anxiety hierarchies with our clients and had them rate each item for anxiety, avoidance, and confidence in their ability to cope in the situation. The behavioral test involved having subjects attempt each item in the hierarchy during a one-week period. Their score on the behavioral test was equal to the number of items completed. The advantage of this type of test is that it allows for the inclusion of items that could not be attempted during a one- to two-hour meeting with an evaluator. Items such as going to the movies, attending church services, or sitting through an Alcoholics Anonymous meeting can be included in the hierarchy and attempted during the week. Often it is precisely these types of situations that are most difficult for the client and most closely related to the goals of treatment.

Standardized behavioral tests have been used extensively in clinical research with agoraphobics (Barlow, O'Brien, & Last, 1984; Burns, Thorpe, & Cavallaro, 1986). Typically, the test will involve a "behavioral walk" (Barlow, 1988). Burns (1977), for example, used a walk that took clients from the clinic to a downtown store. Clients are instructed to walk along the course until they cannot proceed further or until they complete the walk. It is usually best to instruct clients simply to "do the best that you can." This general instruction is preferable to telling clients to return if they experience excessive anxiety because it avoids the confound between the client's interpretation of "excessive anxiety" and her true behavioral capacity (Barlow, 1988). Dependent measures that can be drawn from the behavioral walk might be distance traveled or time away from a safe place.

In clinical practice, behavioral tests do not play as central a role as they do in clinical research. Typically, clinicians rely on their clients' self-report to assess their level of mobility and progress in therapy. In addition, questionnaire measures that have clients rate their ability to engage in certain activities frequently avoided by clients with agoraphobia have been developed (see the following section). We do not recommend using behavioral tests as a standard component of clinical practice unless the clinician suspects that an agoraphobic client is over- or underestimating her level of impairment. We prefer instead to ask clients to attempt specific target situations during the week and report on these during the next therapy session.

QUESTIONNAIRE MEASURES

Structured questionnaires can be a useful adjunct to careful clinical interviews and behavioral tests. The advantage of questionnaires is that they allow us to compare a client's responses against a normative data base of other anxiety disorder clients and nonanxious people. The disadvantage, of course, is that questionnaires rely on the client's memory and her ability to translate an emotional state or behavioral tendency into a numerical value. Responses to questionnaires can be influenced by factors other than the client's status. Probably the greatest concern is that as the client proceeds with treatment, she may want to report her condition as improved so as not to disappoint her therapist. Keeping these caveats in mind, there are questionnaires available that have demonstrated reliability and validity and can provide useful information for the cognitive-behavioral therapist.

Fear Questionnaire

The Fear Questionnaire, developed by Marks and Mathews (1979), yields a variety of useful ratings. The first part of the questionnaire consists of 15 items describing commonly feared situations. A sixteenth item allows the client to describe the main phobia for which she wants treatment. These items are rated by the client for the likelihood that they would be avoided because of fear. Several scores are derived from these items. The main phobia is the client's rating of the phobia for which she would like treatment. The total phobia score is the sum of the client's ratings on the 15 standard items. Three valuable subscores (agoraphobia, blood–injury, and social phobia) can be derived from the client's ratings of particular items (Marks, 1981b). The second part of the Fear Questionnaire provides ratings of anxiety/depression and a global rating of phobic symptoms. The agoraphobia subscale has been studied very closely. Mavissakalian (1986b) suggests that a score of 30 is indicative of severe agoraphobia and that a score of 10 or lower after treatment indicates significant clinical improvement (Mavissakalian, 1986a). Normative data from the general population have been provided by Mizes and Crawford (1986). The scale is reprinted in Marks and Mathews (1979).

Mobility Inventory

The Mobility Inventory is a self-report questionnaire on which clients rate the degree to which they avoid 26 situations. Each item is rated on a five-point scale from "Never Avoid" to "Always Avoid." Each item is rated twice: once for degree of avoidance alone and once for degree of avoidance when accompanied. The items were developed by Dianne Chambless and her associates from the Fear Survey Schedule (Wolpe

& Lang, 1964) and from interviews with and observations of agoraphobic clients. In addition to rating the situations for avoidance, the client is asked to report the number of panic attacks experienced in the past week. The scale is reprinted in Chambless, Caputo, Jasin, Gracely, and Williams (1985).

The Mobility Inventory has been shown to have adequate test–retest reliability and internal consistency. Support for concurrent and construct validity are also provided by Chambless et al. (1985). The Mobility Inventory has some discriminative powers as well in that agoraphobics score higher than social phobics and nonphobic controls on both the Avoidance Alone and the Avoidance Accompanied scales (Craske, Rachman, & Tallman, 1986). The two avoidance measures are only moderately correlated ($r = .67$) (Chambless et al., 1985).

The Mobility Inventory has several properties that make it a valuable clinical tool. First, it provides a quick survey of the types of situations typically avoided by agoraphobics. Second, it provides a useful distinction between the client's avoidance behavior alone and when accompanied. All this information can be extremely useful in treatment planning. Finally, the Mobility Inventory provides an efficient estimate of change in mobility coincident with treatment. Therefore, it is useful in monitoring progress in treatment without having to arrange repeated behavioral avoidance tests.

Agoraphobic Cognitions Questionnaire and Body Sensations Questionnaire

These companion questionnaires were developed to assess fear of fear in agoraphobics (Chambless, Caputo, Bright, & Gallagher, 1984). The Agoraphobic Cognitions Questionnaire asks clients to rate the frequency with which certain catastrophic thoughts occur when the client is anxious. For example, such items as "I will have a heart attack" and "I am going to die" are included. On the Body Sensations Questionnaire, clients rate how frightened or worried they typically are by certain sensations, such as "feeling short of breath" and "dizziness," which may occur when the client is anxious or frightened.

Both measures have been shown to possess adequate reliability, and some support for discriminant and construct validity has also been found (Chambless et al., 1984). Craske et al. (1986), however, found that the Agoraphobic Cognitions Questionnaire did not discriminate a group of agoraphobics from a group of social phobics, and similar observations were made by Thorpe et al. (1987).

In a clinical setting, these questionnaires can help the clinician focus on thoughts or physical sensations that are particularly troublesome for an individual client. Fears surrounding particular body sensations or specific concerns about the consequences of anxious feelings can be identified with these questionnaires and may be worthwhile targets for intervention.

Anxiety Sensitivity Index

This measure was developed by Reiss, Peterson, Gursky, and McNally (1986) on the basis of earlier work by Epstein (1982). It is a 16-item questionnaire designed to measure the construct of anxiety sensitivity, which is defined as an individual's belief that the symptoms of anxiety will have harmful consequences such as heart attack, loss of consciousness, or mental instability. Like the questionnaires developed by Chambless and her colleagues, the Anxiety Sensitivity Index presumably measures fear of fear or fear of anxiety.

Extensive work has been done with this instrument using college students as subjects. The measure has been shown to have adequate reliability (Reiss et al., 1986), and some promising data on construct validity have been gathered (Peterson & Heilbronner, 1987; Reiss, Peterson, & Gursky, 1987). In clinical studies, subjects with agoraphobia have been found to score higher than subjects with other anxiety disorders (Reiss et al., 1986).

The Anxiety Sensitivity Index can be administered quickly and may prove to be useful in designing clinical interventions, in that fear of anxious feelings appears to be at the heart of panic disorder. This instrument is reprinted in Reiss et al. (1986).

ADJUNCT MEASURES

Integrative theories of agoraphobia and panic disorder, particularly those of Goldstein and Chambless (1978) and of Stampler (1982), call attention to the role of general dysphoria (often depression), marital conflict, and personal styles of dependency and unassertiveness. Alcohol abuse can be a concomitant of panic disorder and may interfere with treatment. These issues may be conveniently assessed by specific self-report questionnaires as well as in clinical interviews.

Assertiveness

The Adult Self-Expression Scale (Gay, Hollandsworth, & Galassi, 1973) is a 48-item inventory designed to assess assertiveness in adults from the general population. Each item is rated by the client on a 0–4 scale, and the items fall into seven subcategories, which include refusing unreasonable requests, initiating conversations, and expressing positive and negative feelings. Items cover a range of interpersonal encounters involving close relatives, friends, authority figures, and the general public. The scale has adequate psychometric properties and can be conveniently included in a pretreatment test battery (Cavallaro, 1987).

Depression

The Beck Depression Inventory (Beck, Ward, Mendelson, Mock, & Erbaugh, 1961; Beck, Rush, Shaw, & Emery, 1979) is widely used as a self-report screening measure for depression. It is designed to cover the client's mood and related symptoms over a one-week period; accordingly, it may be used as a weekly barometer of progress in treatment programs for depression. Each of the 21 items consists of a mini-hierarchy of four statements reflecting progressively severe depressive symptoms. The questions are divided into several categories, including dysphoric mood; problems with sleep, eating, and energy; self-punitive attitudes; and thoughts of death or suicide. The inventory has strong internal consistency and is helpful as an indicator of treatment progress as well as serving as an initial screening measure. Nondepressed people typically record scores in a range from 2 to 18 or so, whereas depressive clients usually score from about 10 to 30 (Cavallaro, 1987). These ranges overlap, of course; many clinicians use a cutoff score of 17 to distinguish depressive from nondepressive clients, but this is somewhat arbitrary.

Marital Satisfaction

Several marital satisfaction questionnaires are available. The Maudsley Marital Questionnaire (Crowe, 1978) has been frequently used by British researchers but is less widely used in the United States. It consists of nine questions, each rated by the client on a 0–8 scale to indicate the level of marital distress. The questionnaire has been shown to have adequate psychometric properties for gauging progress in treatment, but normative data that would allow classification of couples' marriages into distressed or nondistressed categories are lacking.

The Dyadic Adjustment Scale (Spanier, 1976) has been popular in outcome studies on the effectiveness of marital therapy in the United States. It is a 33-item inventory that was developed from careful psychometric work on married and divorced couples. It can be used for any couple living together, whether married or not.

Michigan Alcohol Screening Test

The Michigan Alcohol Screening Test (MAST) (Selzer, 1971) consists of 25 questions to which a client must respond with either "yes" or "no." The items deal with typical problems associated with alcohol abuse (for example, "Have you ever lost a job because of drinking?") A score of 5 or greater on this test has been shown to identify close to 100 percent of a group of diagnosed alcoholics (Boyd, Derr, Grossman, Lee, Sturgeon, Lacock, & Bruder, 1983). Scores on this measure have been found to be strongly correlated with psychiatric ratings of alcohol-related problems (Moore, 1972).

In the clinical setting, the MAST is best used as an initial screening device. Clinicians should consider more in-depth evaluation of any client endorsing three or more items in the direction suggestive of alcohol abuse.

Minnesota Multiphasic Personality Inventory

The Minnesota Multiphasic Personality Inventory (MMPI) may be the most extensively studied and most commonly used psychometric measure ever developed. It was first introduced in 1943 by Starke Hathaway and Jovian McKinley. The measure was designed to differentiate diagnostic groups on the basis of their responses to a large pool of self-referent statements. In the standard interpretation of the MMPI, scores on three validity scales and ten clinical scales are used to draw inferences about personality functioning and psychopathology. The MMPI has also been used in treatment planning (Meyer, 1989). A revised edition of the standard MMPI has recently been published.

Despite its general popularity, the MMPI has not played an important role in behavioral assessment and treatment planning. The instrument does not yield scores that reliably differentiate one diagnostic group from another, nor does it yield information on specific environmental factors, behavioral deficits, or cognitive styles that might be important in the maintenance of behavioral and emotional problems.

Although we do not use this instrument routinely in our clinical work with panic disorder and agoraphobic clients, we recognize that it is commonly used in mental health and medical settings. Therefore, we will present what is known about how panic disorder and agoraphobic clients tend to score.

Meyer (1989) has suggested that MMPI profiles of panic disorder clients should show a pattern indicative of "anxiety neurosis," which could be suggested by significant elevation on scales 2 and 8 and by the greatest elevation of high scores on scales 1, 3, and 7. Meyer suggests that individuals with this pattern of scores tend to show high anxiety, dependency, and a proneness to develop psychophysiological disturbances. The MMPI profile of panic disorder and agoraphobic clients would be expected to show similar elevation.

Empirical studies of MMPI scale correlates of panic disorder and agoraphobia have been sparse. Recently, however, Woodruff-Borden, Clum, and Broyles (1989) have reported the MMPI scores of a group of 50 panic disorder and agoraphobic subjects as well as those of 46 subjects with other anxiety disorders. The results indicated that panic disorder subjects scored significantly higher on one of the validity scales (L scale) and on scale 1 (Hypochondriasis) than did the other anxiety disorder subjects. The only other significant differences between the two groups were on scales 4 (Psychopathic Disorder) and 0 (Social Introversion). Panic disorder subjects tended to score lower on these scales. Although there were group differences, it should be noted that the average scores for the panic disorder and agoraphobic subjects on all scales tended to be in the normal range.

Comments on Adjunct Measures

Assessing assertiveness, level of depression, marital satisfaction, and alcohol problems is important because problems in any of these areas may require therapeutic intervention if the client is to be treated comprehensively. Another reason for assessing these domains is that successful treatment of an anxiety disorder may concomitantly bring benefits in these other areas of functioning. Positive therapeutic generalization of this kind can be detected only if the relevant areas of functioning are monitored.

PHYSIOLOGICAL MEASUREMENT

Anxiety and panic are known to be associated with activation of certain physiological systems (Barlow, 1988). We know, for example, that an increase in heart rate is associated with anxiety and panic. It would seem worthwhile, then, to measure these physiological responses directly in order to provide a comprehensive picture of a client's anxiety disorder. Unfortunately, developing procedures for the direct assessment of physiological responses indicative of anxiety that possess adequate psychometric properties has proved difficult.

Several approaches to the assessment of physiological indices of anxiety have been developed. Some of these involve measuring physiological responses while the client is imagining himself in an emotionally volatile situation. An agoraphobic, for example, might imagine herself having a panic attack in a crowded shopping mall. Unfortunately, several factors in addition to a client's level of anxiety influence whether or not she will show a physiological response during imagery of a frightening scene. First, there appear to be individual differences in clients' ability to form vivid images (Levin, Cook, & Lang, 1982). Second, as a group, agoraphobics tend to show significantly less physiological activity during imagery than do members of other diagnostic groups (Cook, Melamed, Cuthbert, McNeil, & Lang, 1988). Finally, the type of instructions given to a person regarding how images are to be formed influences whether or not physiological changes occur during imagery (Lang, Levin, Miller, & Kozak, 1983).

The second general type of physiological assessment is carried out when the client is actually in a phobic situation. Portable heart rate monitoring devices have been developed which allow for unobtrusive assessment of heart rate while a client is in a challenging situation (for example, Holden & Barlow, 1986). Unfortunately, these measures have not been shown to be reliable when used as indices of change during treatment. Holden and Barlow (1986), for example, found that heart rate measured during repeated behavioral tests decreased in a group of agoraphobics as they proceeded through in vivo exposure therapy. Unfortunately, the same effects were found for a group of normal control subjects who received no treatment!

At this time there does not appear to be a reliable and valid measure of physiological indices of anxiety that is also practical for use by clinicians.

CHAPTER 5

Panic: Psychological Approaches to Treatment

The past five years have witnessed a dramatic increase in interest in the treatment of panic disorder by cognitive-behavioral theorists and clinical researchers. This is in marked contrast to the first twenty years or so of modern behavior therapy, during which time panic attacks received relatively little attention from this group. This lack of attention was likely due to the fact that panic attacks are relatively lacking in observable "behavior." Avoidance is much easier to see, measure, and hence bring under experimental control. The assessment of panic is dependent to a large extent on clients' self-report of their experience. Physiological assessment can be useful, but it requires catching the panic when it happens; a challenging endeavor when the phenomenon occurs "out of the blue." In recent years, however, the induction of panic has been brought under experimental control (see Barlow, 1988, for a discussion of the induction of panic in the laboratory), which has resulted in a marked increase in our understanding of the problem. Consequently, effective psychological treatments of panic attacks have been developed at clinical research centers throughout the world.

The treatment approaches to panic that we will describe in this chapter represent a compilation of information from various research centers as well as our own clinical and research experience with panic clients. The mode of action for the various interventions can be conceptualized within the cognitive model of panic described in Chapter 3. This model provides the basis for the treatment rationales presented to clients and therefore deserves review. In the cognitive model, a panic attack is viewed as the result of an interaction between a set of normal body sensations and thoughts about those sensations. The attack is triggered by some stimulus that is perceived by the client as threatening. The triggering stimulus can be external (for example, finding oneself confined in a crowded room) or internal (for example, feeling a tightness in one's chest). The experience of threat leads the client to feel apprehensive. This apprehension is predictably associated with changes in some physiological systems. For example, heart rate may increase, sweat glands may become active, and muscles may tense. These bodily sensations are misinterpreted as being indicative of some impending disaster. Most commonly, these sensations are interpreted as indicating some physical malady (for example, heart attack or stroke), or mental catastrophe (for example, going crazy). For panic disorder clients, they are often seen as the first signs of an inevitable panic attack. This interpretation leads to an increase in anxiety, which provides further evidence for the anticipated catastrophe. The cycle of thoughts and feelings (illustrated in Figure 3.1 of Chapter 3) spirals into a panic attack.

The therapies for panic disorder developed at various clinical research centers have three components in common: relaxation training, cognitive therapy, and exposure to panic cues. These interventions have been combined into treatment packages that emphasize one or more of the components over the others. The interventions will be presented separately here for practical reasons. This is not meant to indicate that the treatment components should be presented one at a time or that a clinician must choose one form of intervention over another. In fact, in the clinical research reports to appear thus far, treatments have usually included a combination of interventions that are presented as a package (for example, Barlow, Craske, Cerny, & Klosko, 1989; Gitlin, Martin, Shear, Frances, Ball, & Josephson, 1985). Clinical research trials designed to dismantle the treatment packages are currently underway at various research centers, including our own.

RATIONALE FOR COGNITIVE-BEHAVIORAL TREATMENT OF PANIC

It is important that the client understands the rationale for treatment before launching into any psychological intervention for panic. The treatment rationale serves several functions in therapy. First, it provides the client with a better understanding of the nature of panic attacks and panic disorder. Second, the rationale provides the client with some context within which to understand his role in treatment. Third, when the treatment rationale is skillfully delivered, it can provide the client with a sense of hope by showing him that he can gain control over his problem. We see the presentation of the treatment rationale as an integral part of therapy. We have, in fact, recently had a client who felt no further need for therapy after the treatment rationale was presented. He explained to us that now that he knew that there was nothing to fear from the sensations he experienced during a panic attack, he was no longer anxious about having one. Thus he no longer experienced anticipatory anxiety and felt that he had greater control of his panic. Although we were pleased for this client, we were somewhat disappointed that he was no longer interested in our clinical research study.

The rationale that we use in treatment is based on the cognitive model of panic. Clients are provided with a schematic diagram illustrating the relationship between thoughts and bodily sensations that results in a panic attack (Figure 3.1). Treatment is explained with repeated reference back to this diagram. We have found that the treatment rationale is more acceptable to clients when it is presented as a dialogue between the therapist and the client, rather than as a didactic presentation by the therapist. The client is encouraged to describe how various components of the cognitive model match his own experiences. Therefore, the sample treatment rationale to be presented here is intended to be used as a guideline by the reader. Reading the rationale to the client or reciting it from memory will only bore the client and therapist alike.

We have found David Barlow's (1988) conception of the panic attack as an "alarm" particularly helpful in presenting a treatment rationale to clients. We have found that this analogy makes sense to most clients and provides them with a nonthreatening way of understanding a confusing experience.

> The type of treatment we will be providing you is designed to help you gain control over anxiety. The goal is not, however, to eliminate anxiety from your life. Anxiety is a natural human emotion. To be alive is to experience some anxiety. Anxiety is not a "bad" thing. It is not dangerous. Anxiety is a problem only to the extent that it interferes with our lives. For example, if we avoid doing certain things that we would like to do out of fear that we may feel anxious, then anxiety is a problem. Similarly, if we can't enjoy what we are doing because we are afraid that anxiety will strike us out of the blue, then anxiety is a problem. Anxiety can also be a problem if it interferes with our performance—that is, if we don't do as good a job as we would like because we are anxious. Some people, for example, are not as

successful as they might be in their personal or professional lives because of anxiety. How has anxiety interfered with your life?

When anxiety is at its most extreme form, we call it panic. For some people, panic seems to strike them out of the blue or with no apparent warning. It is as if they have been "attacked" by panic. Thus we use the term *panic attack* to describe this type of anxiety. Based on what we have learned about you, it appears to us that you experience these panic attacks. We understand panic attacks to be a natural reaction in humans to extreme threat. You might view panic as an alarm reaction. The alarm goes off when we are in a life-threatening situation. For example, if we were attacked by a wild animal and it seemed as if there was no chance to escape, we might panic. The alarm is set off by the threat. Sometimes we experience this alarm reaction when there is no real threat. It is as if the alarm was accidentally turned on. The panic attack is just as strong, nonetheless. When this happens, many people assume that they are in danger—after all, this is what their body is telling them—and they search for reasons why. Since there is usually nothing outside of themselves that is threatening, they may decide that the danger is something within themselves. Based on your own experiences with panic attacks, can you guess what reasons people come up with? [*Allow the client time to respond.*] Typically, when a person has a panic attack, he assumes that something terrible is going to happen to him. He may believe that he is going to die. Some people even believe they know how—"I am going to have a heart attack." "Oh no, here comes the big one!" Others think that the feelings they are experiencing are a sign of a mental disorder. It is not uncommon for us to hear people with panic attacks say, "I feel like I am going crazy." What sort of things do you believe will happen to you when you have a panic attack?

Now, from the description of panic that I have gone over, you might be wondering, "If panic attacks are a natural reaction to threat, how come I have them when I am not being threatened and how come no one else I know has them?" Well, the 100 percent truthful answer to these questions is, "We don't know." Now, having said that, I can tell you why we think that some people have panic attacks very frequently and others do not. First, panic attacks are actually not as rare as you might think. Research suggests that probably around 30 percent of adults have experienced at least one panic attack in the most recent year. Not all of these people go on to have repeated panic attacks. In fact, only a small percentage actually do. When a person goes on to have panic attacks frequently or is preoccupied with the fear that he will have another panic attack, we refer to the problem as *panic disorder*. We believe that many people don't go on to develop panic disorder after the first panic attack because of the way that they make sense of the first panic. If a person sees the panic as having been caused by some temporary set of circumstances, we believe that he is less likely to experience further attacks. For example, if a person believes that he had the panic attack because he drank too much coffee, it is less likely that he will continue to panic. Rather, he will modify his coffee intake. In another case, if a student believes that he had a panic attack because of the stress associated with preparing for final exams, the cause is temporary. Come June, finals will be over. We might compare these relatively mundane explanations of panic attacks with the more catastrophic ones we have already discussed. If the panic attack is attributed to some external, temporary cause, then there is no need to fear the next attack. In this case, we think that panic disorder is less likely to develop.

Anxiety in anticipation that one may have a panic attack is the second factor that we think is important in maintaining a problem with panic attacks. When we anticipate some danger, it is natural for us to experience some anxiety. Unfortunately, for people with panic disorder this anticipatory anxiety can be instrumental in causing the next attack to occur. You see, when a person is anxious, it causes some of the same physical sensations that occur during a panic attack. These sensations are seen as signs that the next attack is about to happen. Since the person with panic disorder has interpreted the attack as a very dangerous thing that must be avoided, this causes extreme anxiety, which can result in a panic attack.

Let's look at a diagram of how this works. [*Here the client is provided with a copy of Figure 3.1.*] We see panic attacks as being the result of the interaction between a set of physical sensations and your thoughts about these sensations. The panic attack starts with some trigger, which sets the process into motion. The trigger can be something external. Are there certain situations in which you are more likely to panic than others? [*Allow the client time to respond.*] There is something in those situations that you perceive as threatening. Sometimes, however, the trigger is something internal. It can be a thought or image that comes to mind, or it can be some physical sensation. What are the first signals to you that you are going to have a panic attack? [*Allow the client time to respond.*] We believe that whether or not the trigger is internal or external, people who experience panic attacks perceive it as threatening. A natural response to a threat is to feel some apprehension or anxiety. There are some natural physical sensations that are part of anxiety. These are usually an increase in heart rate, muscle tension, and sweat gland activity. Some people also experience a tightness in their throat when they are anxious. As you can see on the diagram, the next step in the panic cycle is for the person to interpret the physical sensation in some catastrophic way. We have already discussed some of the catastrophic interpretations that are common in people with panic disorder, and you have shared with me some of the things you say to yourself when you panic. This type of interpretation is naturally seen as threatening, which leads to greater anxiety, which exacerbates the physical sensations, which provides support for the catastrophic interpretation, and so on. You can see how the cycle can take on a life of its own.

The various treatment techniques that we will be using in therapy are designed to break down this cycle. Each part of the treatment targets a different part of the cycle. As I introduce each of the treatments, we will discuss how it can be useful in breaking down this cycle of thoughts and feelings. For now, however, I want to know what you think about the things we have discussed so far. What parts really seem to make sense, and what things do you still have questions about? It is very important that you and I understand panic attacks the same way for therapy to be successful.

RELAXATION TRAINING

Relaxation training has been an important component of behavioral treatment of anxiety since Wolpe (1958) first described systematic desensitization. Wolpe adopted a relaxation training procedure developed by Jacobson (1938), who had shown that the induction of a deeply relaxed state tends to reduce emotional reactions. The relaxation procedure first developed by Jacobson has been applied to the treatment of a variety of anxiety- and stress-related problems, and scientific investigations of its effectiveness have verified its utility (Hillenberg & Collins, 1982). Training in relaxation has been shown to have a beneficial impact when applied with clients who have problems with headache, hypertension, asthma, anger control, generalized anxiety, and specific anxiety problems such as speech anxiety.

The most commonly used procedure for relaxation training involves teaching clients to alternately tense and relax specific muscle groups. Bernstein and Borkovec (1973) described procedures involved in teaching progressive muscle relaxation as a skill. The specific procedures we use are a modification of those described by Bernstein and Borkovec.

As an intervention for panic disorder, relaxation training has typically been applied as part of a more comprehensive treatment package (Gitlin et al., 1985; Barlow et al., 1989). Ost (1988) has demonstrated that when relaxation is taught as a strategy for coping with the first signs of a panic attack, it can be an effective treatment of panic disorder. Other research findings suggest that relaxation may have its strongest impact on generalized anxiety rather than on panic per se (Barlow et al., 1989).

The clinician utilizing relaxation training in the treatment of any anxiety problem needs to be aware that some clients may actually become more anxious during the procedure (Heide & Borkovec, 1983, 1984) and others may even panic (Adler, Craske, & Barlow, 1987). These phenomena have been referred to as relaxation-induced anxiety (RIA) (Heide & Borkovec, 1983) and relaxation-induced panic (RIP) (Adler et al., 1987). RIA tends to be seen most often in clients with generalized anxiety and tension. One study found that about 30 percent of subjects complaining of general tension experienced an increase in tension during relaxation training (Heide & Borkovec, 1983). RIA usually occurs early in relaxation training, most often during the first session. Several theoretical explanations of RIA have been offered: Clients may fear loss of control, which they associate with a deeply relaxed state; clients may fear their own anxiety, to which their attention is drawn during the procedure; clients may worry about matters not specifically related to the relaxation procedure; or clients may fear attending to their internal experience because of a general dissatisfaction with themselves (Heide & Borkovec, 1984). None of these theoretical notions has been empirically verified, and it is possible that the observed phenomena may result from different mechanisms.

RIP tends to occur in clients with panic disorder. Like RIA, RIP may result from different mechanisms. However, following from the cognitive model, it would seem likely that relaxation results in panic because of some internal trigger that occurs with relaxation. Likely candidates include changes in physiology associated with relaxation and thoughts or images that come to the client as he relaxes.

When RIA or RIP occurs during treatment of a panic disorder client, we recommend the following guidelines for dealing with the problem. First, the therapist should not seem surprised by the phenomenon. Rather, he or she should offer calm assurances to the client, pointing out that it is not uncommon for panic clients to have this experience when learning to relax. Second, he or she should have the client describe the thoughts, images, and physical sensations he experienced before and as he became anxious. The therapist and client can then work together to make sense of the anxiety or panic in terms of the cognitive model. This process can be therapeutic in itself and may be viewed as a form of exposure to panic cues, which will be discussed in detail later in this chapter. Finally, in most cases progressive relaxation exercises can be resumed. Quitting relaxation training after RIP would send the countertherapeutic message that panic-inducing experiences should be avoided.

Rationale for Relaxation Training

The rationale for relaxation training follows from the general rationale already discussed with the client. Relaxation is explained as a skill that the client can learn in order to manage the physical sensations that can trigger a panic attack or that occur early in the cycle. We emphasize to the client the active role he plays in relaxation. The procedure is described not as something the therapist does to the client but, rather, as a skill that the client will learn with practice. The goals of relaxation training need to be made clear to the client. It is not reasonable, and would be countertherapeutic, for the client to expect that he will always be relaxed. For therapy to be successful, the client must allow himself to experience some reasonable level of anxiety. Relaxation skills are used not to eliminate anxiety but as a coping mechanism for maintaining anxiety at a reasonable level.

Again, the following example of a rationale should be considered only a general guideline. We encourage clinicians to adapt this example to their own personal styles.

The focus of today's session will be on teaching you the skill of relaxation. Now, it may sound odd for me to use the word *skill* in describing relaxation. The commonsense view of relaxation is that it is a passive process. Most people don't think of relaxation as something they do but, rather, as something they just let happen. We prefer to view relaxation as a skill because we believe that people can learn to actively relax. Once you have learned the skill, you can apply it in managing your anxiety. Learning to put yourself into a deeply relaxed state can be very helpful in managing anxiety and controlling panic attacks.

Let's go back to our diagram of a panic attack and see how this can work. As we have already seen, the panic cycle begins with a trigger. The trigger can be some physical sensation. These sensations are often those associated with anxiety. By learning to relax, you can decrease the physical sensations that trigger a panic. So relaxation can interfere with the process where it starts. [*Here the therapist might point to the "trigger stimulus" on the diagram.*] A second way in which learning to relax can interrupt the cycle of thoughts and feelings that constitutes the panic attack is here at the body sensations. [*The therapist can point to "body sensations" on the diagram.*] The body sensations that occur when we begin to feel apprehensive can be managed using the relaxation procedure. Once you learn that you can control these body sensations, it will no longer make sense to view them as dangerous. Therefore, you will be less likely to interpret them in a catastrophic way. So you will have interfered with the cycle here. [*The therapist can point to body sensations on the diagram*]. Do you see how relaxing interferes with the panic cycle?

Relaxation Training Procedures

The relaxation training procedure we use is a modification of Bernstein and Borkovec's (1973) progressive relaxation training. We have also recently modified our procedures to incorporate specific techniques from Barlow and Cerny (1988). The procedure involves having subjects alternately tense and relax individual muscle groups, thereby learning to distinguish between muscle tension and relaxation. We conduct deep muscle relaxation training in six phases: (1) full fifteen-muscle-group relaxation; (2) discrimination training with fifteen muscle groups; (3) eight-muscle-group relaxation; (4) four-muscle-group relaxation; (5) relaxation without tension; (6) cue-controlled relaxation. Typically, one or two sessions are spent at each phase, although more may be necessary with some clients. Progression to the next phase is dependent on the client's achieving a state of deep muscle relaxation at the earlier phase. At each phase of relaxation training, clients are instructed to practice the procedure at home once or twice a day.

As outlined on the following pages, relaxation training should take between six and twelve sessions to complete. Normally the procedure does not fill up an entire therapy session, and the amount of time devoted to relaxation training exercises should decrease as the client and therapist progress through each phase. The therapist is free to work on other treatment issues during relaxation training sessions.

Phase I: Fifteen-Muscle-Group Relaxation

During this phase of relaxation training, clients are directed by the therapist to alternately tense and relax fifteen different muscle groups. The therapist first demonstrates the muscle groups that will be used in the exercise, showing the client how to tense and then relax each group. The fifteen muscle groups and the ways to create tension in them are as follows:

1. Hand and lower arm—right
2. Hand and lower arm—left
   (make a fist and squeeze your fingers tightly together)

3. Upper arm—right
4. Upper arm—left
   (bring hand up to shoulder and tighten bicep)
5. Lower leg and foot—right
6. Lower leg and foot—left
   (extend the leg and point toe upward toward self)
7. Thighs
   (press legs together from the knees up)
8. Abdomen
   (draw abdominal muscle in and tighten)
9. Chest
   (take a deep breath and hold it for five seconds)
10. Shoulders
    (hunch shoulders up toward ears)
11. Neck
    (press head backwards against head rest)
12. Lips
    (press lips together)
13. Eyelids
    (close eyes tightly)
14. Lower forehead
    (draw eyebrows together and down)
15. Upper forehead
    (raise eyebrows and wrinkle forehead)

Following are the verbatim relaxation instructions that we use the first time we go through the exercise.

Relaxation training involves alternately tensing and relaxing major muscle groups throughout your body. The reason I want you to first tense your muscles before you relax them is that I want you to learn to recognize muscle tension and distinguish it from relaxation. Achieving a state of deep relaxation is a skill that you can learn with practice. Just like any skill, it takes practice to master it. With practice you will begin to be more aware of the tension in your body. You will recognize it earlier and be able to relax it away.

In order to gain the maximum benefit from relaxation training, you should practice the exercise at least once a day and preferably twice.

Before we start with the actual exercise, let me show you the muscle groups we will be tensing and relaxing. [*The therapist should go through the fifteen muscle groups and demonstrate how to tense and relax each.*]

Let's begin the exercise. First, I want you to get comfortable in your chair, loosen any restrictive or uncomfortable clothing. You might want to take off your shoes if you think that will make you more comfortable. Now that you are situated in your chair, I want you to clear your mind of any worries or concerns. I would like you to turn your attention to my voice. I will instruct you as to which muscle group I want you to turn your attention. Close your eyes, pay attention to my voice, and we can begin.

[*Right hand and lower arm*]   Let's start with the right hand and lower arm. You can create tension in these muscles by squeezing your hand tightly into a fist. Hold it for a moment [*wait 5 to 10 seconds*]. Now, relax those muscles. Let your hand rest gently on the arm rest. Let your fingers spread out naturally. Actively let go of the tension in your right hand and lower arm.

[*Left hand and lower arm*]   Now, let's try the same thing with your left hand and arm. Pull your left hand tightly into a fist and hold it for a moment [*wait 5 to 10 seconds*]. Now, relax those muscles. Allow your left arm to rest comfortably on the chair. Try to notice the tension leaving your left hand and arm.

[*Both hands and lower arms*]   This time I want you to tense both your hands and arms at the same time. Go ahead and create fists with both hands and arms. Allow the tension to build [*wait 5 to 10 seconds*], then release the tension. Just let both arms relax. Allow those muscles to become heavy, comfortable, and relaxed.

[*Right upper arm*]   Now let's create some tension in your right upper arm. Trying to leave your right hand and lower arm relaxed, I want you to bend your arm at the elbow and create some tension in your right bicep. Flex it as if you are showing off your muscle. Hold the tension for a moment [*wait 5 to 10 seconds*]. Now, release the tension. Actively let it go. Allow your arm to rest comfortably. Notice the tension leaving your arm. Allow the muscle to go loose and relaxed.

[*Left upper arm*]   Let's try the same thing with your left arm. Create some tension in your left bicep. Hold it [*wait 5 to 10 seconds*]. Now, release the tension. Allow your left arm to feel heavy, comfortable, and relaxed.

[*Both upper arms*]   Now do the same thing with both arms. Bend both arms at the elbow. Create some tension and hold it [*wait 5 to 10 seconds*]. Release the tension. Actively let it go. Just let your arm muscles give in to the pull of gravity. Notice the difference between the tension a moment ago and the relaxed state your muscles are in now.

[*Right lower leg*]   This time I want you to create some tension in your right lower leg. You can do this by straightening your leg and bending your foot back so that it points toward your face. Feel the pulling tension in your right calf [*wait 5 to 10 seconds*]. Now, relax those muscles. Allow your right leg to rest gently against the floor. Just let those muscles go loose and slack.

[*Left lower leg*]   Let's try the same thing with the left lower leg. Create some tension by pointing your foot up toward your face [*wait 5 to 10 seconds*]. Now, release the tension. Allow the muscles in your left lower leg to go heavy, comfortable, and relaxed.

[*Both lower legs*]   Let's repeat that exercise, only this time I want you to create tension in both legs. Go ahead and create some tension. Hold it [*wait 5 to 10 seconds*]. Now, release the tension. Once again, I want you to notice the difference between relaxation and muscle tension.

[*Thighs*]   This time we are going to create some tension in your thighs. You can create some muscle tension in both your thighs by pressing your legs tightly together from the knees up. Go ahead and create some tension in your thighs [*wait 5 to 10 seconds*]. Now, release the tension. Just let your thigh muscles go heavy, comfortable, and relaxed. Allow your legs to give in to the pull of gravity.

[*Abdominal muscles*]   Now I want you to create some tension in your abdominal muscles. You can do that by drawing those muscles in slowly and holding the tension. Pretend that someone is about to punch you in the stomach [*wait 5 to 10 seconds*]. Study the tension for a moment and release it. Let your abdominal muscles go soft, smooth, and relaxed.

[*Chest*]   Now I want you to turn your attention to your chest. You can create some muscle tension in your chest by taking a deep breath and holding it. Go ahead and take a slow breath. Hold it [*wait 5 to 10 seconds*]. Now blow the air out slowly. Feel the muscles in your chest relax. Let's try that again. Take a nice slow deep breath and hold it [*wait 5 to 10 seconds*]. Now, release it. As you return to your natural rhythmic breathing, I want you to feel yourself becoming more and more deeply relaxed with each breath that you exhale.

[*Shoulders*]   Now I want you to create some tension in your shoulders by hunching them up toward your ears. Hunch them tightly and hold it [*wait 5 to 10 seconds*]. Now relax. Let go of the tension in your neck and shoulders. Notice the contrast between the tension you experienced a moment ago and the relaxation you feel now. See how relaxation is just the opposite of tension.

[*Neck*]   Now let's create some tension in your neck. You can do this by gently pushing your head back against the chair behind you. As you push your neck back, notice the tension building in your neck [*wait 5 to 10 seconds*]. Study the difference between the tension you experienced a moment ago and the relaxation you feel now.

[*Lips*]   Now I want you to focus your attention on your facial muscles. We will start with the muscles around your lips. Create some tension in the muscles around your lips by pressing them tightly together. Study the tension for a moment [*wait 5 to 10 seconds*] and then release the tension. Allow the muscles that control your lips to go loose and relaxed. You might allow your mouth to open slightly or remain closed, whatever is more comfortable for you.

[*Eyelids*]   Now let's create some tension in the muscles that control your eyelids. You can do that by pressing your eyelids tightly together. Feel the tension building around your eyes [*wait 5 to 10 seconds*]. Now release the tension. Feel the tension leaving the muscles around your eyes. Allow your eyelids to rest comfortably over your eyes.

[*Lower forehead*]   Now I want you to tense the muscles of your lower forehead. You can do this by drawing your eyelids in and furrowing your brow as if you are very mad [*wait 5 to 10 seconds*]. Now relax. Just do the opposite of tension—allow those muscles to go smooth and relaxed. Actively release the tension.

[*Upper forehead*]   The last set of muscles I want you to tense are the muscles of the upper forehead. You can do that by raising your eyebrows and wrinkling your forehead. Study the tension that is building in your upper forehead [*wait 5 to 10 seconds*], and relax it away. Allow your forehead to go smooth and relaxed.

Now I want you to relax your whole body. Just let yourself sink into a comfortable and relaxed state. Note the pleasant sensations that accompany deep muscle relaxation. I am going to help you achieve a deep state of relaxation by counting from 1 to 5. As I count, you will feel yourself becoming more and more deeply relaxed. One— you are becoming more deeply relaxed; two—down into a very deeply relaxed state; three, four—more and more deeply relaxed; five— deeply relaxed.

Now, as you remain deeply relaxed, I want you to pay attention to your breathing. Breathe through your nose. Notice what the air feels like as you breathe in and out. Feel the cool air come in as you inhale and the warm moist air as you exhale. Use your stomach muscles as you breathe. Now, each time you exhale, I want you to mentally repeat the word *relax.*

[*Allow the subject a minute or two to enjoy the state of deep muscle relaxation.*]

I am going to help you return to your normal level of wakefulness. I will count backwards from 5 to 1. As I count, I want you to gradually emerge from the state of deep muscle relaxation. When I reach 2, I want you to open your eyes. At 1, you will reach your normal state of alertness. Ready?

Five . . . four . . . three . . . two . . . your eyes are open and you are nearly back to your normal state . . . one.

When guiding the client through the relaxation exercise, the therapist should speak slowly, using a calm, soothing voice that is low but clearly audible. It is best to wait about 10 to 15 seconds between muscle groups. Sometimes the therapist will observe a client creating tension in muscles that have already been relaxed by, for example, twitching a foot back and forth. When this happens, the therapist can diverge from the set procedures and repeat instructions to relax one or more muscle groups.

Phase II: Discrimination Training

The second phase of progressive muscle relaxation training is discrimination training. The goal of this exercise is to help clients learn to detect low levels of muscle tension. The idea that should be conveyed to clients is that muscle tension is not an all-or-none phenomenon. Muscle tension can occur at different levels. For the client to obtain maximum benefit from the relaxation procedure, it will be important for him to identify even low levels of muscles tension and to learn to relax this away. In discrimination training the client creates different levels of tension in various muscle groups and then releases that tension. The rationale and procedures for discrimination training are as follows.

> Today we will be repeating the same relaxation training procedure that we have done before, only this time we will be adding a new component—discrimination training. The goal of discrimination training is to teach you to identify lower levels of muscle tension. This will help you to detect and release muscle tension before it reaches

high levels. We call this phase of the procedure discrimination training because we want you to discriminate or distinguish different levels of tension. You will eventually be able to identify and counteract muscle tension when it is at a low level. This will be a positive step toward managing tension before it reaches a level that might trigger a panic attack.

The therapist begins the relaxation/discrimination training procedure in the same manner as the full fifteen-muscle-group relaxation. The client should be instructed to close his eyes and get comfortable in the chair. The therapist then instructs the client to create tension in the right lower arm and hand as in fifteen-muscle-group relaxation. Then the therapist proceeds with discrimination training, as follows:

> I want you to create tension in your right lower arm and hand again, only this time I want you to tense the muscle half as much as you did before. Concentrate on what it feels like for these muscles to be half as tense as they were last time [*wait 5 to 10 seconds*]. Now release the tension. Relax it away.
> Let's try to tense these muscles one more time, only this time I want you to create one-fourth as much tension as you usually do. Notice what it feels like for these muscles to be tensed only one-fourth as much [*wait 5 to 10 seconds*]. Now, relax your right lower arm and hand.

The therapist repeats the procedure with the left lower arm and hand, then asks the client to open his eyes and inquires as to whether or not the client could distinguish different levels of muscle tension. If so, the therapist congratulates the client and continues with relaxation training. If not, the therapist repeats the rationale and the exercise. As relaxation training proceeds, it is not necessary for the therapist to do discrimination training with every muscle group. This would be very time-consuming and boring. Instead, he or she should pick two other muscle groups and go through the discrimination training procedure. Some clinicians focus on the back of the neck and eyes (Barlow & Cerny, 1988). The therapist can instruct the client to try discrimination training with different muscle groups as he practices relaxation during the week.

Phase III: Eight-Muscle-Group Relaxation

Eight-muscle-group relaxation is very similar to the full relaxation training procedure, only the client is taught to tense several muscle groups at a time. The procedure is quicker and is described to the client as the first step toward making relaxation a portable skill. The first step in this phase is to demonstrate for the client the eight muscle groups to be relaxed, as follows:

1. *Both arms:* The client is told to hold both arms out slightly bent at the elbow and is instructed to flex the bicep muscle and create fists, thus tensing the hands and lower arms.
2. *Both lower legs:* The tensing exercise is exactly the same as in fifteen-muscle-group relaxation, only both legs are tensed at the same time.
3. *Abdomen:* This is the same as in full relaxation training.
4. *Chest:* This is the same as in full relaxation training.
5. *Shoulders:* This is the same as in full relaxation training.
6. *Back of neck:* This is the same as in full relaxation training.
7. *Eyes:* This is the same as in full relaxation training.
8. *Forehead:* The client is instructed to create tension in the forehead using the same exercise as in creating tension in the lower forehead during full relaxation training.

The instructions for eight-muscle-group relaxation follow the same format as in fifteen-muscle-group relaxation except that the client is allowed more time to relax each set of muscles. The therapist should allow the client 20 to 30 seconds to relax each muscle group after creating tension for about 10 seconds. After going through the eight muscle groups, the therapist should guide the client through the counting and breathing procedures described in the full muscle relaxation procedure.

The therapist should discuss with the client the level of relaxation he was able to achieve using the eight-muscle-group procedure. The client should be instructed to practice the eight-muscle-group procedure at home.

Phase IV: Four-Muscle-Group Relaxation

Teaching the client to tense and relax four sets of muscles is the next step in teaching him to relax quickly. The procedures are the same as in eight-muscle-group relaxation, only the subject is instructed to tense, then relax, the following sets of muscles.

1. *Both arms:* This is the same as in eight-muscle-group relaxation.

2. *Chest*: This is the same as in eight-muscle-group relaxation.
3. *Neck and Shoulders:* The client is taught to hunch his shoulders and draw his neck back, thus creating tension in the neck and shoulders simultaneously.
4. *Face:* The client should create tension throughout the facial muscles by closing his eyes tightly, pressing his lips together, and furrowing his brow.

After completing the exercise, the therapist should guide the client to a state of deeper relaxation by using the counting technique described earlier. Once relaxed, the client should focus his attention on his breathing and say a word like "relax" or "calm" each time he exhales.

The therapist should discuss with the client the level of relaxation he was able to achieve with four-muscle-group relaxation. The client should be asked to try this at home. At this phase of progressive relaxation training, the client should begin trying to apply the relaxation procedure in less than optimal circumstances. The therapist can instruct the client to try obtaining a state of deep relaxation in various less comfortable positions at home (for example, in a hard chair, standing). Learning to relax in these relatively uncomfortable circumstances is an important step in teaching the client to apply muscle relaxation when he experiences tension in real life.

Phase V: Relaxation without Tension

The goal of this phase of relaxation training is to teach the client to achieve a state of deep relaxation without first tensing the muscle groups. This is the next step in making relaxation a portable coping skill.

This phase also starts with the client getting comfortably situated in his chair. The therapist then instructs the client to focus his attention on his arm muscles, identifying any tension that exists in these muscles and relaxing it away. The therapist then repeats this procedure for the other three muscle groups used in the last phase of training. Once again, the therapist should assist the client in deepening his relaxation by counting to five, asking the client to become more and more relaxed as he progresses through the procedure. The client should also be instructed to repeat the word "relax" each time he exhales when he is in a deeply relaxed state.

This phase of training can be challenging for some clients who have a difficult time relaxing their muscles if they have not purposely tensed them. If a client has a particularly difficult time relaxing without first tensing, the therapist should consider repeating discrimination training for the muscle groups in question.

Phase VI: Cue-Controlled Relaxation

In the final phase of relaxation training, the goal is to teach the client to associate a certain cue word with the state of deep muscle relaxation and to use that word as a cue to relax. In a sense, cue word training has occurred throughout the procedure, when the therapist had the client repeat the word "relax" as he exhaled in a deeply relaxed state. The order is reversed in this phase of training. The client starts relaxing by focusing on his breathing and thinking the cue word, "relax." As the client repeats the word to himself, he scans his body for low levels of tension and relaxes it away.

This procedure should be practiced in the session, after which the therapist discusses with the client the level of relaxation he was able to achieve. Trouble spots of tension should be identified. It may be necessary to repeat discrimination training for certain muscle groups in order to help the client obtain a state of deep muscle relaxation with the cue procedure.

Once the client has mastered cue-controlled relaxation, he will have a portable coping mechanism that he can apply to deal with tension and anxiety as it builds. The therapist can then work with the client on designing homework assignments in which the client places himself in progressively more anxiety-producing situations and applies the cue-controlled relaxation procedure to cope with the tension that arises. Caution should be exercised in warning the client not to attempt to master the most anxiety-producing situations too quickly. Mastering lower levels of anxiety should precede advancing to more challenging situations.

COGNITIVE THERAPY OF PANIC DISORDER

Cognitive therapy of panic disorder has been developed by clinical researchers in the United States and Great Britain and has been tested, by itself or in combination with other methods, in clinics and research laboratories throughout the world. In contrast to the relatively discouraging findings in studies of cognitive therapy in the treatment of agoraphobic avoidance, early research reports suggest that cognitive therapy can be a powerful and effective treatment for panic disorder. Much of the credit for the development of cognitive therapy for the anxiety disorders goes to Aaron Beck and his colleagues at the Center for Cognitive Therapy in Philadelphia, who have been pioneers in the treatment of emotional disorders. The cognitive therapy procedures we will describe here were very strongly influenced by the work of Beck and Emery (1985), and we recommend this book to the reader.

Effective application of cognitive therapy to the treatment of panic disorder requires that the therapist be thoroughly familiar with the cognitive model of panic disorder and with the techniques of cognitive therapy. Previous supervised experience and training in cognitive therapy are prerequisites to treatment. Therapy requires more flexibility on the part of the therapist, who often must think on his or her feet during a session. We will provide an overview of the procedures for cognitive therapy of panic disorder. The therapist should not consider this a step-by-step approach. Rather, in cognitive therapy the therapist moves between procedures within a single session. The order in which we present the phases of cognitive therapy is meant as a general guideline, therefore, and it is expected that the therapist will move back and forth between phases as necessitated by the demands of the individual therapy session.

Rationale for Cognitive Therapy

The rationale for cognitive therapy follows directly from the cognitive model of panic. The therapist has already discussed the relationship among thoughts, anxiety, and physical sensations in discussing the general rationale for cognitive-behavioral therapy. In providing the rationale for the cognitive therapy component, several additional points can be made. First, the client is introduced to the notion that thoughts are not facts. The therapist should convey to the client the idea that the best way to conceptualize thoughts is as hypotheses, which can be tested against available data. Second, the therapist will want to discuss with the client how he can learn to interfere with the cycle of thoughts and sensations that make up the panic attack (Figure 3.1) by applying cognitive techniques. Finally, the general procedures for cognitive therapy should be made clear to the client so that he knows what to expect. Once again, the following rationale is intended to be used as an example by clinicians, who are encouraged to modify it so that it matches their own styles.

Let's take another look at our diagram of the panic attack. [*Here the therapist and client both look at Figure 3.1.*] As we have discussed already, in this model, thinking plays a central role in generating a panic attack. Initially, believing that something either outside of you or within you is a threat to your safety or even your life begins the process. An example of this might be the thought that tightness in your chest is the first sign of a heart attack. This belief causes you to be apprehensive, which leads to a whole other set of body sensations. Based on our earlier discussion, it seems that one of the things that you frequently perceive as threatening is . . . [*Here the therapist can fill in an example from the client's own experience. The example is then discussed in terms of the cognitive model.*]

The second point in the cycle where your thoughts play a crucial role is here, where you interpret body sensations. [*The therapist points to the appropriate spot on the diagram.*] How you interpret the sensations associated with your apprehension influences whether or not you panic. When these sensations are seen as further evidence for the original threat or as signs of some new threat, you are more likely to panic. Alternatively, if these sensations are interpreted in a more neutral fashion, it is unlikely that you will panic.

In therapy we will help you to identify the thoughts that exacerbate your anxiety. We will then explore how realistic these thoughts are and look at alternative ways of interpreting the same sensations. We know from our work with anxious clients that many of these thoughts are based on faulty logic and that when people are anxious they tend to concentrate on the worst possible interpretation. We will examine methods you can use to discover the logical errors that result in these catastrophic interpretations. Together, we will generate alternative ways to view body sensations and the triggers that initiate the panic cycle. We find it helpful to view the thoughts that are central to panic as guesses about the best way to interpret situations or physical sensations. Sometimes we guess wrong. In therapy we will try to find the guesses that are most accurate and that reduce, rather than exacerbate, anxiety. You and I will work together like two scientists. We will design experiments to test different guesses to see how well they match up with the available data.

Let me illustrate with a simple example. Let's say that when you feel warm and flushed, you see this as the first sign that you will have a panic attack. The warm feeling is the trigger in this example. Your thought that you will have a panic attack is your guess about why you feel flushed—"I feel warm, therefore I must be about to have a panic attack." This interpretation may make sense to you because of your past experience with panic attacks. However, there are alternative explanations. It is quite possible that you feel warm because it is hot and stuffy in this room. If I were to tell you that I also feel warm and flushed, you might have an alternative explanation for your feeling. The alternative is less threatening than the thought that you are going to have a panic attack. The new thought might be, "My therapist is also warm and looks flushed, therefore it must be hot in this room." By coming up with a less threatening alternative, you have interfered with the process that leads to a panic attack.

Procedures in Cognitive Therapy

Didactic Overview of Cognition and Emotion

In the earliest phase of cognitive therapy, the therapist takes the role of teacher. He or she will be teaching the client a new way of understanding heretofore mysterious experiences—anxiety and panic. Furthermore, the therapist will be teaching the client a set of skills that he can use to manage anxiety. Although the therapist is in the role of teacher throughout treatment, this role is most obvious early in cognitive therapy.

If the therapist is to function as a teacher, it is important that the client is ready to learn. Beck and Emery (1985) emphasize that clients should be "learning to learn" in therapy. Many clients view therapy as analogous to medical treatment, in which something is done to them by a specialist and their ailment is cured. This misconception needs to be addressed early. If a client seems resistant to learning, the therapist should not forge ahead until this problem has been dealt with. One way of addressing this is to discuss explicitly the teacher–student analogy with the client. Drawing on the client's personal experiences as a student, the therapist can ask the client to recall the classes in which he learned the most from his instructors, to describe the attitude he had in these classes, and then to adopt this same attitude in therapy. A second way to deal with this problem is for the therapist to challenge the client to learn what the therapist has to offer as a way of testing its value.

In the didactic phase of therapy the relationship between thoughts and feelings should be the first topic discussed. We have found Albert Ellis's (1962) A-B-C model to be an easy one for clients to learn. In this model A stands for the *antecedents* to anxiety, B for *beliefs,* and C for emotional *consequences.* This can be diagrammed on a chalkboard or paper. The consequences of interest are anxiety and panic. The client is asked to describe what causes him to feel anxious or panicky. These are the antecedents. Typical antecedents for panic are certain situations, such as a crowded room, or certain physical sensations, such as lightheadedness or heart palpitations. The view held by most people is that anxiety is caused by these antecedent events—that A causes C. But the cognitive viewpoint holds that there is an intervening variable—B, or the client's beliefs about the activating events. The therapist can then discuss some of the types of beliefs that lead to or exacerbate anxiety. The goals of therapy are to identify the beliefs, examine their logical bases, and replace them with more logical and hence less anxiety-producing alternatives.

Once the client seems to understand the A-B-C model, the therapist can introduce examples of the types of beliefs and faulty reasoning that tend to result in anxious feelings or panic. Providing the client with names for the distorted beliefs can help him identify his own distortions and create a common language shared by the therapist and client, which will facilitate communication. Here are examples of distorted styles of thinking that the therapist can present to the client early in cognitive therapy.

Catastrophizing: When a client perceives that he is in danger, he will tend to focus on the most catastrophic outcomes. Panic disorder clients most commonly believe that they will die, go crazy, or lose control of their behavior when they have a panic attack. They ignore the evidence to the contrary—that is, their own experience of having had many panic attacks and never having died or gone crazy as a result.

Overgeneralizing: Clients frequently generalize from a single experience to their lives in general. Because a client has, for example, had a panic attack while alone with his children, he may assume that he is a terrible father or cannot cope with the responsibilities of parenthood.

All-or-none thinking: Thinking in black-and-white or all-or-none terms can set a client up for a panic attack. Believing, for example, that feeling any anxiety means a panic attack is forthcoming can work as a self-fulfilling prophecy.

Exaggerating: Blowing out of proportion the consequences of some negative event is another error of thinking that can exacerbate anxiety. For example, exaggerating the impact of a panic attack on one's physical and mental health can lead to anticipatory anxiety, which may itself be a trigger for a panic attack.

While going over these distorted styles of thinking, the therapist should try to use examples already provided by the client and challenge the client to generate examples of these types of logical errors from his own experience.

Identification of Irrational Beliefs and Faulty Logic

Distorted beliefs about anxiety and panic are sometimes not obvious to clients or can be identified only in retrospect. The beliefs are often poorly articulated in the client's mind and sometimes occur as images or pictures. The thoughts and images often occur very quickly and appear to be automatic responses to certain situations or feelings. Teaching the client to identify his own anxiety-producing beliefs and faulty logic is the first step toward changing this style of thinking. The idea that should be conveyed to the client is that he needs to learn to catch these beliefs as they occur in order to disrupt the cycle that results in a panic attack.

The place to start in identifying panic-producing thinking styles is with the Daily Self-Rating forms described in Chapter 4. The therapist can discuss with the client recent panic attacks, focusing on the client's thoughts before and during the attack. To facilitate the client's recollection of the panic, the therapist can instruct the client to recall the attack in imagination during the session. The client can be asked to describe the situation he was in and what he was thinking and doing when he experienced the attack. The therapist's role is, first, to listen carefully in order to identify the automatic thoughts and faulty logic that are evident in the client's description of the experience. Then the therapist can ask the client to describe the panic attack in terms of the diagram of the panic cycle (Figure 3.1). The therapist and client then work together to identify illogical beliefs and distorted logic in the client's thinking. It can be helpful for the therapist to write these down or to have the client write them down so that a record can be kept of the kinds of thoughts that occur during a panic attack.

A second method of identifying illogical thinking is in vivo thought sampling. In this procedure the therapist samples the client's thoughts when the client appears to be anxious during the therapy session. This is a valuable technique because it allows for identification and discussion of distorted beliefs as they are happening. The therapist can induce anxiety in the session by using role plays and imagery of panic experiences, and by producing some of the physical sensations of a panic attack during the session. The latter technique will be discussed in more detail later.

Homework can also be used to help the client learn to identify the irrational thoughts associated with panic attacks. By recording his thoughts during or immediately after a panic attack, the client can improve his skill at identifying distorted beliefs. As an adjunct to the Daily Self-Rating, the therapist can have the client record in detail his thoughts before and during a panic attack and have him also identify and record the distortions in his thinking. The therapist can review the homework during the session in order to help the client fine tune his skills at identifying and labeling cognitive distortions.

Insight into Illogical Thinking

The next set of skills that the client needs to master involves challenging his own thoughts and disputing these thoughts on logical grounds. We describe this as teaching the client to gain insight into his own thinking. The therapist teaches the client to challenge his own irrational thoughts through modeling in the therapy session. During this phase of therapy, the therapist adopts a Socratic approach. He or she asks the questions that lead the client to see the unhelpful and illogical nature of his thoughts. The therapist needs to strike a balance between achieving an empathic understanding of how the client views his world and challenging the client to think about his interpretations of the world in a different way. This can be the most challenging component of treatment for the therapist.

There are many techniques that the therapist can use to help the client gain insight into his unhelpful style of thinking. These techniques can be organized into three basic approaches (Beck & Emery, 1985), which can be summarized into the following questions:

1. What is the evidence?
2. What is an alternative way of looking at this?
3. So what if it happens?

EXPLORING THE EVIDENCE   Having a client explore the evidence for his belief is a useful method of helping him see the faulty logic he uses in arriving at the catastrophic conclusion. Simply asking the client to describe the evidence that led him to conclude that he will die, for example, can help him see that typically the only evidence is his own feelings. One of our clients was convinced, each time she had a panic attack, that she was having a heart attack. When the therapist asked her to describe the evidence that led her to this conclusion, she could only offer the physical sensations she had when she panicked as evidence that she was having a heart attack. She could come up with no other data to support her conclusion. The therapist asked the client what she knew about the risk factors for heart attack. She could say only that she knew that smoking was a risk factor and that she had formerly smoked, although she had quit about two years before. The therapist then discussed with the client the other known risk factors for heart attacks, including obesity (she was of normal weight), family history (no one in her family had died of heart failure), and age (she was 24 years old). The evidence against her being at risk for heart attack was weighed against the evidence in favor of this catastrophic outcome—her feelings. Eventually this client was able to see that in fact it was very unlikely that she would suffer a heart attack any time soon. This set the stage for exploring alternative ways of interpreting her physical sensations.

Hypothesis testing can also be used to help the client examine the evidence for and against his catastrophic belief. The therapist and client can write out the client's predictions about some horrible outcome, which can then be tested. For example, if a client believes "I can't cope with any anxiety," the therapist and client can design an experiment to test this idea. The client would identify a mildly anxiety-producing task, which he would try during the week. In the next session, the therapist and client review the accuracy of his prediction. If the client experienced some anxiety but was able to get through the situation, this is evidence against his prediction. Even if the experiment fails—perhaps the client does panic in the situation—it has still provided useful data. The therapist and client can examine the thoughts the client had during the panic attack and can realistically examine how he coped in the situation.

There are several types of questions the therapist can use to help the client explore the evidence for and against his belief. Here are some examples:

Explain the logic that led you to this conclusion.
Because this happened once, does that mean it will always happen?
Is that phrase the most accurate way to describe what happened, or does it exaggerate the negative?

EXPLORING ALTERNATIVES   The second general method of helping clients to gain insight into irrational styles of thinking involves challenging the client to explore alternative ways of viewing the triggers for panic attacks and the catastrophic interpretations of body sensations (see Figure 3.1). In the therapy session, the therapist can use a blackboard or a blank sheet of paper to write out the client's anxiety-producing thoughts. The therapist and client then work together to generate as many alternative ways of viewing the situation as possible. This has been called the two-column technique (Beck & Emery, 1985) and can be practiced by clients between sessions. The process of generating alternative ways of understanding a single situation or physical sensation can be therapeutic in itself, because anxious clients typically have a very narrow focus of attention. The process of generating alternatives helps the client to broaden his perspective and recognize that his catastrophic expectations are not the only, or even the most likely, possibility. Initially it can be very difficult for some clients to generate feasible alternatives because their attention is so narrowly focused on the possible threat. The therapist who is flexible in his or her own thinking is often the most helpful because he or she is able to produce alternative explanations quickly and easily.

Once the client develops some skill at generating alternatives and begins to accept the idea that his interpretations are not the only possibilities, the therapist can move on to help the client choose the interpretation that is most helpful for him. In helping a client to choose among alternative explanations, the therapist can ask two types of questions. The first has to do with the probability of occurrence of each alternative. The probability of the catastrophic interpretation can be compared with the likelihood that one or more of the alternative explanations is accurate. Typically, the irrational belief is found to be weak on this criterion. Next, the therapist and client can explore which of the alternative beliefs it most behooves the client to accept. In other words, the therapist teaches the client to choose a belief that will be most helpful to him. Examining the helpfulness of beliefs can involve having the client think through the consequences of accepting each alternative. The consequence of accepting the irrational belief is always anxiety or panic, whereas accepting another alternative is usually not associated with a negative mood state.

EXPLORING THE CONSEQUENCES   Anxiety-producing cognitions have in common the underlying assumption that some terrible consequence is about to befall the client. Typically, panic disorder clients believe that the consequences of feeling anxious or of having a panic attack will be horrendous. The expected outcome is often poorly articulated in the client's mind but is believed to be terrible. Panic disorder clients will often report, for example, that if they were to have a panic attack in a public place, they would not be able to "handle it," or they would "fall apart." The therapist can help the client to decatastrophize the outcome by having him explain what he means by terms such as "handle it" and "fall apart." Typically, these are not clearly understood. Asking the client to describe how he "handled" previous panic attacks often elicits evidence that the client did in fact cope quite well with the experience.

In exploring the consequences of anxiety with a client, the basic question the therapist is asking is, "So what?" How bad would it really be if the client became anxious or even panicked? Usually panic disorder clients ignore data that are readily available to them and which show that their dire predictions are inaccurate. Each time he has a panic attack and survives, the panic client is given evidence that is inconsistent with his expectation that he will die. Most panic clients ignore these contradictory data, and it is the therapist's job to help them to recognize this evidence.

According to Beck and Emery (1985), four issues can be addressed when examining the question, "So what if it happens?" These are "(1) the probability of the feared event; (2) its degree of awfulness; (3) the patient's ability to prevent it from occurring; and (4) the patient's ability to accept and deal with the worst possible outcome" (p. 209).

Rehearsal of Coping Self-Statements

The last phase of cognitive therapy for panic disorder involves strategies designed to provide the client with a set of coping statements that he or she can use when feeling anxious. We generally introduce these strategies after the client has gained some insight into the irrational nature of his automatic thoughts. The rationale for this progression is that since the client now understands that his automatic thoughts are not necessarily helpful or logical, he needs to develop a new set of thoughts that will help him cope with anxiety rather than exacerbate it.

Meichenbaum (1977) introduced several procedures in which clients rehearse helpful, adaptive, or coping self-statements as part of an overall treatment plan to reduce unwanted extremes of emotion. In the rehearsal phase of Meichenbaum's "stress inoculation training," the client rehearses coping self-statements while imagining himself progressing through a four-part sequence: (1) preparing for a stressor, (2) confronting and coping with a stressor, (3) coping with arousal while confronting the stressor, and (4) reflecting on the experience.

We have used Meichenbaum's procedure in treating panic attacks in clients with panic disorder. Rather than having the client imagine feared situations or external stressors, we have him imagine experiencing the sensations that are associated with the onset and development of a panic attack. In this procedure, the client rehearses rational statements he can think to himself when these feelings occur.

In self-instructional rehearsal it is important that the client and therapist work together to generate coping statements so that they are meaningful for the client. Therefore, prior to the imaginal exposure, the therapist should talk through a situation with the client and generate several coping statements for each of the four phases: preparing for the challenge, confronting the feared sensations, coping with the feeling of being overwhelmed, and reflecting on the experience. Here are some examples of coping self-statements generated by panic disorder clients.

1. *Preparing for the challenge:*
   —"I can cope with anxiety if it occurs."
   —"There is no sense in worrying about whether or not I'll panic."
   —"I have been anxious before, and I've always lived to tell the tale."
   —"I may not be perfectly calm, but I know I can handle the situation."
   —"Remember, just think rationally."

2. *Confronting the feared sensations:*
   —"I am feeling some anxiety, but that's O.K."
   —"A little anxiety never hurt anybody."
   —"These feelings don't necesssarily mean something awful will happen. They are normal."
   —"Relax. I can handle this."
   —"Remember, anxiety is part of everyone's life."
   —"Just stay calm."
   —"Worrying about these feelings won't help anything."

3. *Coping with the feeling of being overwhelmed:*
   —"This will pass. It always does."
   —"When anxiety goes up, it always comes down."
   —"I've felt this way before and I know I can handle it."
   —"There is no point in saying I shouldn't feel this way. I do."
   —"This doesn't mean I will die or go crazy. It's just another one of those annoying panics."
   —"Keep the focus on what I have to do right now."

4. *Reflecting on the experience:*
—"That wasn't pleasant, but I handled it."
—"Once more I've proved I can cope with anxiety."
—"Let's look at that realistically. Was it really as bad as I expected?"
—"Hey, I was anxious and didn't panic—that's great!"
—"I didn't let my negative thoughts get the best of me that time."

In applying self-instructional rehearsal in the treatment of panic attacks, the therapist has the client generate a set of situations in which he anticipates that panic attacks are most likely. The client then imagines himself prior to entering the situation, experiencing some panic symptoms in the situation, feeling overwhelmed in the situation, and reflecting on it later. The therapist guides the client through these stages and has the client practice saying the coping statement generated earlier, first aloud and then to himself. Homework assignments during this phase of cognitive therapy involve having the client enter situations that tend to be associated with anxiety and utilize the coping self-statements in vivo.

COGNITIVE THERAPY: SOME COMMON PROBLEMS

There are some common stumbling blocks that we have encountered in applying cognitive therapy techniques with panic disorder clients. These problems occur with enough frequency that we feel they merit individual attention.

Many clients quickly recognize that their thoughts during a panic attack are not rational and are able to see how they contribute to the development of panic attacks. Because they recognize the irrational nature of their beliefs, they see no need to explore this with the therapist. These clients will typically say something like, "I know rationally that it's not true, but I still feel like I am going to die." Here the client is confusing *thinking* and *feeling*. It is common for these two terms to be used interchangeably in everyday language, but in therapy it can cause problems. The client who says that he *feels* he is going to die is really saying that he *believes* he is going to die. The therapist can point this out and explain that the difference between his rational belief and his feeling (irrational belief) is the strength of his conviction in each. During a panic attack, he believes very strongly that he will die. By exploring the basis for this belief and examining alternative methods of interpreting the same data, the client can chisel away at the degree of conviction with which the catastrophic interpretation is held.

A second common problem encountered in cognitive therapy is that it seems too simple to many clients. As they construe it, the therapist is telling them simply to "think happy thoughts." Recently, one of our clients compared cognitive therapy to the popular song by Bobby McFerrin, "Don't Worry, Be Happy." The therapist who encounters this problem needs to make clear the distinction between thinking positively and thinking rationally (see Beck, Rush, Shaw, & Emery, 1979). In cognitive therapy the client is taught to examine his experiences objectively. This is not simply a matter of replacing negative distortions with positive ones. The goal, in cognitive therapy for panic disorder, is to teach the client to interpret physical sensations as realistically and accurately as possible.

EXPOSURE TO PANIC CUES

The final component of the cognitive-behavioral treatment of panic disorder is exposure to the cues that trigger panic attacks. Although panic triggers can be thoughts and images, noticeable physical sensations of some type are invariably part of the beginning phases of a panic attack. Systematic exposure to these sensations occurs at this stage of treatment. Producing the sensations of panic is a central component in each of the treatment packages for panic disorder developed at the major clinical research centers (Barlow & Cerny, 1988; Beck, 1988; Clark, 1988).

In this stage of treatment, the therapist and client develop ways of reproducing some of the physical sensations that are associated with a panic attack. Therapy sessions are devoted to systematic exposure to these sensations. This component of treatment gives the client an opportunity to apply the relaxation and cognitive coping skills he developed earlier in therapy. Furthermore, by creating the sensations of a panic attack himself, the client learns experientially that he has some control over the feelings that had previously seemed unpredictable. Finally, repeated and prolonged exposure to certain physical sensations such as choking will result in extinction of conditioned fear responses associated with these sensations.

We will describe some standard methods of inducing panic sensations in the consulting room. In the clinical setting, however, it is important that the clinician attempt to reproduce the physical sensations that are most meaningful to his or her client. If, for example, the client reports that the first sign of a panic attack is shortness of breath, exposure should involve rapid breathing, running in place, or some other method of producing that sensation. It would be of little value to spin this client in a chair in order to produce dizziness, for example, if this sensation is not associated with panic. For another client, exposure to dizzy feelings may have powerful therapeutic effects. Researchers have found some evidence that the effectiveness of exposure to panic cues is related to the extent to which clients perceive a similarity between the effects of the exposure intervention (for example, voluntary overbreathing) and their own naturally occurring panic attacks (Salkovskis, Jones, & Clark, 1986).

Research studies examining the effectiveness of exposure-based treatments for panic disorder have always combined other interventions with exposure treatment, such as cognitive therapy (Barlow et al., 1989) or breathing retraining (Clark et al., 1985). Therefore, we recommend introducing exposure after a client has gained some skill at implementing anxiety management strategies.

Rationale for Exposure to Panic Cues

The rationale for exposure treatment of panic disorder follows from the general rationale for cognitive-behavioral intervention. Once again, the client is referred to Figure 3.1. Several key points should be made in the treatment rationale. First, it should be explained that a central component of panic disorder is a learned fear of the physical sensations that are part of an attack. Through exposure therapy, clients will learn that there is no basis to this fear. Second, exposure trials will provide clients with the opportunity to practice cognitive therapy and relaxation skills. Third, by learning to produce some of the sensations of a panic attack themselves, clients will gain a sense of control over these feelings. In the following verbatim rationale, we endeavor to make these three points.

> Today we will begin the last component of treatment. In a sense this is what we have been working up to all along, since you will have a chance to utilize the relaxation techniques and cognitive strategies that you have already learned. This component of treatment, although challenging for many clients, has been shown to be a highly effective method of treating panic disorder.

Let's start by looking back at our diagram of a panic attack. [*Therapist and client look at Figure 3.1.*] As we have already seen, the panic attack is initiated by some trigger stimulus. This trigger is often something inside of you, such as feeling your throat constrict or dizziness. Since you have experienced panic attacks after feeling these sensations, you have come to fear them. This fear has been learned through the association of these sensations with panic attacks. Similarly, you have learned to fear the body sensations associated with panic since they are an important part of the panic cycle. [*Therapist points to "body sensations" in Figure 3.1.*] These sensations are not dangerous in and of themselves. It's just that you have learned to fear them through their association with panic attacks. As we have already discussed, these are normal physical sensations. They are frightening to you because of their association with panic attacks. The goal of this part of treatment is for you to relearn that these sensations are not dangerous. We will do this by actually creating the sensations in the therapy session. By repeatedly creating these sensations, you will learn through experience that they are not dangerous.

You will likely experience some anxiety when you create these physical sensations, based upon your past learning experiences. Having some anxiety right here in the session will give you the opportunity to practice coping with anxiety by using the relaxation procedures and cognitive strategies that we have discussed. I will be here to assist you and to help you fine tune the skills that you already have. Learning to manage anxiety without panicking during our therapy session will help you manage anxiety in the real world. Furthermore, when you create and then control the sensations of a panic attack, these feelings become far less mysterious than they once were, and you will learn that these sensations are under your control. Do you see how this would work?

We will experiment with different methods of creating the sensations of a panic attack in the therapy session. There are some things that we can do, such as breathing very rapidly for two minutes, that I know tend to produce the sensations of a panic attack in most people. I will need your help in figuring out what is the best way that we can reproduce the sensations that you feel during a panic attack. Your daily record of anxiety and panic may provide us some help here.

Procedures for Exposure to Panic Cues

Exposure sessions follow a general three-step format, which includes induction of panic sensations, focusing of attention on those sensations, and discussion of the exposure experience. For any type of exposure therapy to be effective, the client must be engaged in the exposure experience. That is, he must actively attend to and interact with the feared stimulus for exposure to have its beneficial effects (deSilva & Rachman, 1981). This appears to be true for simple phobia as well as for panic disorder. The procedures we use are designed to maximize the client's involvement with the panic cues elicited in the session.

There are no set procedures for inducing the sensations of a panic attack that are demonstrably more therapeutic than others. The key guideline is to produce sensations that are as close to those of the client's panic attack as possible. There are some procedures, however, that are known to produce sensations similar to those of a panic attack in most clients.

Hyperventilation is known to cause some of the same physical sensations as a panic attack, and clients can be taught to hyperventilate voluntarily quite easily. When a person hyperventilates, there is a decrease in partial pressure of carbon dioxide and an increase in pH in the blood. It is these changes in blood chemistry that produce the unpleasant sensations associated with hyperventilation, including dizziness, blurred vision, heart palpitations, nausea, shortness of breath, and a tingling in the hands and feet. A quick perusal of this list reveals that these are also many of the physical symptoms of a panic attack. Shallow, rapid breathing for an extended period of time will produce the changes in blood chemistry that cause the unpleasant feelings. When using voluntary hyperventilation as an exposure method, we start by giving the client a brief description of the known effects of hyperventilation. The desired sensations can usually be produced by having the client take quick, shallow breaths through his mouth and nose for two minutes.

Vigorous exercise can also produce some panic-like sensations, such as shortness of breath, heart rate acceleration, and sweating. Running in place, jumping jacks, and deep knee bends are all exercises that can be carried out easily in most therapy rooms. Dizziness and mild nausea can also be produced in the consulting room by spinning a client in a chair. Inhalation of carbon dioxide (35 percent carbon dioxide, 65 percent oxygen) has also been used as method of inducing the autonomic symptoms of a panic attack in exposure therapy (Griez & van den Hout, 1986). Carbon dioxide inhalation is not widely used, however, and requires special equipment and training.

In our clinic we have found that two minutes is usually a sufficient amount of time to produce the panic cues. Whenever possible, the therapist will participate in the exposure exercise him- or herself along with the client. This serves several purposes. First, the therapist is able to demonstrate the appropriate way to induce sensations such as involuntary hyperventilation. Second, the client sees first hand that the exercise is not dangerous. Third, the therapist is able to share with the client the sensations that he or she experienced during the exposure induction, thus providing further evidence that these sensations are normal. Fourth, it clearly demonstrates the point that the therapist and client are working on the problem together.

Once the desired physical sensations have been produced, clients are asked to sit down in their chair, close their eyes, and focus their attention inward onto the thoughts and feelings they are experiencing. We have clients concentrate in silence for five minutes. The goal here is to ensure that the client is engaged in the exposure experience. This period of time also gives them the opportunity to practice managing any anxiety they might experience using the relaxation technique and to dispute any automatic catastrophic thoughts they may notice.

After the five-minute period of focusing attention on physical feelings, the client and therapist discuss the exposure experience. There are several important questions that the therapist should ask: Can you describe the physical sensations experienced during exposure? How similar were these to the feelings you have during a panic attack? Did you notice any catastrophic automatic thoughts? How did you handle these? How anxious did you feel? How did you manage your anxiety? In the discussion, the therapist assesses the client's proficiency at applying cognitive strategies to cope with catastrophic thoughts that are triggered by the panic sensations. The therapist should praise the client for successful efforts at coping with anxious feelings.

These three steps—inducing panic sensations, focusing attention on these sensations, and discussing the experience—are repeated two to three times per session. The therapist and client should refine the exposure technique used so that it more closely approximates a panic attack.

During this third phase of treatment, exposure to panic cues will sometimes induce a panic attack, although this has happened far less frequently than we expected when we first began using these techniques. When a panic attack does occur, the therapist should remain calm and wait it out. Far from being a therapeutic setback, the panic attack provides an opportunity to work on anxiety management skills when the experience is still fresh in the client's mind. First, the therapist and client should dissect the panic attack with respect to the panic attack model used throughout treatment (Figure 3.1). The client is encouraged to identify the trigger, the body sensations he was aware of, and the automatic thoughts he noticed. Using the cognitive strategies discussed earlier, the therapist can help the client to dispute and replace the anxiety-producing thoughts. If at all possible, at least one exposure trial should be conducted after the panic attack. Although this will likely prove difficult for the client, additional exposure trials after a panic attack drive home the message that panic attacks are not dangerous and that the sensations of panic do not have to be avoided.

Respiratory Control: An Adjunct to Exposure Therapy

Breathing irregularities, including increased respiratory ventilation, occur in many individuals when they are under stress. It has been suggested by several writers that these changes in breathing patterns cause panic disorder clients to hyperventilate, which is instrumental in instigating the panic attack (Clark, Salkovskis, & Chalkley, 1985; Ley, 1985; Lum, 1976). Therefore, treatment programs for panic clients have included instructions and practice in slow, regular breathing, which is inconsistent with hyperventilation, as an additional method of coping with panic sensations. Teaching clients to switch to slow, regular breathing after first hyperventilating has been found to be an effective treatment of panic attacks in a series of clinical trials conducted in England (Clark et al., 1985; Salkovskis, Jones, & Clark, 1986). The clients were chosen for these trials on the basis of having panic attacks in which symptoms were similar to those one would expect during hyperventilation. The client can be taught to take deep breaths by having him breathe in such a manner as to expand his stomach "like a balloon." Sometimes it is helpful to have the client put his hand on his stomach so that he can feel it rise and fall with each deep breath. The client should also learn to breathe slowly by timing his breath so that he inhales every five to eight seconds. Homework assignments in slow, regular breathing can help the subject learn to switch to slow, regular breathing on command. An audio tape on which the therapist has recorded a signal every five to eight seconds can be used by the client to pace his breathing during home practice sessions.

CONCLUDING REMARKS

Clinical trials using cognitive-behavioral techniques in the treatment of panic disorder have been extremely encouraging. The proportion of clients who are panic-free after treatment has approached 100 percent

(Barlow, 1988). Although various combinations of techniques have been applied, the successful treatments have had several ingredients in common. First, clients received a thorough description of the theoretical rationale for treatment. This rationale included the idea that panic attacks are not dangerous but, rather, are the product of an accelerating interaction between normal body sensations and catastrophic thoughts. Second, clients have been provided with some strategies for coping with anxious feelings. These have usually included relaxation training and cognitive strategies. Finally, they have been exposed to the physical sensations of anxiety. They are encouraged to use their coping strategies to handle the fear associated with these sensations. The success of panic attack treatments has led to a flurry of research activity. Questions such as what is the best ordering of treatment methods and what are the essential, as opposed to the helpful but not essential, components of treatment remain unanswered at this time.

Exposure-Based Treatment of Agoraphobic Avoidance

Therapy strategies based on the principles of exposure treatment outlined in Chapter 3 provide the backbone for cognitive-behavioral treatment of agoraphobia. Exposure therapies have their strongest impact on avoidance behavior. In this chapter we will provide an overview of exposure methods. Relevant parameters that should be considered when developing a treatment plan that includes exposure-based intervention will be discussed. The clinical research literature on exposure therapy will also be reviewed.

PROVIDING THE CLIENT WITH A RATIONALE

In vivo exposure therapy is challenging and anxiety-provoking for most agoraphobic clients. In a sense, the client is being asked to do the exact thing she has felt unable to do and for which she is seeking help. It is important, therefore, to provide clients with a thorough rationale and to elicit their cooperation before launching into in vivo exposure exercises. We recommend giving the client an account of agoraphobic avoidance behavior that is based on two-factor theory. Such a rationale gives the client a cognitive set within which she can make sense of the exposure therapy experience. The following is an example of the type of rationale we provide an agoraphobic before beginning in vivo exposure therapy.

> Based upon all that we have learned about you over the previous few meetings, we feel confident that we understand the problem. We use

the term *agoraphobia* to describe the set of problems you have presented. Agoraphobia is not caused by any serious mental illness or any known physical problem. Rather, it is the result of a set of learning experiences. The problem begins when a person experiences the first panic attack. We understand a panic attack to be a natural response to a life-threatening situation. For example, if you were being attacked by a lion, you would be extremely frightened. The fear is a natural part of being human. The panic attacks that begin the learning process that results in agoraphobia are the same type of fear response that you would experience if you were really under attack. The only difference is that there is no real danger. It's as if your fear switch was turned on accidentally.

While it is not always possible to say what caused this first attack, we know that first panic attacks usually occur during a period of physical or psychological stress. It is common, for example, for some people to experience the first panic attack after a pregnancy or while recovering from the flu. Others will experience the first panic episode during some stressful life event such as a divorce or while grieving the loss of a loved one. Whatever initially caused the panic attack, once it has occurred it is often followed by other attacks. The attacks may begin to occur more reliably in certain places or in response to certain thoughts or certain physical sensations. To understand why this happens, we need to understand a special kind of learning called conditioning.

Conditioning takes place when some natural response occurs in the presence of some stimulus or cue that does not naturally cause that response. For example, if a child meets a dog for the first time and the dog barks very loudly so that the child is frightened, the next time the child sees a dog she may again become frightened and run away. The child's fearful reaction was learned through *conditioning,* which occurs automatically. The child learns to run away from or avoid dogs because she feels less anxious when she does. Just as in the case of this child, when you have panic attacks, the terrible fear you experienced may become conditioned to the situations you are in, the thoughts you're having, or even other physical sensations. Later, when you are in the same situation or having the same thoughts, your fear may recur automatically. You have learned that certain situations, thoughts, and feelings are associated with panic attacks, and you learn to avoid these to escape the anxiety.

Unfortunately, avoiding the situation associated with the panic attacks only makes the problem worse. If we have avoided a situation for a long time, we will often worry about whether or not we can handle the situation the next time. Fear over encountering a phobic situation because it might produce a panic attack has been called fear of fear. The ironic thing here is that being afraid of having a panic attack can actually cause some of the physical sensations of a panic.

The panic attack is such a powerful experience that many people worry that they may become sick, faint, or lose control of themselves in public. This is why many people with agoraphobia will travel only with a person who knows about their condition. The idea is that this "safe" person will be able to rescue them if they should become incapacitated with a panic attack.

Now, given that this is how the problem develops, you might wonder how you can get over it. Remember the example of the child who was frightened by the barking dog and begins to be frightened by and to avoid all dogs. What would you do to help this child learn that all dogs are not dangerous? [*Allow the client time to answer.*] Right, you would have the child meet and get to know other dogs. Now, she may be frightened when she first meets the new dogs, but this fear will subside in time. You can learn to overcome your agoraphobia in the same way—by going into the exact situations you have been avoiding.

The treatment we are recommending involves gradually practicing entering the places and doing the things that you have feared. In time your fear will be overcome. As you might expect, you will experience some anxiety along the way to conquering your phobia. It will not be necessary for you to push yourself to the point of having a panic attack each time you practice entering difficult situations. But it will be important for you to challenge yourself to cope with some fear.

IN VIVO EXPOSURE THERAPY

Graduated-exposure therapy involves having the client place herself in contact with the situations that typically provoke anxiety. Empirical research has not found elicitation of maximum emotional arousal during exposure to be a necessary component of treatment. Intensive in vivo exposure is more difficult for clients, and studies have found higher dropout rates when intensive exposure methods are used (Barlow, 1988). Furthermore, when exposure therapy is conducted over a brief period (for example, two weeks of daily exposure therapy), it can be difficult for important people in the client's life to adjust to the rapid changes in the client's mobility.

The hierarchy of anxiety-provoking situations constructed during the assessment phase provides a good starting point for exposure therapy. Although standardized exposure exercises can be used, it is usually best to design exposure sessions around the situations presented by the client.

Individual sessions of exposure therapy involve breaking down the challenging situations into a set of increasingly difficult steps. Progression through the steps is usually determined by the client's level of anxiety, as judged by self-report estimates. Typically, clients are asked to remain in the situation until anxiety subsides to a predetermined level. For example, the client may be asked to rate her anxiety at regular intervals during exposure sessions. A typical rating would be from 0 to 8, with 0 indicating no anxiety and 8 indicating maximum anxiety or panic. The client would be asked to stay in the situation until her anxiety reached a level of 3 or less. It may be necessary for some clients to remain in the situation for one to two hours before this level of habituation occurs.

For some clients, remaining in the phobic situation until anxiety reaches this predetermined level may be impossible because of the type of situation feared. We are reminded here of a client treated by one of us (JEH) for whom the target situation was riding in an elevator. Even entering the elevator was extremely anxiety-provoking for this woman. Prolonged exposure to a closed elevator proved impossible to arrange. First, it was difficult to guarantee undisturbed access to an elevator for an extended period. Second, the client was reluctant to tackle her most feared situation in a single session. As an alternative, she and her therapist created a hierarchy of increasingly difficult steps involving the elevator. Exposure sessions were carried out following these increasingly difficult steps.

1. Remain in the elevator with the door open for 10 seconds.
2. Repeat step 1 for 30 seconds.
3. Repeat step 1 for 1 minute.
4. Remain in the elevator with the door closed, then immediately opened.
5. Repeat step 4, but leave door closed for 5 seconds.
6. Repeat step 4, door closed for 10 seconds.
7. Repeat step 4, door closed for 30 seconds.
8. Repeat step 4, door closed for 1 minute.
9. Repeat step 4, door closed for 2 minutes.
10. Repeat step 4, door closed for 5 minutes.
11. Ride the elevator from the third to the second floor.
12. Ride the elevator from the third to the first floor.

The client was allowed to repeat a step as many times as she liked until her subjective anxiety subsided to a level of 3 or lower. Each of these steps was first done with the therapist, than repeated alone. Although therapy proved to be an uplifting experience for the client, this example demonstrates the patience required of the therapist conducting graduated-exposure therapy.

PARAMETERS OF EXPOSURE THERAPY

Session Duration

The clinical research literature supports the use of longer sessions of exposure treatment over treatments of shorter duration. Stern and Marks (1973), for example, found that continuous two-hour sessions of exposure therapy were more effective than four thirty-minute sessions. In general, it has been found that exposure sessions lasting one and a half to three hours are most beneficial (Michelson, 1987).

The decision of whether to end an exposure session before a client's anxiety has subsided to an acceptable level is one often faced by clinicians. According to two-factor theory, it would be countertherapeutic to end an exposure session before anxiety has had a chance to subside. In fact, for years the conventional wisdom among behavior therapists had been that clients should remain in anxiety-provoking situations until their anxiety had habituated, in order to avoid negatively reinforcing escape behavior. Emmelkamp (1982a, p. 69), for example, warned therapists, "It is essential that patients remain in one situation (for example, riding a bus) until anxiety has declined before entering a new situation (for example, shopping)."

Two studies, however, indicate that habituation of anxiety responses may not be necessary for exposure to have its therapeutic effects. Rachman, Craske, Tallman, and Solyom (1986) compared two groups of agoraphobic clients treated with eight sessions of individually administered exposure therapy. Half of their agoraphobics were instructed to stay in fear-evoking situations until their fear dropped to a level at least half of its peak value. Presumably in this group clients' anxiety would have habituated. The other agoraphobics were instructed to "escape" the situation if their anxiety reached a predetermined level (70 on a subjective scale of 0 to 100). In this group, anxiety would not have had time to habituate, and escape would have been reinforced. Contrary to conventional wisdom, both sets of clients showed equivalent levels of improvement at the conclusion of treatment and at three-month follow-up assessment. In an older study,

Everaerd, Rijken, and Emmelkamp (1973) compared a combined imaginal and in vivo exposure technique with a procedure they called "shaping." In the latter, agoraphobics were instructed to enter anxiety-arousing situations until they began to feel uncomfortably tense, at which time they were to return to a place of safety. Both treatments were equally effective.

Spacing of Exposure Sessions

Following from the finding that longer treatment sessions were more helpful than shorter sessions, it has been suggested that massed exposure therapy sessions (daily sessions) may be a more powerful treatment than sessions that take place once a week, as is typical in psychotherapy. Clinical research has lent some support to this suggestion. Foa, Jameson, Turner, and Payne (1980) found that agoraphobics improved more following daily therapy sessions, as opposed to weekly sessions. Features of the experimental design, however, limit the conclusions that can be drawn from this single study. Recently, Chambless (1988) found no benefit for daily exposure sessions over weekly sessions in a study that included 14 agoraphobics.

Given the inconsistencies in the research literature, it seems that clinicians may be on more solid ground if exposure sessions are conducted on a weekly, or twice weekly, rather than a daily basis. There are several advantages to weekly sessions. First, daily sessions are likely to disrupt the client's life. Daily one- to three-hour exposure sessions may be difficult to arrange around employment, child care, and other responsibilities. Second, given the powerful influence exposure therapy can have on avoidance behavior, such large changes may have a negative impact on the client's interpersonal system. Clinical research studies that have found a deterioration in the marital relationship coincident with exposure therapy have tended to employ time-limited intensive exposure treatment (for example, Hafner, 1977).

The Therapist's Role

Graduated-exposure therapy can be carried out either from the client's home or from the clinic, with varying degrees of therapist involvement. The therapist's role varies during the course of treatment. Early in graduated-exposure therapy, the therapist's role is to ensure that the client understands the rationale for treatment, to provide structure to the session, and to encourage and support the client. As the client challenges herself with increasingly more difficult situations, the therapist should praise each step liberally. Clinical researchers have found that when verbal praise is made contingent upon agoraphobic clients traveling increased distances on a specified route or spending greater amounts of time in exposure exercises, clients tend to make more rapid progress (Agras, Leitenberg, & Barlow, 1968).

Programs have been devised that involve either no therapist contact (self-help books) or minimal contact with the therapist (programmed practice). Using self-help manuals, agoraphobics can construct their own self-directed exposure exercises. Research on the effectiveness of self-help manuals suggests that these can be helpful with some clients (for example, Weekes, 1968). However, self-help books may be helpful for only the least impaired agoraphobics. Holden, O'Brien, Barlow, Stetson, and Infantino (1983) treated six severely agoraphobic clients by providing them with self-help manuals that contained instructions for a self-directed exposure program and some suggestions for cognitive restructuring. The self-help manual itself was not an effective treatment. Examinations of possible reasons for treatment failure revealed that after an initial burst of interest in exposure exercises, the client's compliance with direct exposure practice dropped to near zero by week 2 of the program. When these six clients were treated by a therapist who followed the same program outlined in the self-help manual, they demonstrated moderate improvement.

Programs that involve minimal therapist time have been shown to be effective in clinical research studies. Mathews, Gelder, and Johnston (1981) developed programmed practice manuals to be used by clients and their spouses (or significant others) with very little therapist involvement. These programs emphasized the following six points:

1. It is made clear to the client from the start that she, rather than the therapist, will be responsible for running the program.

2. A suitable person, usually a spouse, is recruited to help with the day-to-day operation of the program.

3. Detailed but simple manuals that describe the nature of agoraphobia, the principles of graded exposure, and the methods of coping with anxiety and of encouraging regular practice are provided to the client and her partner.

4. The therapist describes his or her role as that of an advisor and does not take an active role in exposure practice.

5. The meetings with the therapist usually take place at the client's home and take the form of a discussion among the therapist, the client, and the partner about the practice program and any problems that may have arisen.

6. The time spent with the therapist is limited to about five visits over a month, after which the meetings are phased out. The client and partner continue the program after the therapist has stopped making scheduled visits.

In an intriguing study, Ghosh and Marks (1987) treated three groups of agoraphobics with various forms of self-exposure instructions. Clients received either instructions from a psychiatrist, a self-help book (*Living with Fear;* Marks, 1978), or a computer program. The average total times spent with the therapist in each condition were 4.6 hours (psychiatrist instructions), 1.5 hours (book instructions), and 2.7 hours (computer instructions). These average times include a 1.5-hour initial evaluation of each client. Ghosh and Marks found that all groups improved and that there were no significant differences in improvement rates. The work of Mathews et al. (1981) and of Ghosh and Marks (1987) indicates that self-directed exposure can be beneficial to some clients and may lead to improvement comparable to that achieved with more therapist-intensive interventions.

Despite these findings, clinicians need to guard against prematurely removing themselves from the exposure therapy. Self-directed treatment may have beneficial effects only with agoraphobics who are experiencing milder forms of the disorder. A recent study has found a combination of self-directed exposure and therapist-directed exposure to be superior to self-directed exposure alone (Mavissakalian & Michelson, 1986a). The latter intervention led to significant improvement in fewer than one-third of the clients, whereas the combined treatment resulted in significant improvement in two-thirds of the clients.

There has been relatively little empirical research into the relationship between therapist characteristics and outcome of behavioral therapies. The few studies examining the relationship between therapist characteristics and outcome of exposure therapy of agoraphobia have tended to be retrospective and have suffered from other methodological weaknesses (see Williams & Chambless, 1990, for a review). Recently, however, a prospective and methodologically improved study of therapist characteristics and outcome of in vivo exposure treatment of agoraphobia has been published (Williams & Chambless, 1990). In this study, significant and positive relationships were found between agoraphobic clients' ratings of two therapist variables (self-confidence and caring/involvement in treatment) and outcome on a behavioral test.

Drawing from this body of research literature and from our own experiences, we offer these general guidelines for therapists conducting graduated exposure. The therapist's role is most important early in graduated-exposure therapy. He or she needs to ensure that the client understands the rationale for exposure exercises and that self-directed exposure sessions have the necessary structure. This can be accomplished by helping the client develop her individualized exposure exercises and actually accompanying her on her earliest excursions. While on exposure excursions, the therapist should strike a balance between responding empathically to the client's emotional reactions and confidently encouraging the client to persist. Sharing the client's excitement over progress and disputing the client if she downplays her achievements are important as well. The therapist should assess the impact of exposure exercises on the client's interpersonal environment. It may be necessary to meet with clients and spouses together, as outlined by Mathews et al. (1981) to ensure that both are working toward a common goal. As the client's efficiency at developing and carrying out exposure exercises increases, the therapist should withdraw from exposure sessions. The message that should be conveyed to the client is that she is capable of overcoming her problem and developing independence. By decreasing his or her role in exposure exercises, the therapist can facilitate the development of a sense of control in the client (Barlow, 1988).

Client's Role: What Do I Do?

The rationale for exposure therapy presented to clients before the initiation of treatment can be helpful in providing a framework within which the client can understand the purpose of the exposure exercises. In addition to having a general rationale, however, clients frequently want to know what to do when they are in the phobic situation. Scanning the clinical research reports, one encounters a variety of brief descriptions of the instructions given to clients. Often these are cryptic—for example, remain in the situation until your anxiety subsides to a level of 3 or less. In our experience, clients frequently want to know more. Marks (1981b) describes some general guidelines for instructing clients as to how to use time in the phobic situation constructively. He suggests that clients deal with anxiety first by accepting that it will occur. The implicit message is that anxiety can be withstood and that it will subside with time. Second, clients should attend to the cues that indicate the presence of anxiety. Physical sensations that indicate the onset of anxiety should not be ignored. Third, clients should be taught to rate their anxiety without exaggerating its magnitude. Finally, clients are encouraged to observe how long it takes for anxiety to subside. By following these general guidelines, the clients can begin to understand the topography of their anxiety.

A relatively common question asked by clients who are initiating exposure exercises has to do with panic attacks. In fact, after we carefully explain the rationale for in vivo exposure, one of the first things we frequently hear from clients is, "But what if I have a panic attack?" The best responses to this question usually include the following components. First, the client can be reassured that the success of treatment does not depend on her experiencing a panic attack in therapy. On the other hand, if she should panic, it will not cancel out the benefits of therapy. The message is that if a panic happens, it happens. Therapy will progress nonetheless. Second, to help the client reconstrue the attacks, the therapist can point out that she has experienced them in the past and that she has always survived the experience—she is here to "tell the tale." Experiencing a few more panic attacks in the course of therapy, though clearly unpleasant, will be worth the cost given the long-term benefits she can expect to gain. Third, the therapist should convey to the client the idea that avoiding future panic attacks at all costs is not the goal of therapy. It would be countertherapeutic for the therapist to concur with the client in her perception that a panic attack is the most dreaded of outcomes. The metamessage here is basically this: *Panic attacks are not dangerous!* The client will not die, nor will she be taken away, bound in a straitjacket, to the local mental hospital. Instead, panic attacks should be discussed as if they are inconvenient annoyances.

In vivo exposure exercises can, of course, be used in the treatment of panic attacks as described in Chapter 5. An excursion into a phobic situation can be a reliable method of inducing the physical sensations of a panic attack. Clients can be encouraged to use applied relaxation and cognitive strategies to cope with the anxiety associated with those sensations.

COGNITIVE THERAPY OF AGORAPHOBIC AVOIDANCE

In studies directly comparing cognitive therapy with in vivo exposure therapy, the latter intervention has been found to be more effective in treating agoraphobic clients' avoidance behavior (see Chapter 3 for review). Nonetheless, cognitive techniques can be used as an adjunct to exposure methods. We continue to use cognitive restructuring along with in vivo exposure despite the disappointing empirical findings. We justify our time spent in teaching clients cognitive coping strategies on the following grounds. First, the cognitive interventions follow logically from the general account of panic disorder we provide clients (see the rationale for cognitive-behavioral treatment of panic in Chapter 5). Second, in our experience clients seem to like the cognitive strategies. We have been pleased by recent empirical findings that have found support for using cognitive interventions in treating agoraphobia (Michelson & Marchione, 1989).

The rationale for cognitive therapy of agoraphobic avoidance follows from the intervention of cognitive therapy of panic. However, a greater emphasis is placed on identifying and disputing catastrophic misinterpretations of the consequences of panicking in a public place. We have used the following verbatim rationale with agoraphobic clients.

As we have already seen, these sudden attacks of anxiety, or panic attacks, are a central component of agoraphobia. These attacks are difficult to understand, so people come up with a variety of explanations, such as, "I must be going crazy," or, "There is something terribly wrong with me." People will often leave the situation in which the panic attack struck and return home as soon as possible, with great relief. Oftentimes, people with agoraphobia will draw the inaccurate conclusion that they can't return to the situation where they panicked. They will often think, "I'll panic if I go there," or, "I can't handle that situation." These types of beliefs make it harder to go back to the surroundings in which the attack was experienced. Of course, a person would not want to go to the mall, for example, if she believed that she would not be able to cope while there and would panic. The ironic thing here is that by repeatedly going back to the situation and refusing to leave it regardless of fear, she would eventually overcome the phobia. However, it is hard to alter the habit of avoiding or escaping from the situation, and it is also hard to stop brooding about the negative aspects of the problem. These brooding, worrisome thoughts actually keep the problem going, because there is a vicious circle in which anxious thoughts create anxiety, which encourages further worrying, and so on.

In this part of the treatment, we will help you to overcome the negative and unhelpful thinking that contributes so importantly to your fear and makes it difficult for you to travel as freely as you would like. Therapy will involve discussing the unhelpfulness of typical phobic thoughts. We will also practice a method of building confidence so that you can *cope* with the anxious feelings you will have as you practice exposing yourself to the situations you have avoided.

Ellis (1979) has identified a set of irrational beliefs that are particularly prevalent among agoraphobics. Especially poignant for agoraphobics is the sense that the integrity of one's self, one's personal worth, or one's comfort is threatened. Related irrational ideas are that one must always perform well, be approved by others, and have things go one's own way; if not, catastrophe! As Ellis puts it, the agoraphobic mobilizes self-statements like: "I *must* not experience this kind of exceptionally painful reaction! It's *awful* to get that uncomfortably anxious! I *can't stand* that amount of inconvenience!" (Ellis, 1979, p. 163).

The therapist helps the client to identify these kinds of automatic thoughts and to see how they exacerbate anxiety. The therapist then challenges the client to examine how well these statements match up with objective facts. Finally, the client is encouraged to generate alternative ways of thinking about the same situation. The following case vignette illustrates this approach.

Therapist: When you said, "I just couldn't deal with that," did you mean you couldn't handle feeling panicky if you were with your children at the restaurant?

Client: Yeah . . . I just couldn't deal with it if I panicked with the kids.

Therapist: Yet you had told the children you would take them out for pizza . . . so on the one hand you've said, "I will go to the restaurant," and on the other hand you've said, "I can't handle being at the restaurant." How did it feel to make these two conflicting statements—one to the children and one to yourself?

Client: It felt terrible. I felt like I was trapped because I had told the kids I would take them but I knew that I couldn't handle it.

Therapist: How do you know you couldn't handle it?

Client: What do you mean? I mean, what if I panicked?

Therapist: Let's look at that. First, what is the probability that you will have a panic attack at the restaurant?

Client: There is a pretty good chance.

Therapist: Is it 50/50?

Client: More like 70/30.

Therapist: O.K. Let's say there is a 70 percent chance that you will have a panic attack at the restaurant. O.K. So what if you do?

Client: I couldn't handle it. I mean, what am I supposed to do, take the kids to the emergency room with me?

Therapist: Wait a minute. Who said anything about the emergency room?

Client: Well, I was just thinking that if I had to go there, who would take care of the kids?

Therapist: When was the last time you went to the emergency room?

Client: About a year ago.

Therapist: How many panic attacks have you had in the last year?

Client: I don't know. A hundred maybe.

Therapist: So, in the last hundred panic attacks, you have never had to go to the emergency room. So the odds are at least 100 to 1 against your having to go there if you panicked at the restaurant.

Client: I guess so.

Therapist: In looking at your panic diary, it seems that your average panic attack lasts about 15 minutes. Is that right?

Client: That's about right, but I'm usually shook up for the rest of the day.

Therapist: O.K. . . . . So if you panic, you really feel bad for about 15 minutes.

Client: I feel bad and I would have to get out of there. I mean, I couldn't stay in the restaurant if I panicked.

Therapist: You feel like, if you panicked, you would have to leave.

Client: I know that I don't have to leave. I mean . . . I know it's like you said, the attack will pass. But it feels like I have got to get out of there.

Therapist: What about at the restaurant? You would feel like you had to get out of there, but might you be able to stay anyway?

Client: I know I could if I really pushed myself. I know I could do it for the kids. It's just that I feel terrible.

Therapist: O.K. Let's look at this situation again. There is a 70 percent chance that you will have a panic attack in the restaurant. If you did have a panic attack, you would want to leave, but you think you could make yourself stay for the children. And if you stayed, our prediction would be that the attack would be over in 15 minutes. So you would be very uncomfortable for about 15 minutes. The attack would be unpleasant, but nothing you couldn't handle—you have had plenty of experience.

Client: That's for sure. I don't know. When you describe it that way, it doesn't sound so impossible.

Therapist: You said there is about a 30 percent chance that you won't have a panic attack at the restaurant. How would you feel if you took the kids to the restaurant and you did not have a panic attack?

Client: That would be great. I mean, I would feel like a normal mommy.

Therapist: So that would be great. I guess that means that there is a 30 percent chance that you will have a great experience if you go to the restaurant. What are the chances of having a great time if you don't take the kids?

Client: Oh, that would be awful. They would be disappointed and I would feel like a failure.

Therapist: Is it worth the risk, then, to go to the restaurant?

Client: I think so.

In the preceding vignette, the therapist is trying to help the client gain insight into her unhelpful style of thinking and to examine the situation objectively. It can also be helpful to have clients think of coping self-statements that they can use while practicing exposure exercises. We follow Meichenbaum's (1977) stress inoculation training model in helping clients develop and practice coping self-statements. In the therapy hour, the therapist and client will pick one or more self-exposure homework assignments that the client will practice in the ensuing week. Coping self-statements that the client can use as she prepares to face the challenge, confronts the feared situation, copes with anxious feelings, and reflects back on the situation are generated by both the client and the therapist. Next, the client imagines proceeding through the four steps and practices using the coping self-statements. The client is instructed to use the coping statements during the week as she practices her in vivo exercises.

Here are some examples of coping self-statements generated by one of our agoraphobic clients.

1. *Preparing for the challenge:*
   —"One step at a time."
   —"I'll be able to cope with the situation even though I may not feel perfectly relaxed."

2. *Confronting the feared situation:*
   —"One step at a time."
   —"I can handle this situation."
   —"I may be anxious, but I can cope."
   —"It's not dangerous; I will just feel uncomfortable for a while."

3. *Coping with the feeling of being overwhelmed:*
   —"It will be over soon; it will not be the worst thing that can happen."
   —"I've gone through this before; I can do it again if I need to."
   —"Even if this is a full-blown panic attack, 10 on a 10-point scale of fear, it will soon come down to 9 if I hold my ground."

4. *Reflecting on the confrontation:*
   —"No matter how well it went, I tackled a really challenging situation."
   —"I am proud of myself."
   —"Each time I confront a situation like that, it gets better than the time before."
   —"I am on my way."

INVOLVEMENT OF THE SPOUSE IN TREATMENT

The interpersonal context in which agoraphobic avoidance develops has been highlighted by several theorists (for example, Goldstein & Chambless, 1978). Whether or not certain interpersonal dynamics are important in the development of the disorder, as these theorists have suggested, there is no question that the problem impinges on the social system in which the client lives. That system needs to accommodate the changes in the agoraphobic client as she progresses through exposure treatment. One method of facilitating integration of the improving client into the social system would be to include important parts of that system in treatment. Most clinical research has concentrated on the inclusion of the spouse in treatment. Utilizing the home-based treatment program described above, Mathews and his colleagues in England have demonstrated the value of a home-based treatment program in a series of uncontrolled clinical trials (Mathews et al., 1981).

Spouse-assisted treatment programs have also been compared to exposure treatment without the spouse and have fared well (Barlow, O'Brien, & Last, 1984). The husbands of 14 agoraphobic women participated in small-group treatment with their spouses. Treatment focused on teaching cognitive restructuring procedures in order to eliminate negative attitudes and dispute thought processes that contribute to anticipatory anxiety and panic, and on self-paced exposure exercises to be carried out from the client's home in a structured fashion. Fourteen agoraphobics received the same treatment but without their spouse's participation. Both groups improved significantly, which is, of course, not surprising given that in vivo exposure exercises were a large part of the treatment. Including the spouse in treatment appeared to have a beneficial influence on the clients. In the spouse-assisted group, 12 of the 14 clients were "treatment responders," which these investigators specified as a 20 percent improvement on at least three of five measures of agoraphobic severity. Only 6 of the 14 agoraphobics treated without their spouses met criteria as treatment responders.

Although these results support the inclusion of the spouse in exposure treatment, they must be interpreted with caution. Other investigators have found no advantage for including spouses in a home-based treatment (Cobb, Mathews, Childs-Clark, & Blowers, 1984). The Barlow, O'Brien, and Last (1984) study does, however, point to the need for therapists to consider the marital relationship when treating agoraphobic clients. We will take up the topic of marital therapy in the treatment of agoraphobia in more detail in Chapter 7.

GROUP EXPOSURE TREATMENT

Exposure therapy has been successfully adapted to treating groups of agoraphobic clients. Group treatment has several intrinsic advantages. The first is the obvious savings in the therapist's time. Second, group treatment provides clients with the opportunity for observational learning. Clients can observe other agoraphobics struggling with and overcoming anxiety. In doing so, they may be more motivated to tackle their own challenging situations. Finally, if a group of clients is socially cohesive, they may encourage one another and subsequently achieve greater individual success.

Several clinical research studies have demonstrated the efficacy of group treatment (Hafner & Marks, 1976; Hand, Lamontagne, & Marks, 1974; Teasdale, Walsh, Lancashire, & Mathews, 1977; Watson, Mullet, & Pillay, 1973). Levels of improvement following group exposure therapy compare favorably with those for individual treatment (Hafner & Marks, 1976), with group treatment showing some advantage on nonphobic measures of adjustment. The level of social cohesion experienced by the group appears to have an influence on treatment outcome. Hand et al. (1974) controlled the level of social cohesion achieved by two groups of agoraphobics undergoing exposure therapy. High group cohesion was achieved by presenting the treatment rationale to the group together and by allowing group members to discuss problems before the initiation of exposure exercises. The low-cohesion group was not allowed to discuss problems, and members were presented with the treatment rationale individually. An independent assessment of social cohesiveness confirmed the effect of the manipulation. Cohesive and noncohesive groups improved to a similar degree at the end of treatment. However, at three- and six-month follow-up assessment the cohesive group showed further improvement and the noncohesive group did not. Furthermore there were fewer treatment dropouts in the cohesive group. Informally, the investigators observed that members of the cohesive group kept in touch with one another after treatment and appeared to support each other's continued efforts at overcoming the problem.

In a replication study of the influence of group cohesion on treatment outcome, continuing improvement during the follow-up interval was not observed (Teasdale et al., 1977). This failure to replicate the positive influence of group cohesion on treatment outcome may have been due to the level of group cohesion achieved in the replication study. The amount of group cohesion achieved in the Teasdale et al. (1977) study was actually midway between the high- and low-cohesion groups studied by Hand et al. (1974). Taken together, these results seem to suggest that although group cohesiveness may lead to continued improvement after treatment, high levels of social cohesiveness may be difficult to achieve.

SAFETY SIGNALS: THERAPY IMPEDIMENTS
OR THERAPY TOOLS?

The presence or absence of safety signals can have a significant impact on the degree of mobility demonstrated by an agoraphobic client. As we indicated in Chapter 4, the identification of safety signals is important when assessing avoidance. In the course of exposure therapy, it is necessary repeatedly to evaluate the extent to which clients continue to rely on safety signals when confronting anxiety-provoking situations. It is not uncommon for clients to develop new safety signals in the course of therapy. A scrap of paper on which the client has written coping self-statements can take the place of an empty medicine bottle or an umbrella. There is some disagreement among clinical researchers over what steps therapists should take when safety signals are identified. Unfortunately, there is little in the way of empirical research findings to guide the clinician.

David Barlow, an eminent researcher and thinker in the area of anxiety disorders, has stressed the importance of weaning clients from their safety signals as a part of exposure therapy (Barlow, 1988). Barlow argues that the danger of ignoring or overlooking safety signals lies in increased relapse after therapy. If the former agoraphobic loses or forgets her safety signal item, she may become anxious, avoid situations that she had previously entered with her good-luck charm, and perhaps panic. A full-blown relapse may follow such an experience. Barlow recommends that clinicians wean clients from their safety signals in the context of structured exposure exercises.

S. Jack Rachman, another eminent clinical researcher and theoretician, recommends an approach to safety signals that is somewhat divergent from that of Barlow (Rachman, 1983, 1984). Rachman suggests that we might view agoraphobia as maintaining a balance between danger and safety signals. Safety signals might be exploited by therapists, according to Rachman, in order to facilitate exposure exercises. Rather than arranging exposure sessions so that the client is encouraged to move further and further away from safety, the clinician might have the client move toward her safety signals. Take, for example, the client for whom a trusted friend serves as a safety signal and for whom entering a shopping mall is a dangerous situation. Rather than weaning the client from her friend, as Barlow would presumably suggest, the client might be allowed to go to the friend but only by passing through the mall. The safety signal in this way becomes an incentive for the client to engage in previously avoided situations. The exposure experience would then provide the client with the opportunity to develop new and less restrictive safety signals. Conceptualizing agoraphobia as a balance between danger and safety signals leads to alternative ways of viewing exposure therapy. From this perspective, the goal is not to eliminate safety signals but to change the signals from those that are restrictive to those that allow the client a greater range of movement. Therapies based on Rachman's safety signal perspective have yet to be put to empirical test.

Our own view of the best therapeutic approach to the problem of safety signals falls somewhere between those suggested by Barlow and Rachman. In our work with agoraphobic clients, we collaborate with the client in identifying which safety signals need to be eliminated and which ones the client might choose to keep. When another person is the primary safety signal for a given client, we will usually encourage the client to wean herself from that person given the limitations inherent in relying on the presence of another person when doing such routine activities as shopping or taking the bus. However, when the safety signal is unobtrusive and can be reliably carried with the client (for example, an empty medicine bottle), we tend to be less strident in our recommendations. The responsibility for deciding which safety signals are acceptable and which need to be eliminated is, in our view, primarily that of the client. For example, the client described in Chapter 4, for whom having a six-pack of beer in the trunk of his car was a powerful safety signal, chose not to wean himself from his security six-pack. Until empirical findings emerge regarding the impact of untreated safety signals on posttreatment functioning, we do not see the need to impose on the client the elimination of safety signals as a necessary treatment goal.

IMAGINAL EXPOSURE METHODS

The first widely used behavioral procedure in the treatment of phobic disorders was systematic desensitization (Wolpe, 1958). Desensitization involves presentation of a hierarchy of phobic scenes while clients remain in a deeply relaxed state. As typically applied, systematic desensitization involves developing a hierarchy of situations that the client avoids or that are associated with anxiety. Clients are then taught a method of progressive muscle relaxation. Once this is mastered, the client is asked to relax and the least frightening scene is presented. If the client feels any anxiety at all as she imagines the scene, she is to signal the therapist who instructs her to stop imagining the scene and to regain a state of relaxation. Progression to the next item in the hierarchy occurs only after the client imagines the scene without any anxiety. Instructions for teaching clients deep muscle relaxation are described in detail in Chapter 5. Clients are instructed to practice relaxation exercises at home so that they can master this skill. Sometimes it is necessary to provide the client with an audio tape of the relaxation procedure to assist with home practice.

Early clinical reports of the use of systematic desensitization in the treatment of agoraphobia were encouraging. However, positive effects were not reliably found, and the benefits obtained could often be attributed to instructions given to clients to practice in vivo exercises between therapy sessions. The weight of the evidence has led investigators to conclude that desensitization by itself is not an effective treatment for agoraphobia (Emmelkamp, 1982b; Thorpe & Burns, 1983).

Imaginal flooding is similar to systematic desensitization except that the client is not encouraged to remain completely relaxed as she imagines phobic scenes. This procedure usually involves prolonged presentation of phobic scenes until the client's anxiety subsides. Imaginal flooding does not require the presentation of fear-producing scenes of maximum intensity. Frightening scenes can be presented in a graded fashion. Flooding simply implies exposure to "high-intensity . . . stimuli for prolonged periods" (Marshall, Gauthier, & Gordon, 1979, p. 215). Several studies have compared the efficacy of imaginal versus in vivo flooding in the treatment of agoraphobia (Chambless, Foa, Groves, & Goldstein, 1982; Emmelkamp & Wessels, 1975; Mathews, Johnston, Lancashire, Munby, Shaw, & Gelder, 1976; Stern & Marks, 1973; Watson, Mullett, & Pillay, 1973). Most reviewers have concluded, on the basis of these studies, that in vivo treatment yields results superior to imaginal flooding (Emmelkamp, 1982a; Jansson & Ost, 1982; Mavissakalian & Barlow, 1981; Wilson, 1982). This conclusion may not, in fact, be warranted (James, 1986). Better outcome with in vivo flooding has not been consistently found. When it has, the studies tend to have suffered from methodological problems. We have examined this literature and agree with James's (1986) conclusion that it would be premature to discard imaginal exposure methods (Hecker & Thorpe, 1987). Our review suggests that imaginal and in vivo flooding techniques may operate via the same fear reduction mechanism.

We recommend that clinicians familiarize themselves with the imaginal exposure methods and keep them in their arsenal of interventions. There are circumstances in which imaginal exposure procedures provide the only reasonable method of exposing clients to important anxiety-provoking situations. Clients often fear situations that cannot be predicted, such as encountering an acquaintance at a crowded shopping mall, or that are so brief that it is impossible to implement prolonged in vivo exposure. Writing a check at a supermarket might be an example of the latter.

An agoraphobic client treated by one of the authors (JEH) provides an interesting example of a case in which imaginal exposure procedures were called for. Cathy had made significant progress in decreasing her avoidance of public places through in vivo exposure therapy. One target situation had been attending Sunday mass. Therapy included graduated exposure to Sunday mass by having Cathy at first arrive late to mass so that she had to stand in the back. Each week she was given the homework assignment of going to mass earlier than the previous week and obtaining a seat closer to the altar and hence farther from the exit. Therapy sessions focused on other situations she avoided, such as the supermarket and the bookstore. Eventually, Cathy was able to attend mass and sit almost anywhere in the church. The stumbling block proved to be receiving holy communion. It was not possible for us to break this task down into a graded series of steps. Cathy believed that once she stood in line to receive communion, she would be trapped and could not escape if she were to have difficulty. There was clearly a component of social anxiety for this client in that she was concerned about how she would appear to the rest of the congregation if she were to panic while standing at the altar to receive communion.

Graduated imaginal flooding was used to treat this problem. A series of four scenarios involving progressively more disastrous attempts at receiving communion were created by Cathy and her therapist. In the first scenario she was anxious but did not panic. In the fourth, she panicked after taking communion and vomited up the communion wafer. The imaginal flooding sessions lasted about 90 minutes. The beginning of each session was devoted to a review of the previous week's homework assignments and presentation of the rationale for imaginal flooding. The therapist explained that in this procedure Cathy would be asked to imagine herself in an extremely difficult situation for an extended period of time. She was told that she would likely feel anxious but that her anxiety would subside with time. Eventually she would be able to imagine herself engaged in the worst possible scenario without experiencing excessive anxiety. Because she had experienced her worst expectations without fear, actually taking communion in real life should prove much easier. About 45 to 60 minutes of each session were actually spent in imaginal flooding. The therapist described the scene using a script constructed by himself and Cathy, which included descriptions of Cathy's physiological and behavioral responses in the situation (Lang, 1979). After the scene had been described, the therapist would prompt Cathy with lines from the script about once every minute. Cathy also rated her anxiety level periodically. Each scene was imagined until Cathy's anxiety rating dropped below 3 on a 0–8 scale. After three sessions of imaginal flooding, she was able to take communion.

Another common use for imaginal exposure methods is in preparing clients for important events that arise infrequently, such as attending a wedding. Another of our clients, David, contacted us several months after therapy had terminated. David had been moderately agoraphobic but had made rapid progress with a combination of cognitive therapy and in vivo exposure. He reported that although therapy had been very helpful in getting him to the point at which he could carry out the routines of his daily life, he was concerned about attending his son's high school graduation. David reported that the graduation was to take place in June in the high school gymnasium, which was not air-conditioned. He was fearful that the heat and the crowds would cause him to panic. Furthermore, his anticipatory anxiety was exacerbated by the knowledge that his ex-wife would also be attending the ceremony. He reported that if he panicked and had to leave the ceremony, his ex-wife would think he was self-centered and did not care about his son.

A coping desensitization (Goldfried, 1971) procedure was used to help David prepare for the graduation ceremony. Coping desensitization is similar to standard systematic desensitization in that a hierarchy of anxiety-provoking situations is developed with the client. In this case the hierarchy included items such as entering into the crowded gymnasium, finding a seat, encountering his ex-wife, feeling warm as the ceremony progressed, and experiencing difficulty breathing (an early sign of panic for this client). In coping desensitization, rather than maintaining complete relaxation, the client is encouraged to allow some anxiety to arise, but learns to practice dealing with the anxiety with strategies developed in therapy. David was taught progressive muscle relaxation exercises and cognitive coping strategies for managing anxiety. As each item in the hierarchy was presented, David practiced using relaxation and cognitive self-statements to control his anxiety.

David was able to attend his son's graduation with little difficulty.

We will never know for sure how much of his success can be attributed to the exposure therapy and how much to the fact that his ex-wife missed the ceremony because of illness.

SOME GUIDELINES FOR IMAGINAL EXPOSURE THERAPY

As we have seen, imaginal exposure therapy can take a variety of forms. Regardless of the particular type of imagery procedure used to expose the client to anxiety-provoking situations, we suggest that clinicians consider the following guidelines. First, allow the client to take the lead role in developing the situations to be presented in imagery, including the scripts to be used when presenting scenes. There are particular words and phrases that may have specific meaning for the client, which would be lost if the therapist decides to paraphrase using his or her own language. One way to conceptualize imagery is to view it as an active process in which the image is constructed from information that is stored in long-term memory (Lang, 1979). Certain descriptors may cue or activate some information in memory. If the therapist uses descriptors that have a specific meaning for him or her, they may cue nothing for the client. Therefore, it is best to use the client's own language whenever possible. A second guideline to consider when presenting scenes to clients is to include in the description information pertaining to how the client will respond in the situation. Again, it is best to rely on the client to provide this type of information. Simple questions—"How do you think you would feel if this were to happen to you in real life?" or "What would you typically do in a situation like this?"—can be useful in gathering this information. Finally, we recommend that clinicians allow clients to experience some anxiety during imaginal exposure therapy. We have argued (Hecker & Thorpe, 1987) that activation of anxiety responses during exposure therapy is crucial to fear reduction.

Some clinicians use audio tape recordings of imaginal flooding scenes so that clients can practice imaginal exposure at home. This offers the obvious advantage of providing larger amounts of exposure than can be provided in weekly therapy sessions. Furthermore, when using audio tapes the client can record the imagery scene in her own voice and using her own words. This should provide descriptions that most closely match the information stored in the client's memory. The clinician needs to exercise caution when assigning imaginal flooding homework. He or she should develop with the client structured times for practicing imaginal exposure. Furthermore, the client should be encouraged to make exposure trials long enough so that anxiety that is activated during imagery has enough time to habituate.

HOW EFFECTIVE IS EXPOSURE THERAPY?

A great deal of enthusiasm was generated by the early success achieved through the application of behavioral techniques to the problem of agoraphobia. The syndrome had proved resistant to change via more traditional approaches to psychotherapy. With the discovery of exposure therapy, clients who had confined themselves to their homes, sometimes for several years, were able to make significant gains in mobility with relatively time-limited intervention.

As with many new discoveries, the enthusiasm that was generated by the early successes of behavior therapy has subsided with time. Clinicians and researchers have taken a cold, hard look at the gains made by agoraphobic clients and at the number of clients who drop out of treatment. The results of this reexamination, while clearly showing that exposure therapy is beneficial and results in superior outcome when compared with credible alternative treatments, has tempered the initial enthusiasm for exposure treatments. As we stated in Chapter 3, clinical research studies indicate that 60 to 70 percent of agoraphobic clients who complete a course of exposure treatment reap clinically significant gains. This conclusion is based on a compilation of data from many studies. Typically, improvement is defined as a reduction of 50 percent or greater in agoraphobic anxiety and avoidance that is maintained for at least six months (for example, Jansson & Ost, 1982).

The reliable production of clinically meaningful improvement in 60 to 70 percent of treated clients is a success story in the history of psychotherapy. Nonetheless, the converse finding that 30 to 40 percent of clients fail to benefit is cause for concern. Furthermore, when posttreatment levels of functioning in the improved clients are examined, it can be seen that "cure" is still the exception rather than the rule. McPherson, Brougham, and McLaren (1980), for example, found that only 18 percent of clients who improved in the course of exposure treatment were completely free of agoraphobic problems at follow-up assessment.

An additional factor to consider when evaluating the efficacy of any form of treatment is the rate at which clients refuse or drop out of treatment. The dropout rates across several studies of exposure therapy of agoraphobia, reviewed by Jansson and Ost (1982), ranged from 0 to 35 percent. The median dropout rate was 12 percent. When clients who drop out of treatment are included in estimates of the percentage of improved clients across studies, the success rate drops to 50 to 60 percent.

Given these findings, it is clear that although in vivo exposure remains the treatment of choice for agoraphobic avoidance, it is not a panacea. Clinicians need to assess each client carefully before applying exposure therapy. Some form of in vivo exposure should be central to any treatment plan. Nonetheless, the use of additional treatment procedures should also be considered. Treatments that appear to have roles as adjuncts to exposure therapy will be presented in the next chapter.

CHAPTER 7

Adjuncts to Cognitive-Behavioral Treatment of Panic Disorder and Agoraphobia

Alice had just described to her new therapist what sounded like a typical case of agoraphobia. She had frequent panic attacks and avoided stores, public buildings, formal occasions of any kind, and traveling more than five miles from home. Her symptoms had become worse recently, after her husband had left her and she had found herself in the involuntary role of single parent, with five young children to care for. Only a few months earlier, the family had moved into a home with barely adequate amenities, in a rural part of a rural state. Having established at least the tentative diagnosis of agoraphobia, the therapist entered the final phase of the initial interview by asking Alice what were the most distressing or handicapping aspects of her anxiety disorder in her everyday life. She responded as follows:

> It's being taken advantage of. It's bad enough having to look after my own kids, but all my neighbors have started using me as a free babysitter. Since I'm always at home anyway, they figure I won't mind if they leave their kids with me every time they want to go out. I don't like to hurt their feelings, so of course I can't tell them I would really prefer not to run a volunteer day-care center all the time. But it's driving me crazy! The only way I could get here at all today for this appointment was because I managed to sneak out early, before anyone came by the house. Please help me!

Brett had responded well to exposure therapy and had made some definite practical gains. But after one particularly successful session, he told his therapist he needed to get advice on something that threatened to undo all of his progress.

157

As I told you in our first meeting, my marriage isn't the best, and I guess I have come to accept it that way. But every time I achieve something new in the therapy, my wife has something negative to say about it. She's so negative I end up believing her. "Big deal, so you went to the library all by yourself," she said the other day. "If you would only pull yourself together, you wouldn't need a therapist to hold you by the hand. Just my luck to have married a mental case who's afraid of his own shadow. Anyway, I'm fed up with driving you to your therapist's office. You'll just have to make it on your own in the future." What can I do? I have made a lot of progress, but I'm not ready yet to make it here on my own. Besides, she would find a way of interfering even if I could make it on my own. She says she wants me to be well, but I don't think she really wants me to get better.

When Donna began therapy, she was nearly house-bound. She left her home only with her spouse. She decided to get help for her problem when her youngest child started school, because this left her home alone all day. Therapy sessions took place early in the morning, before her husband went to work. A course of in vivo exposure was initiated. Therapy sessions were devoted to helping the couple plan weekly exposure exercises, presenting the cognitive model of panic, and developing cognitive coping strategies. During the sixth therapy session, Donna asked if she could talk about some things that had been on her mind for a couple of weeks.

I just get discouraged. I know you are qualified, and deep down I want to believe that this treatment can work for me. It's just that every day, sooner or later, I get thinking "Will I ever get better?" I mean, last week I went into the grocery store alone and it was such a big deal. Steve was excited and you were excited. But I think, "Hey, a 34-year-old woman goes into the supermarket—big deal." I mean, will I ever just be able to do something like that without it being such a huge effort? Sometimes I just feel like there is no point in going on. I just can't get myself up to do the exposure homework. Then I get irritable and snap at Steve when he tries to make me do it. Then I feel guilty about that. I just feel like I hate myself sometimes.

Ted, a junior business major, was referred to us from the university's student counseling center for treatment of social phobia. He had requested help because he needed to take a required course in which all students had to deliver several speeches in front of the class.

He had put off taking the course as long as he could. During the initial interview, Ted presented as a charming young man who joked about his fear. He asked his therapist whether he could be rid of his concerns about public speaking through hypnosis.

It was while completing the ADIS-R with Ted that the therapist discovered a history of panic attacks. Ted's first attack occurred on a Saturday morning when he was a senior in high school. He had been up late the night before and had consumed a fair amount of alcohol and smoked some marijuana. When he had the panic attack, Ted worried that the marijuana he had smoked was laced with some other substances, which had caused permanent damage to his brain. Ted experienced his second panic attack while at a high school dance. He had come to the dance alone but expected to meet friends there. He was anxious about being seen alone, which was considered "uncool." The dance was in the school cafeteria, which was very crowded and hot. Ted recalled that he began to feel he could not draw a full breath and worried that he would pass out. When he began to feel the attack come on, he left the dance and went out to his car, where he drank several beers. He reported that the alcohol helped him to feel more relaxed.

Ted began to use alcohol regularly before going out on dates or out with his friends. This was acceptable to his friends, and he gained a reputation as a heavy drinker. When Ted came to college, his panic attacks increased in frequency. He began to carry a bottle of peppermint schnapps in his book bag and would sneak drinks between classes to reduce his anxiety. Occasionally, Ted would feel a panic attack come on in class and would slip out with his book bag to have a drink. Ted reported that he preferred peppermint schnapps because he could tell anyone who asked that he had eaten a mint. Ted's fear of giving a speech centered around his concern that should he panic while speaking, he would not be able to escape and would pass out. Ted's social drinking was also excessive. He reported that he drank every weekend night, and on any other evening when he went out socially.

Wendy, a 38-year-old accountant, was seen for therapy in the context of a clinical research study that compared two forms of cognitive-behavioral therapy of panic disorder. At initial evaluation, Wendy met diagnostic criteria for panic disorder and social phobia. Wendy had made good progress in developing a sense of control over panic attacks by the conclusion of the study. Although she continued to experience occasional limited-symptom panic attacks, Wendy was much less bothered by these than she had been before treatment. At follow-up, Wendy continued to have problems with social anxiety, and therapy was initiated to address these concerns.

Wendy lived alone and had never married. She had one close friend, Ann, whom she had met during her freshman year in college when they had been assigned to share a dormitory room. Both women had taken jobs in the town where they had attended college. Ann had married, had children, and divorced in the years that Wendy had known her. Other than occasionally attending movies or having lunch with Ann or babysitting for her children, Wendy had minimal social contacts. She was an avid reader, primarily of mystery and romance novels.

The treatment plan for addressing Wendy's social anxiety utilized a combination of social skills training, exposure therapy, and cognitive techniques. During one therapy session, Wendy was given the homework assignment of having lunch at a restaurant where several of her co-workers regularly ate. She was also asked to pay attention to the thoughts and images that came to mind as she carried out the assignment and to record these later. Wendy was not able to carry out the in vivo exposure exercise. She reported at the next session that she had felt a rush of anxious feelings as she approached the restaurant and had turned and fled to her car. But the assignment turned out to be an important exercise for Wendy nonetheless.

Wendy: As I was walking toward the restaurant, this image flashed through my mind. It happened so fast, I don't think I would have noticed if you hadn't told me to keep track of my thoughts. I remembered a birthday party I had attended when I was about four or five years old. It was just an image of it that flashed by.

Therapist: Tell me about the birthday party.

Wendy: I don't remember much about it. I just remember that at one point each child was supposed to do something. You know, like sing a song or say a poem. The child could pick whatever. When it came to my turn I just froze. I didn't say anything. Everyone just stared at me. I couldn't speak.

Wendy then recalled a whole series of times in her life when she had gone to great lengths to avoid being evaluated or scrutinized by others. In elementary school and high school, although she received very good grades, she always feigned illness or skipped school on days when honor students received special recognition or awards. In college, Wendy always waited until the last minute before she went to the dormitory cafeteria to get dinner. She did not want to have to carry her tray when the cafeteria was crowded for fear that she might drop it and draw attention to herself. She also dreaded the thought of approaching a crowded table to sit with a group of students. She generally ate alone or with Ann. Although she was an attractive woman, Wendy rarely dated when she was in school. Typically, if she did go out, it was with Ann and her boyfriend on a double date. Since finishing college, she never dated. Wendy stated, "If I went out with a man he could just see how worthless I am."

As these clinical anecdotes illustrate, the course of therapy does not always go strictly according to the textbook. In earlier chapters we reviewed a long series of impressive studies that attest to the value of exposure in vivo in the treatment of agoraphobia. Yet these studies, understandably, have dealt mainly with the discovery of important treatment elements in uncomplicated cases. Usually, the client in a research trial is given a single treatment technique for a fixed number of sessions. This is defensible as a research strategy because the researcher does not want to make confounded comparisons; but however enlightening the study is in establishing treatment effectiveness, it does not approximate the usual clinical situation, in which a more holistic treatment approach is necessary. Similarly, clients in research trials are carefully selected to represent relatively pure cases of panic disorder or agoraphobia; again, it would confound the study if the participants had a mixture of diagnoses. A client with agoraphobia, alcoholism, and depression who made disappointing gains in a research trial would leave the researcher with more than one possible explanation for the treatment failure. Although it is understandable for researchers to use pure cases and study one treatment technique at a time, the practicing clinician often wonders whether the clients seen in routine clinical work have much in common with the research participants. Complex cases for whom several treatment strategies are necessary are the norm in clinical practice. Accordingly, in the absence of research studies of multiple treatments in clients with multiple problems, clinicians find few practical guidelines in the literature and must use their own judgment in treatment planning.

The case vignettes that introduced this chapter are paraphrases of actual issues presented by clients. Panic disorder clients are not immune to assertiveness difficulties, depression and discouragement, marital difficulties, or substance abuse. They also may present with long-standing personality traits that interfere with therapy. In this section we shall present some ideas for treatment planning for complex cases.

THE SOCIAL CONTEXT

Clinicians are amply justified in paying serious attention to agoraphobic clients' social situations and social functioning. As we have indicated in Chapter 3, theorists like Goldstein and Chambless (1978) and Brehony and Geller (1981) have formulated agoraphobia as a response to interpersonal conflict in the context of low assertiveness and self-sufficiency. Others have pointed out that people diagnosed with agoraphobia are predominantly female and may have developed their disorder partly because of the powerful social influence of sex-role stereotyping (Fishman, 1980; Fodor, 1978). Research findings that agoraphobic clients may respond particularly well to group treatment and to treatment conducted with the cooperation of the spouse (see the review by Thorpe, Burns, Smith, & Blier, 1984) also encourage attention to the social context of agoraphobia. We have reviewed evidence on the benefits of including spouses in treatment in an earlier chapter; in the following sections we shall discuss assertiveness training and behavioral marital therapy as adjuncts to exposure in vivo for agoraphobia.

Assertiveness Training

The literature reviewed in Chapter 3 indicates that many people with agoraphobia have assertiveness deficits, and that treatment of assertiveness problems improves the general adjustment of those clients. There are some indications that assertiveness training actually has a positive impact on the fear and avoidance patterns of agoraphobia, but not as efficiently as exposure in vivo. Among the few studies available, however, some have provided assertiveness training in the context of a general set of recommendations and guidelines for self-initiated exposure.

What, then, does the clinician do in the case of an obviously unassertive agoraphobic like Alice? Fortunately, the clinician does not have to choose between exposure in vivo and assertiveness training; both can be implemented as part of the treatment plan. The research literature provides few guidelines as to how to sequence these interventions—that is, whether to begin with assertiveness training and then proceed with exposure, or vice versa. In the absence of clear guidelines, clinicians must use their own judgment.

In the case of Alice, it appeared that her assertiveness difficulties were not only at the forefront of her immediate concerns, but were potentially detrimental to her efforts to initiate home-based practice. She could hardly spend time each day vigorously confronting her avoidance of travel away from home if she was tied to the household by her involuntary child-care responsibilities. The therapist proceeded as follows. First, the rationale for self-initiated exposure was given. The client was told that a general policy of confronting, not avoiding, feared situations is most helpful, and that it is usually best to begin with easier items, and gradually progress to more difficult ones. This rationale was given during an early treatment session and was repeated in later sessions. Also in that early session, the client was asked to consider the common elements in (1) avoiding specific phobic surroundings because of fear and anxiety and (2) avoiding appropriate assertive behavior toward people because of fear, anxiety, lack of social skill, or self-defeating thinking patterns. The client was asked to identify a particular problem involving assertiveness that typically arose more than once a week. The therapist ensured that the item selected was at the easier end of the spectrum.

Alice chose a situation in which an acquaintance telephoned to ask if she would be available for babysitting (Alice found a telephone conversation less threatening than a face-to-face encounter). Next, she was asked what was difficult about the situation—knowing what to say, fearing the consequences of a refusal, doubting her ability to be assertive, and so forth. Alice said that the chief problem was the notion that she would be acting selfishly and unkindly if she were to refuse the request, but that it was also difficult to be assertive because she was not used to it and it made her nervous. The therapist explained the rationale for role playing or behavior rehearsal as a treatment tactic. The session proceeded as follows.

Therapist: It would help me to begin with if you could take the role of yourself, and say just what you usually would say if this took place in real life, and I would take the role of the acquaintance making the phone call. O.K.?

Alice: It'll feel a bit strange, but O.K., I'll try it!

Therapist: "Hi, Alice, hope I'm not calling too early, but I was wondering if you were going anywhere today?"

Alice: "No, I guess not . . ."

Therapist: "Oh, good. I was wondering if you wouldn't mind watching the kids for me while I go shopping. I could drop them off in about five minutes, if you like."

Alice: "Oh, O.K., I guess so."

Therapist: Thank you, that was helpful. Is that pretty much how it would usually go in real life?

Alice: Yes, I'm afraid so!

Therapist: O.K., so it sounds as if you were dissatisfied with the way you handled the situation. What would you rather have done?

Alice: Be assertive, of course! I suppose I could have made an excuse; I do that sometimes.

Therapist: Can we role-play it that way, then? I'll be the friend once more. "Alice, could you babysit for me today?"

Alice: "Well . . . actually, I have to go shopping, and I think I have a dentist's appointment."

Therapist: "No problem! Tell you what, I'll drive you to town for half an hour so you can do your shopping and see the dentist, and then we'll come back and you can take the kids then. O.K.?"

Alice: "Well, maybe I don't need to go to town today. I guess I'll take the kids" [*ending role-play*]. Oh. I guess that won't work, will it?

Therapist: The problem with making an excuse is that the other person might call your bluff, right? How about simply saying "no" to the person?

Alice: Yes, I really should, but it's so difficult.

Therapist: My idea is that if we practice it here, there's really nothing that can go wrong. You will have a chance to try assertiveness on for size, and if you end up deciding you don't want to be assertive in real life, that's up to you. But if we practice it here for a few minutes, you might even become more comfortable with the idea of being assertive. Shall we try it?

Alice: O.K.!

Therapist: O.K., I'm the friend again. "Alice, will you look after my kids this morning?"

Alice: "No, I'm sorry, I can't, because I have to go out . . . I mean, there are some other things I have to do and . . ."

Therapist: That was great! You said "no" very plainly. How did you feel?

Alice: It wasn't too bad, but I don't know how the conversation would have ended. I was starting to explain to her why I couldn't, and then all I could think of was a bunch of excuses again.

Therapist: Do you mind if I have a shot at it? You act as the friend, and I'll be you. There's the phone ringing now . . . "Hello, this is Alice."

Alice: [*in role as the friend*] "Oh, good, I'm glad I caught you in . . . can you look after my kids this morning?"

Therapist: "No, I'm afraid that won't work out today."

Alice: "Oh, why not? I mean, later would do fine, if that's better."

Therapist: "No, not today; I have other plans. We can probably work something out for another time, if we set it up in advance."

Alice: "Oh, shoot. Well, O.K., I guess I'll try someone else for today."

Therapist: How did I do?

Alice: Fine. I wish I could just say "no" like that.

Therapist: I was assuming that you might be willing to babysit another day, provided that it was set up in advance at a time convenient to you.

Alice: Oh, yes, I really don't mind helping her out; but I would like to have more control over the situation.

Therapist: Would you like to try it again, as yourself?

Alice: O.K. I'll try to be like someone on TV who is really assertive.

Therapist: Excellent! Here goes. "Alice, can you look after the kids this morning? I have to go out."

Alice: "No, not today, I'm afraid."

Therapist: "Oh, why not?"

Alice: "I have other plans, and in any case I would like to have more notice. I'll do it another time if we set it up ahead of time."

Therapist: "O.K. I guess I can ask someone else for today. Thanks anyway." That was just fine! You were assertive without being unpleasant about it, and you persisted after she questioned you. Well done!

Alice: Yes, if I could just say that without thinking too much about it, it would work, I know it would.

In this brief series of role plays, the therapist was trying to get the client started on making assertive responses in a safe environment. It seemed important to keep the exchange simple and not to get embroiled in the details of what the other might say, what circumstantial factors might complicate the picture, and so forth. The therapist deliberately congratulated the client on the positive aspects of her performance, and decided to defer until a later time comments on her initial passivity, indecisiveness, and tendency to respond defensively. The therapist's motto was: Keep it simple, reinforce liberally at first, and emphasize the benefits of simply saying "no." Repeated role plays of this kind took place in the next few sessions, and the simulated encounters grew more similar to real-life situations in a series of graduated steps. Eventually Alice learned to be appropriately assertive in these situations and began to reap practical rewards from this in the form of greater autonomy and an increased sense of personal control.

Before proceeding to further role plays, the therapist had addressed the issue that Alice felt she was being selfish and unkind in not helping her acquaintance. This issue was handled by means of cognitive restructuring procedures. Alice was asked to consider the idea that, being unassertive and unable to say "no," she was not able to make a free choice when confronted by a request. It was as if the acquaintance were making a demand with menace rather than a request that could be accepted or rejected as Alice saw fit. As a result, when confronted by a request, Alice felt she had no choice but to say "yes," because otherwise she would be acting unethically. Therefore, she felt forced into agreeing with any request, regardless of the circumstances and regardless of her own preferences. Here are Alice's responses in later, more challenging role-playing sessions.

> **Therapist:** This time, let's suppose I am a close friend who has just shown up on your doorstep with three preschool children. Let's also suppose that you definitely do not want to do any baby-minding today. "Hi, Alice, I know this is short notice, but you have always been someone who will help a friend; could you look after the kids while I go into town?"
>
> **Alice:** "No, that won't be convenient right now, I have plans. Perhaps you could ask somebody else."
>
> **Therapist:** "Alice, this is unlike you! Have I done something to offend you? It will really put me in a difficult position if I have to ask somebody else."
>
> **Alice:** "No, you haven't offended me. I don't mind you asking me to do you a favor. Sometimes I can oblige, sometimes I can't. Today just isn't convenient."

Therapist: "Look, there's something behind this, isn't there? You are normally so decent about everything. Now you are suddenly being unfriendly. I don't like the new Alice."

Alice: "I'm sorry you feel that way. There are times when I will be glad to help you out. It simply isn't convenient today. Next time, I would prefer it if you would ask me ahead of time, so you won't be disappointed if I can't help you."

Therapist: "Gee, what has got into you? With friends like you, who needs enemies?"

Alice: "Again, I'm sorry you feel that way. Feel free to ask me another time, but give me a few days' notice and I will tell you if it's convenient or not."

Therapist: "O.K., I guess."

Alice found that what she had learned in the sessions devoted to assertiveness training also applied to her agoraphobia. Learning to take the plunge and act assertively despite initial anxiety helped her to do the same thing in her counterphobic ventures in vivo. It seems likely that similar therapeutic processes are at work in assertiveness training and exposure in vivo, so that treating assertiveness difficulties and agoraphobia in the same client is not a piecemeal approach but a coherent strategy (Cavallaro, 1987).

In Alice's case, the therapist focused on the assertiveness difficulties first because, untreated, they would interfere with her exposure treatment program. Being able to say "no" to requests as Alice saw fit was the facet of assertiveness addressed first, for similar reasons. Generally, clinicians must choose whether to deal with assertiveness issues before, after, or concurrently with in vivo exposure. It is helpful to deal first with problems that have the greatest impact on the client's life. In Alice's case, learning to refuse unreasonable requests was necessary before she could gain sufficient control of her time to allow her to work on exposure. In another client, it may be more helpful to reverse the order of the treatments. A client who had had a successful work history before becoming house-bound by agoraphobia cited assertiveness difficulties as a significant concern. But because these difficulties were specific to work situations, therapist and client agreed to work on increasing her mobility before beginning the assertiveness training. Being able to get out and about enough to seek employment again was the priority.

Assertiveness is not a unitary trait, and a client who has trouble refusing requests is not necessarily unassertive in other ways. Assessment of the range of difficulties experienced by an unassertive client usually involves interviewing and the administration of a self-report questionnaire. Typical areas of assertive behavior to be assessed include being able to insist on one's rights, to refuse unreasonable requests, to express opinions and emotions freely, to praise or reprimand others as appropriate, to initiate conversations and end them, and to give and accept compliments. The Adult Self-Expression Scale (Gay, Hollandsworth, & Galassi, 1975) is a convenient inventory for use with adults from the general population; as noted earlier, we have found that many agoraphobics score lower than general population norms on this measure.

Reseachers have identified several appropriate techniques for assertiveness training. The modeling and role-playing format as followed in the treatment of Alice is popular and realistic; it gives the therapist a sample of the client's assertive behavior and provides opportunities for feedback, practice, and reinforcement of assertive responses. In addition to imparting assertive skills, the technique also appears to reduce anxiety about assertiveness and to reveal any dysfunctional cognitions mobilized by the client that may interfere with assertive behavior. Specific cognitive restructuring methods are also effective in assertiveness training; in addition to rehearsing assertive responses, the client can rehearse appropriate self-statements that will facilitate assertiveness (Thorpe, 1975). A client who knows what an assertive response would be, but fails to make it because of an "internal dialogue of conflict" (Schwartz & Gottman, 1976), can benefit from practicing helpful self-instructions in therapy. Instead of saying to herself, "What if I hurt the other person's feelings?" or, "Suppose I try to be assertive, but fail and embarrass myself?" Alice could practice self-statements like, "Remember, it's my perfect right to say 'yes' or 'no' as I choose; this is a request, not a demand," or, "Even if I do not stand up for my rights perfectly competently in a flawlessly executed speech, it's better to make the attempt than to remain passive indefinitely." Convenient guides to assertiveness, helpful for clients and therapists, are found in the books by Galassi and Galassi (1977) and (for women especially) Baer (1976). Galassi, Galassi, and Fulkerson (1984) have provided a convenient summary of relevant research and practice for clinicians.

Behavioral Marital Therapy

In Chapter 3 we reviewed some of the evidence concerning the impact of marital maladjustment on agoraphobia, and the desirability or otherwise of including the spouse in treatment sessions. There are several issues here. Successful treatment of agoraphobia may provoke resistance, or even the emergence of psychopathology, in the client's spouse. Alternatively, the active cooperation of a supportive spouse may boost the effects of therapy on the client. When the agoraphobic client's marriage is known to be troubled, it is appropriate to offer martial therapy for the reasons that (1) if the bad marriage somehow causes or worsens the client's agoraphobia, improving the relationship may improve the agoraphobia; (2) changing a conflict-ridden relationship into a mutually supportive one can positively enhance the client's efforts to overcome the anxiety disorder; and (3) improving the marital relationship may offset a spouse's tendency to thwart or obstruct the client's progress in treatment.

In designing marital therapy interventions, behavior therapists have been influenced by *social exchange theory* and, to a lesser extent, by *systems theory*. The techniques of behavioral marital therapy include contingency contracting, communication skills training, and problem-solving training. These theories and techniques will be briefly summarized next.

Social Exchange Theory

Behavioral marital therapy has been influenced significantly by the social exchange theory of Thibaut and Kelley (1959; Kelley & Thibaut, 1978). The social interaction of two people in a close relationship may be seen as a reciprocal phenomenon in which each person presents stimuli to the other and responds to stimuli from the other. Each partner tries to obtain as much satisfaction as possible from the relationship. In any particular interaction between the partners, the consequences for either of them can be positive *(rewards)* or negative *(costs)*. A general prediction from social exchange theory is that more satisfying interactions will be repeated, whereas less satisfying ones will be avoided. If the costs for a partner exceed the rewards, the partner may seek to leave the relationship, or at least to end the particular interaction.

Whether or not the person actually leaves the relationship depends on what rewards or costs are expected outside the relationship. The alternative to an unsatisfying relationship could be an even less satisfying life of isolation and loneliness, for example.

Brett, introduced at the beginning of this chapter, is an example of an agoraphobic currently experiencing an unsatisfying relationship. The costs of being married to his wife include her repeated insults and complaints about his anxiety problems. The rewards could include her availability as a trusted companion while he deals with his agoraphobia, even if she is beginning to abandon this role. Whether or not the costs for Brett exceed the rewards, he will be likely to remain in the relationship if he believes that there would be even greater costs involved in leaving his wife.

Social exchange theorists predict that the most satisfying relationships are those based on *reciprocity*—in other words, those in which the partners act so as to obtain rewards from each other. Research has shown that partners in successful marriages usually exchange positive reinforcement at a high rate, whereas distressed relationships are marked by low rates of positive exchange (Weiss & Wieder, 1982).

Unsatisfying or distressed relationships are typically associated not with reciprocity but with *coercion*. Relationships based on coercion are characterized by the use of unpleasant stimuli, such as nagging and threats, in an attempt to obtain rewards from the partner. As in a reciprocal relationship, a coercive relationship is one in which the two people involved control each other's behavior. Brett's wife controls his behavior if he makes progress in treatment as a result of her withdrawal of support. At the same time, Brett's improvement reinforces his wife's coercive strategy.

Systems Theory

According to systems theory, in marriages and other close relationships certain forces operate to maintain a sense of balance. Suppose that Brett lacks ambition at work, and his wife tends to get overinvolved in her job. He may be able to accept her strong commitment to her work as long as she accepts his inertia. The partners may adopt certain behavior patterns that further entrench these roles—for example, Brett taking responsibility for looking after the children (he spends more time at home), and his wife making sure the car gets serviced (she drives to town each day).

In this model, a problem is created when one of the partners makes a change in the usual behavior pattern. If the wife begins to work shorter hours outside the house, for example, the spotlight is thrown on the husband, who may feel pressured to work longer hours and take up the financial slack. Or if Brett begins to recover from agoraphobia, he may be available for more activities than staying at home with the children, and his wife may feel pressured to change her routine in some way. In systems theory, changing one aspect of the system is predicted to have repercussions on other aspects (Stuart, 1980).

The *assortative mating* pattern described by Hafner (1977) provides an example of how equilibrium may be maintained in a marital relationship. In assortative mating, put simply, each partner chooses the other on the basis of having roughly the same overall level of mental health. A man with agoraphobia and a woman who is compulsively perfectionistic may team up because each of them might feel threatened by a spouse who is the very picture of mental health. However, if one of the partners receives successful treatment for his or her disorder, the systems theory principles operate so as to lead the other to attempt to preserve balance. The untreated spouse may try to thwart the other's efforts to improve, for example. This may be what is happpening when Brett's wife stops driving him to his therapy sessions.

The chief treatment procedures used in behavioral marital therapy are communication skills training, problem-solving training, and contingency contracting. These will now be discussed.

Communication Skills Training

To help partners improve their communication, therapists urge them to take responsibility for their own feelings (instead of blaming the other for "making" them feel that way), to avoid saving up examples of each other's undesirable behavior, and to encourage the honest expression of feelings rather than categorical demands for the other party to change his or her ways. Therapists usually explain the reasoning behind the therapy first, then proceed to use role-playing methods to help clients practice, and eventually adopt, more constructive ways of communicating with each other (Gurman, 1980).

Problem-Solving Training

Problem-solving training is aimed at helping couples resolve problems by acquiring certain new skills, which include defining problems in the relationship, proposing solutions, suggesting compromises, and being willing to accept responsibility (Weiss & Wieder, 1982). Research has shown that satisfied couples can usually negotiate compromises once they have aired their differences, whereas unhappy couples tend to continue to disagree. Unhappy couples are good at suggesting ideas for change but are not good at settling on an agreement on which changes to make (Gottman, 1979). Treatment procedures include behavior rehearsal, feedback, and homework assignments (Weiss & Wieder, 1982).

Behavioral Contracting

In a behavioral contract (Stuart, 1980), the partners make a commitment to each other to attempt to do things that please each other. With the help of the therapist, each partner makes a list of positive activities that the other could do that would bring pleasure (for example, helping with a household chore, spending a few minutes talking about something that interests the other, smiling and expressing affection without being prompted). Each partner's behavior can serve as a reinforcer for the other's behavior. It is especially helpful for partners to use more holistic contracts in which the aim is a shared goal, rather than a series of particular individual goals. This is known as a *good faith* contract, in which each person hopes that the other will make changes but does not wait for that to happen before proceeding with individual efforts to change. Stuart (1980) recommends that the partners use a "caring days" technique in which they begin to act *as if* they care for each other a great deal. Each partner tries hard to act in this way and to make changes quite independent of the other. The partners record their preferences as to what the other could do to show caring. Ideally, these behaviors will be specific, realistic, repeatable ones that avoid areas highly charged with conflict.

Examples

The provision of marital therapy for agoraphobics with troubled relationships is supported by research that has shown continued improvement after exposure therapy in clients who subsequently received communication training (Arnow, Taylor, Agras, & Telch, 1985). Although it is desirable to offer behavioral marital therapy to the couple when marital conflict is an issue for an agoraphobic partner, clinicians often encounter difficulties in effecting this. An obvious problem is the spouse's unwillingness to cooperate in marital therapy. Initially, Brett's wife was not interested in attending sessions with him unless the focus was clearly on his problems, not those of the relationship. Yet, with tact and persistence, clinicians are often able to earn the trust of an agoraphobic's spouse if it is explained clearly that neither partner is to be singled out for blame. Typically, the therapist will be able at least to meet the spouse, who may, of necessity, accompany the client to therapy sessions when the client cannot make it alone; when the therapist must conduct treatment at the home of a house-bound client, the spouse may well be present.

To take a positive example first, one severely agoraphobic elderly woman was distressed by her husband's sometimes overbearing efforts to get her to confront feared situations. She perceived him as having a basically supportive attitude; both retired, they spent practically all of their time together, and he was quite willing to drive her to the therapy sessions. However, he challenged her mercilessly to practice confronting feared situations, to the extent that he would drive her for long distances against her protests and would deliberately abandon her for long periods when they were shopping together. The client also reported that her husband often criticized her for being weak-willed when she balked at highly anxiety-provoking in vivo exploits. Because the husband was essentially supportive and cooperative, it was a fairly straightforward matter for the therapist to help the couple plan a more suitable, graduated approach to exposure in vivo. Contingency contracting and communication skills training were used to help each partner identify specific behaviors that were mutually rewarding, and to make a deliberate policy of adopting these behaviors for the sake of the relationship.

A less desirable outcome was seen in the case of a house-bound agoraphobic woman whose husband sought to protect her from emotional discomfort of any kind. He was present during the initial interview at the client's home. Whenever the therapist asked the client about areas of distress in her life in general, the husband would intervene and try to change the subject or, if that failed, to put the most benign construction upon any incident that had caused the client discomfort. As it happened, the therapist recommended that the client work on assertiveness issues as part of the treatment plan, but the husband was adamantly opposed to this because he thought it would upset his wife. Eventually he succeeded in putting a stop to the therapy by intercepting telephone calls to his wife from the therapist and even appropriating letters addressed to her, so that further appointments could not be made. The therapist's impression was that the client's husband was strongly invested in keeping his wife unassertive, phobic, and house-bound, and that he apparently had the power to do so.

TREATING CONCOMITANT PROBLEMS

Depression

As we have seen in Chapter 4, people with panic disorder and agoraphobia frequently show signs of depression along with their anxiety and avoidance problems. Depression will sometimes abate as the client's anxiety disorder improves. In other cases, however, depression merits treatment on its own. The case of Donna, presented at the beginning of this chapter, illustrates how depression can interfere with the course of treatment.

Donna described how difficult she found it to motivate herself to do exposure homework. Problems with motivation are, of course, a central component of depression. Depressed people are also often irritable and difficult for others to be around. They will often strike out at others and then feel guilty for their actions, a pattern Donna aptly described in herself.

Besides impeding clients' efforts at practicing exposure exercises, depression can also influence how clients evaluate their performance accomplishments (Telch, 1988). When an agoraphobic client practices exposing herself to a challenging situation, negative thoughts about her performance may limit the impact her accomplishments have on her self-confidence. If the client minimizes her accomplishments, she will likely not derive from the exposure a strong sense of her ability to handle similar situations. We have even seen instances where clients will interpret progress as further evidence of their own inadequacy. For example, when the therapist congratulates the client on a performance accomplishment, the client thinks to herself, "I am such a pitiful case that my therapist is excited just because I went to the shopping mall." Donna reported a similar, though perhaps not as severely self-critical, attribution when she stated, "A 34-year-old woman goes into the supermarket—big deal."

When depression is identified either during the initial evaluation or in the course of therapy, the clinician may choose one of several courses of action. Depression can simply be monitored to see if mood improves as the client makes progress with panic and phobic problems. This course of action would seem most appropriate when depression is in the mild to moderate range. Alternatively, the therapist may wish to treat the depression directly, in its own right. Effective pharmacological interventions for depression are available, and there are some empirical findings that suggest that a combination of antidepressant medication with exposure therapy is an effective package for treating panic disorder with agoraphobia (Telch, 1988). A brief review of antidepressant medication and the treatment of panic disorder and agoraphobia is provided in Appendix B.

As a third alternative, the therapist may choose to use cognitive-behavioral procedures to treat the depressed mood while also treating the anxiety disorder. The cognitive-behavioral procedures for treating anxiety and depression are very similar, and the skilled therapist can move from focusing on one problem to the other without disturbing the integrity of therapy.

In the case of Donna, the therapist opted to shift the focus of the session to address Donna's negative beliefs about herself and therapy. Cognitive therapy procedures similar to those described in Chapter 5 for disputing "panicogenic" cognitions were used.

Therapist: It sounds like you're really feeling discouraged and you're wondering will you ever get better.

Donna: I just feel like its hopeless sometimes . . . like things will never change.

Therapist: You think sometimes that things will never change. Let's take a look at that now . . . that things will never change. How do you feel when you think that things will never change?

Donna: I feel lousy. I feel like giving up.

Therapist: O.K., so you feel lousy and you want to give up. What would happen if you gave up?

Donna: I guess I'd just stay in the house all the time like a slug. I'm not saying I want to give up. I'm just saying that I feel like it sometimes.

Therapist: I understand. You think you want to give up sometimes because you feel so lousy. But let's go back and look at why you feel lousy. What caused you to feel lousy?

Donna: What do you mean? I feel lousy because I've got this problem and I am making everybody's life miserable.

Therapist: We'll come back to whether or not you are making anybody's life miserable. Just a minute ago you told me you feel lousy when you think that things will never change. I am suggesting that it's that thought—that things won't change—that causes you to feel so lousy. You don't like the way you are living your life right now, but you believe that things will never change. Of course you feel lousy. But that thought is not an indisputable fact. In fact, I would argue that your thought that things will never get better is really just your guess, or hypothesis, about the future. The problem is you treat it like a fact.

Donna: Are you saying I don't want to get better?

Therapist: Not at all. I'm just saying that your belief that you won't get better is making you feel lousy, which is making it more difficult for you to get better. How do you know you won't get better? What evidence did you use to draw that conclusion?

Donna: Just look at the way that I am now. I'm pathetic.

Therapist: So because you are the way you are now, you will never change?

Donna: I'm not saying I can never change, I'm just saying that I feel like I can never change.

Therapist: Right. I would argue that when you say you "feel like" you won't change, you really mean you *believe* that you will never change. It's that belief that we need to examine if you are going to start feeling better about yourself. Last week you went to the grocery store. How long had it been since you had been there?

Donna: I don't know . . . I don't think I've been in there by myself since before Tyler was born.

Therapist: So that would be at least six years. And how long have you been coming here for therapy? About two months.

Donna: Yeah.

Therapist: So in about eight weeks of working on the problem, you have been able to do something you haven't done in six years. Is that consistent with your idea that you will never change?

Donna: No, I guess not. It just seems like I'm not changing fast enough. I guess I'm just impatient.

Therapist: O.K., so you're not changing as fast as you would like. That's very different than believing that you will never change.

In cognitive therapy of depression, the depressed client is taught to identify negative thoughts, explore the objective evidence for the thought, and generate alternative ways of thinking about the same situation. There are certain types of errors in thinking, or cognitive distortions, that are identified in cognitive therapy of depression. Examples include the following:

Selective abstraction: The client will select out of a situation small negative details and ignore neutral or positive ones. One of our clients described this distortion by saying, "I'm a magnet for things that reflect negatively upon me." An example might be that of an agoraphobic client who feels moderately panicky during 5 minutes of a 60-minute exposure session and concludes, "I couldn't handle it. I freaked out."

Arbitrary inference: This refers to drawing a conclusion from irrelevant evidence. An example of this distortion was offered by a client whose therapist was five minutes late to their session. The client concluded that he was the therapist's least favorite client and that the therapist dreaded meeting with him. In reality, the therapist had been delayed by a lack of available parking spaces.

Aaron Beck and his colleagues have developed a comprehensive manual describing cognitive therapy of depression, which we recommend to the reader (Beck et al., 1979).

Behavioral conceptions of depression have focused on the role of loss of social reinforcement in the development and maintenance of depression. Peter Lewinsohn (1974) has argued that a low rate of positive reinforcement for social behavior results in a decrease in the frequency of such behaviors. As the person's behavioral output decreases, fewer and fewer social rewards are available, which results in even less social behavior. Depression results in turn from this loss of response-contingent reinforcement. Given the limits that people with agoraphobia place on their environment, opportunities for rewarding social interactions can be minimal. According to the behavioral model, the frequency of social behavior decreases because it is not reinforced. Donna's depression may have developed in this manner. When her youngest son went to school, she was home alone with few opportunities for engaging in pleasurable activities. As her depression worsened, she became more irritable, which in turn made it less pleasurable for her husband to be around her. He began to work late during the week and to take the children places on weekends that "Mommy couldn't go" because of agoraphobia.

The therapist identified this pattern in Donna's relationship with her husband. He outlined the behavioral model of depression for Donna and her husband and helped them to plan pleasurable activities that they could engage in together. As it became easier for Donna to engage in a wide variety of activities, the couple began to schedule one night a week when they did something fun together without their children.

Depression, Panic Disorder, and Suicide

One very serious factor of which clinicians always need to be aware is the risk of suicide in depressed and anxious clients. The relationship between suicide and depression has long been recognized (Hamilton,

1982). Depressed people often view their futures as hopeless and see no end to their suffering except death. Recently, some very disturbing findings have been published regarding the risk of suicide in people with panic disorder. People with panic disorder and people who experience panic attacks but don't meet criteria for panic disorder are at an increased risk for suicidal ideation and suicide attempts compared to people with other psychiatric disorders (Weissman, Klerman, Markowitz, & Ouellette, 1989), including people with major depression (Coryell, Noyes, & Clancy, 1982). About 20 percent of people with panic disorder have attempted suicide. Factors that are associated with increased risk of suicide attempts in panic disorder clients include coexisting alcohol or drug abuse, female sex, and early onset of panic (Weissman et al., 1989).

Evaluating a client's risk for suicide is a difficult and uncertain enterprise. The risk factors are well known to most clinicians (see Monk, 1987). Women are about three times as likely to attempt suicide as men, although when they try, men are much more likely to succeed. Successful suicide attempts are associated with increased age, alcohol and drug abuse, recent losses through death or divorce, unemployment, and being unmarried. A history of one or more suicide attempts is also associated with suicide. Approximately 35 percent of people who commit suicide have made previous attempts.

Signs of suicidal ideation can be identified during initial assessment and in the course of therapy. Statements that suggest hopelessness or apparent jokes about death or suicide should be followed up by the clinician. Suicide attempts may be unplanned, however, and may evolve rapidly in the context of a panic attack. We prefer to err on the side of caution when working with potentially suicidal clients. At the very least, we share our concerns and develop a plan with the client as to what steps he will take should he experience suicidal ideations. Local hotline and emergency room numbers are sometimes provided. In cases where the risk factors are greater (for example, an alcohol-abusing client, who lives alone following a recent divorce and who has lost his job because of panic attacks), we will recommend inpatient hospitalization. In rare cases, involuntary hospitalization procedures need to be initiated to protect the suicidal client.

Alcohol Abuse

Alcohol abuse is a serious and prevalent problem in our society, and people with anxiety disorders may be at greater risk than the general population for developing alcohol-related problems. In the case of Ted, presented at the beginning of this chapter, the development of excessive alcohol use appears to have been related to panic attacks and social anxiety. When alcohol abuse and panic disorder are present in the same individual, the complexity of the clinician's task is multiplied. Active alcohol use interferes with treatment in several ways. Intoxication during exposure exercises may nullify the benefit of therapy. Activation of anxious responses may be inhibited during exposure, which would interfere with emotional processing (see Hecker & Thorpe, 1987). Clients may attribute decrements in anxiety to alcohol rather than to the anxiety management skills acquired in therapy. In addition, the physical sensations of a hangover may be misinterpreted as signs of an impending panic attack or of some physical disorder, thus initiating the panic cycle (see Figure 3.1). Alcohol may, in fact, exacerbate anxiety rather than reduce it as is commonly believed (Thyer & Curtis, 1984). Finally, alcohol abuse and panic disorder both appear to be risk factors for suicide, and alcohol or drug abuse increases the risk of suicide attempts in clients with panic disorder.

When alcohol abuse and panic disorder present themselves in the same client, the clinician will need to make a series of decisions regarding treatment options and prioritization of presenting problems. Referral for inpatient treatment of the substance abuse problem may be necessary if the client is alcohol-dependent or there are medical risks associated with alcohol withdrawal (for example, seizures, delirium tremens). In some cases, social or familial functioning may be so chaotic that inpatient treatment provides the only reasonable alternative. The decision to refer for hospitalization should be made only after careful consideration of the negative consequences of an extended (usually around 30 days) hospital stay. There are many advantages for outpatient treatment over hospitalization (Lewis, Dana, & Blevins, 1988). When seen on an outpatient basis, clients are able to maintain supportive social ties, and there is significantly less disruption of their occupational and family lives. Furthermore, the client may be more likely to retain a sense of responsibility for making constructive changes in his life.

If immediate hospitalization does not appear to be necessary, the clinician needs to decide whether concomitant treatment of alcohol abuse and panic disorder is appropriate or whether addressing one problem should take precedence over the other. We usually recommend concomitant treatment, as the two problems can be related, as in the case of Ted, and there are common elements to cognitive-behavioral treatment of both problems. There are instances in which we will utilize self-help groups or other treatment facilities to help the client address substance abuse, while we focus on the anxiety disorder, but this is not the preferred treatment plan. Self-help groups typically use an addiction model for helping alcohol abusers remain abstinent from alcohol. Alcoholics Anonymous (AA) is the most widely available self-help organization. AA is not, however, a treatment program. Rather, it exists to support alcoholics in their efforts to remain sober. The philosophy of the program is strongly based in acknowledging one's powerlessness over alcohol. We recommend AA only when the client has previous experience with this model and subscribes to its basic philosophy. We also tend to be reluctant to use other outpatient treatment facilities, unless we have a thorough understanding of the approach to treatment used at the facility and can coordinate treatment planning.

Panic disorder and alcohol abuse can be treated together on an outpatient basis. We make this statement recognizing that we cannot cite a body of clinical research literature to support it. Instead, we make the statement on the basis of our experience in working with panic disorder clients who also have mild to moderate problems with alcohol abuse.

Individualized treatment planning is necessary for addressing the complexities of working with an anxiety disorder client who also abuses alcohol. We will use the case of Ted to illustrate the integration of therapy for these two problems.

Initially, treatment focused on teaching Ted to manage his anxiety by using progressive relaxation. Cognitive therapy of anxiety and panic was then introduced. Ted automatically interpreted any uncomfortable physical sensation as a sign that he was going to pass out. He worried that he would embarrass himself terribly should this happen. As therapy progressed, Ted admitted that he still worried about what had caused the attacks to start in the first place. He continued to hold onto the idea that he had caused himself permanent brain damage by his experimentation with illicit drugs when he was younger. Ted also held strongly to the belief that alcohol prevented panic attacks. Access to alcohol had clearly become a safety signal for Ted. He believed that he could deal with most situations as long as he had access to booze. These three issues were dealt with using various forms of exposure and cognitive therapy.

Exposure to panic cues was used to address Ted's belief that certain physical sensations indicated that passing out was imminent. Voluntary hyperventilation, running in place, doing jumping jacks, and spinning in circles were used separately to induce unpleasant physical sensations. Ted's therapist helped him to identify and dispute the automatic thoughts elicited by these procedures. Ted's belief that he had caused himself permanent brain damage was addressed by challenging him to provide evidence consistent with this conclusion. He came to see that the only evidence was the panicky feelings. Ted now had a reasonable alternative to this interpretation of these feelings. He could see that the panicky feelings were caused by catastrophic misinterpretation of normal physical sensations. Ted's belief in the anxiety-reducing effect of alcohol and the safety signal properties of access to alcohol were addressed using exposure properties. Ted was weaned from his book bag bottle of schnapps by agreeing to attend classes without the bottle one day a week, then three, then five days a week. He was encouraged to use relaxation skills and cognitive restructuring techniques to cope with the anxiety he felt in the classroom.

Ted was first seen during the fall semester, and sessions were focused primarily on anxiety management, including relaxation training, cognitive therapy, and exposure therapy as described previously. In the spring, Ted registered for the public speaking course he had avoided. The first few sessions of that semester were focused on public speaking anxiety. In vivo exposure exercises were used, in which Ted practiced giving brief speeches, both prepared and spontaneous, in front of a mock audience made up of graduate students in our clinical psychology doctoral training program. Ted's anxiety was much improved after three sessions of in vivo exposure.

At this point in therapy, the therapist shared with the client his concerns about Ted's abusive social drinking. The therapist pointed out that although Ted had learned some useful anxiety management skills in therapy, his excessive weekend alcohol use continued. The therapist speculated that the use of large amounts of alcohol might have developed as a means of coping with anxiety. Ted's pattern of heavy drinking might no longer serve that purpose but might now be maintained by another set of factors. The therapist offered Ted continued therapy focused on significantly reducing or eliminating his alcohol use. Although initially somewhat defensive, Ted admitted that he had been concerned about his alcohol use. He reported that he was sure that his heavy drinking had been the cause of at least one breakup of a dating relationship he had with a female college student.

Individualized cognitive-behavioral assessment and treatment of clients who abuse alcohol is multifaceted (Lewis et al., 1988). In a behavioral assessment of drinking behavior, the therapist identifies the situational and emotional antecedents to drinking, as well as the reinforcing consequences of alcohol consumption. In this type of assessment, the clinician attempts to determine what is reinforcing and punishing for the client and to identify the factors that are related to alcohol abuse (Maisto, 1985). Cognitive-behavioral treatment of alcohol abuse uses a variety of techniques such as relaxation training, assertion training, modeling, and contingency contracting (Lewis et al., 1988). The specific interventions used are determined by the results of the behavioral assessment.

Assessment of Ted revealed a variety of situational determinants of drinking. A theme that ran through many of these situations was the potential for Ted to be evaluated by others—for example, on dates and at parties. In addition, certain friends were associated with alcohol use. Ted stated that he always drank when he socialized with certain friends. The primary reinforcing consequence of drinking for Ted was the relief from anxiety he felt when he drank and the decrease in his concern about being scrutinized by others.

Developing treatment goals proved to be the next stumbling block in treatment. Ted felt strongly that he did not want to quit drinking altogether. Rather, he wished to have a greater sense of control over his drinking so that he did not feel he had to drink when he was in certain situations and felt comfortable in ceasing alcohol use after two or three drinks. Ted's personal goal for alcohol treatment was to become what is known as a "controlled drinker" (Miller & Munoz, 1982). A controlled drinker is a person who has had previous life problems related to alcohol use, has decided that he or she needs greater control over drinking, and chooses to be neither abstinent nor an excessive drinker. Controlled drinking is a controversial concept in the alcohol treatment literature (see Lewis et al., 1988, for discussion) because it is inconsistent with the basic tenets of AA and other abstinence-oriented programs. Controlled drinking can be an exceptionally difficult goal to achieve. Miller (1977, 1980) has developed a behavioral self-control training program that is designed to help the problem drinker achieve controlled drinking status.

Ted's goals for drinking, however, were inconsistent with usual controlled drinking in that he wished to be able to drink until he "had a good buzz" and then stop. The therapist explained the problems inherent in this approach. Once he was intoxicated, Ted's ability to monitor and control his behavior would be impaired. This would significantly reduce the likelihood of successful controlled drinking. Appropriate limits for alcohol consumption were determined using a chart showing alcohol consumption by body weight in a given amount of time. An appropriate goal would be for Ted to have one ounce of alcohol (one beer or one mixed drink) per hour when he drank. Ted agreed with this goal, although continued compliance proved to be a problem.

Each week Ted and the therapist set goals for drinking on the following weekend. Contingency contracting, a technique that is used to tie some reward or reinforcement with some behavior, was used to reinforce Ted for compliance with his specified goals. Ted and the therapist developed a contingency contract for Ted's drinking behavior. If he stuck to his one drink per hour limit on weekends, Ted would reward himself by buying himself a new compact disc—one CD for each night he succeeded in controlled drinking. As an added incentive, Ted agreed that for each night he drank more than his stated goal, he would donate an amount equal to the price of a CD to the Campus Republicans, an organization that supported political interests diametrically opposed to his own.

Therapy sessions with Ted were focused on helping him to develop alternatives to drinking behavior and assertive refusal skills. The therapist and Ted developed strategies for decreasing the rate of alcohol consumption. Ted reported that he felt awkward if he did not have a drink in his hand when he was at a party, so he began to use glasses of club soda or water or cans of soda as a replacement. The therapist used modeling and behavior rehearsal to help Ted develop skill at assertively refusing drinks when offered.

Ted's progress in therapy was uneven. He had some initial early successes with controlled drinking but then slipped and became intoxicated on both weekend nights. Ted did not comply with the contingency contract; he argued that he knew he had "screwed up" and that there was no reason to punish himself further by giving money to the Campus Republicans. The therapist responded to this by reviewing the rationale for contingency contracting. The goals of controlled drinking were reviewed, and Ted was encouraged to recall why he had set these goals in the first place. During the session, Ted became angry and stated that he would make the donation to please the therapist. After two canceled appointments, Ted returned to therapy and complained of problems with anxiety. Anxiety management skills were reviewed and self-instructional rehearsal was used to help Ted prepare for an upcoming speech. During the last several weeks of the semester Ted's attendance was sporadic, and at the end of the semester he left campus and discontinued therapy.

Personality Disorders

As we indicated in Chapter 4, there has been a recent emergence of interest in personality disorders among cognitive-behavioral clinicians and researchers. Cognitive (Freeman & Leaf, 1989) and behavioral (Linehan, 1987) models of therapy for these problems have been presented. These treatments have not yet been subjected to series of empirical tests, and their efficacy in the treatment of personality disorders is not known. But mental health clients are not patient. They don't wait for the clinical researchers to develop, test, and replicate innovative treatment strategies before presenting themselves to clinicians in the field.

Clients with personality or Axis II (DSM-III-R) (American Psychiatric Association, 1987) disorders seldom present themselves asking to change their maladaptive personality styles. Rather, they tend to present with other complaints such as depression and anxiety, or they are referred by family members or other significant people in their lives (Freeman & Leaf, 1989). We tend to be very conservative about making the diagnosis of an Axis II disorder. We prefer to address problems with depression or anxiety directly first. Data on the possibility of a personality disorder are gathered in the course of treatment.

Freeman and Leaf (1989) suggest the following diagnostic signs as potential indicators of an Axis II problem:

1. The client or a significant other reports that the client "has always been this way." In the case presented at the opening of this chapter, Wendy's recollection of social avoidance at a very early age suggests the possibility of a personality disorder.

2. Persistent noncompliance with treatment regimens can sometimes suggest personality disorder.

3. When progress in therapy abruptly stops for no apparent reason, it may indicate the need for exploration of Axis II disorders.

4. Clients with personality disorders can appear to be oblivious to the impact of their behavior on others.

5. The client's motivation to change becomes highly suspect. Although the client may give lip service to the desire to change, he or she seems to manage to avoid changing.

6. The problems that the client presents seem to be an inextricable part of who the client is.

7. Axis II clients often see problems as "out there" or as something that the world is doing to them.

The model of personality disorders on which cognitive therapy is based views schemata as the organizing structures of personality. A *schema* is a stable cognitive pattern for attending to, organizing, and interpreting environmental events. More colloquially, schemata are attitudes and assumptions about the world (Beck et al., 1979). Schemata can be *active* or *dormant*. An active schema influences our daily behavior. A schema can govern what we choose to wear, whom we choose to talk to, or how we interpret the comments of others. Dormant schemata are usually out of our awareness but become active when an individual is stressed. Schemata are the basic rules that people use to make sense of their experiences. In personality disorders, the schemata are not functional. Freeman and Leaf (1989) have suggested that in personality disorder clients, schemata that were appropriate in childhood have not changed but continue to be utilized as the person moves into adulthood: "The schema that are [sic] basically functional in this earlier part of life are being applied during later, more demanding times. These schemata become fixed when they are reinforced and/or modeled by parents" (p. 408).

The personality disorders most frequently present in individuals diagnosed with panic disorder and panic disorder with agoraphobia are avoidant and dependent personality disorder (Brooks et al., 1989). Other Axis II disorders, including borderline personality disorder (Modestin, 1989), have also been diagnosed, though less frequently. Freeman and Leaf (1989) have speculated, on the basis of their clinical experience, that there are types of schemata that are associated with each personality disorder. Schemata typical of avoidant personality include the following:

1. I must be liked.
2. I must not look foolish to myself or others at any time.
3. The world is a dangerous place.
4. I must depend on others to take care of me.
5. Isolation is better than being put at risk of being hurt.
6. All criticism is the same. The slightest criticism is the same as massive condemnation.
7. People must offer me unconditional guarantees of acceptance before I commit myself to relating to that person (Freeman & Leaf, 1989).

The schemata associated with dependent personality disorder center around the belief that one is not capable of functioning independently.

In the case of Wendy, presented in the introduction to this chapter, her memories of childhood indicated that social avoidance was a life-long pattern, which suggested to her therapist the presence of an avoidant personality disorder. A basic assumption that Wendy held about herself was that she was worthless and that she must disguise this lack of value from other people. The therapist helped Wendy to explore the origins of these beliefs. She was raised in a family where there was consistent tension between her parents, both of whom were alcoholic. Wendy's mother was extremely critical of her. Her earliest and strongest memories were of being yelled at by her mother and searching unsuccessfully to find ways to please her. She adopted a style of "trying to be invisible" in order to avoid her mother's wrath.

Cognitive therapy of personality disorders follows the same steps and uses the same procedures as cognitive therapy of other disorders (Freeman & Leaf, 1989). The therapist helps the client to identify distorted styles of thinking. The client's beliefs are then scrutinized against the available facts. Options and alternatives are examined on the basis of their match with the available data as well as the advantages and disadvantages they present compared to the client's typical beliefs. Behavioral techniques are also used to change self-defeating patterns of behavior, allay skills deficits, and test out cognitions (Freeman & Leaf, 1989).

With Wendy, the transition in therapy away from a focus on managing anxiety and toward addressing basic assumptions she held about the world was a very natural one. The basic premises on which cognitive therapy are based had already been presented and accepted by Wendy when cognitive therapy of panic attacks was applied. She readily accepted the notion that thoughts are not facts, and she had seen the benefits of challenging automatic thoughts when she learned to interfere with the panic cycle. After exploring the origins of some of Wendy's beliefs about herself, the therapist and Wendy developed a list of her basic assumptions (schemata). Three basic beliefs were identified: "I am worthless," "Others must not see that I am worthless," and "I must not place myself in a position where others can discover that I am worthless."

In the therapy sessions, the consequences of holding these beliefs were explored. Wendy could see that many of her automatic thoughts sprang from these more basic assumptions. For example, the most common type of automatic thought Wendy had always started with "I can't . . ." She described how she would think to herself, "I can't walk across the room," when she was at work. Despite thousands of experiences to the contrary, this automatic thought persisted. Wendy and the therapist hypothesized that this belief sprang from her basic assumption "I am worthless." The behavioral consequences of operating under her general rules were, of course, devastating. She never placed herself in any situation that would put her at risk of being evaluated.

The therapist used the analogy of a faulty experiment to help Wendy see how her behavior repeatedly provided support for the negative beliefs she held about herself. Each time she avoided doing something (for example, avoided having lunch with her colleagues), she concluded from the experience that she could not do it. Like a naive experimenter, Wendy continually proved her hypothesis.

As therapy progressed, a series of more challenging tests of her basic assumptions was designed. Wendy joined a church, which provided a neutral testing ground. No one knew her at the church, so her past avoidance behavior could not have influenced their opinion of her as it might in other situations such as work. Wendy began attending Sunday services. The therapist used modeling and role plays to help her develop social and conversational skills. Wendy eventually started attending the coffee hour that followed services. Each week she set a new goal for herself, such as introducing herself to small groups. She began to identify catastrophic images that flashed through her mind, causing her to "freeze." Relaxing images were developed in the therapy sessions, and she practiced switching off the catastrophic images and switching on the positive ones.

Eventually, Wendy joined a group of people who were studying to become official members of the church. This gave her the opportunity to form new relationships, and she began to socialize with a few of the group members. Wendy's successes had an interesting impact on her relationship with Ann. Wendy began to detect some hostility and resentment from Ann, sometimes openly, as in sarcastic comments Ann made regarding Wendy's "new-found religion," and other times less directly. Wendy feared losing Ann's friendship, but she was determined to continue to branch out. Using the metaphor of a box to describe her life, she said that she had been trapped in a box by her own actions. She used the phrase "I will not live in a box" as a coping self-statement to help her when facing a new challenge. Wendy began to see that she would have to face some resentment from Ann if she was going to escape from her box.

CONCLUDING REMARKS

As the cases described in this chapter suggest, panic disorder and agoraphobia can be present in clients who are experiencing a variety of other problems. Clinical research studies, by necessity, select the purest cases for treatment. The challenge for the clinician is to apply the findings from those studies in a way that best serves the needs of the client. A thorough and comprehensive assessment is needed to identify concomitant problems. The therapist needs to formulate preliminary hypotheses about the relationship among problems before implementing treatment. These hypotheses are repeatedly tested and reformulated as therapy progresses. Therapy progresses most smoothly when assigning priorities for treatment goals is a joint enterprise between therapist and client.

CHAPTER 8

The Course of Treatment

The cognitive-behavioral approach to panic disorder with and without agoraphobia, described in the preceding chapters, is based on empirical findings of clinical researchers who have systematically developed and studied various methods of assessment and treatment of the anxiety disorders. The anxiety disorders stand out as an area in which a careful experimental approach to developing the most efficacious psychological interventions has led to meaningful advances in clinical practice. Findings from carefully controlled empirical investigations have direct implications for the clinician in a primary-care mental health facility. Nonetheless, integrating research findings into one's day-to-day work with clients can sometimes be a challenging endeavor.

In this chapter we attempt to teach by example. In order to help the reader develop a better understanding of the process of assessment and treatment, we will recount our work with three clients—Louise, Barbara, and Margaret. We have already provided some basic background information about two of these women (Louise and Barbara) in Chapter 2, when we first described panic disorder with and without agoraphobia. The reader is invited to review these case illustrations before proceeding (Louise: pages 30–31; Barbara: pages 31–33). Margaret, the third case we will present, was severely disabled by her anxiety problems and presented a particularly difficult challenge for the therapists.

CLINICAL MANAGEMENT OF PANIC DISORDER WITH AGORAPHOBIA: LOUISE

Louise was seen at our clinic in the mid-1980s, before psychological treatments of panic attacks had been fully developed. Her treatment plan was developed on the basis of the available research findings at the time. No interventions directed specifically at panic attacks were used. Rather, exposure methods were at the heart of the treatment program.

Louise's presentation at our clinic was, with the exception of her age, typical of many agoraphobic clients. She associated the beginning of her difficulties with her experience of an initial panic attack, which at the time she attributed to a life-threatening condition ("I thought I was having a stroke"). Avoidance of public places developed gradually after the onset of panic attacks. It was clear from the initial interview that, in addition to panic attacks and avoidance behavior, certain personal characteristics and interpersonal factors in Louise's life influenced her current level of distress. Clearly, issues of assertiveness and marital harmony would require assessment and possibly intervention.

Diagnosis: Louise

A strong diagnostic impression of panic disorder with agoraphobia was formed during the initial interview. Nonetheless, the ADIS (designed to coincide with the DSM-III) was conducted during the second session in order to form a more comprehensive diagnostic picture. The results clearly supported the diagnosis of agoraphobia with panic attacks (DSM-III classification). The interview revealed that Louise associated riding in an elevator and crossing bridges with panic attacks and that she avoided these two situations whenever possible. Both of these proved difficult to avoid altogether, however, because Louise lived in a rural area with many rivers and streams. In addition, her physician, whom she visited for frequent checkups, had his office on the fifth floor. Many public places that are typically difficult for agoraphobics were also avoided by Louise unless she was accompanied by her husband, one of her children, or a friend who was fully aware of her problem.

Detailed questioning revealed that Louise met diagnostic criteria for dysthymia or a chronically depressed mood, as well as those for panic disorder. Furthermore, it was revealed during the structured interview that Louise suffered from hypertension, for which she was taking Inderal (propranolol). This medical condition appeared to be important to the onset and maintenance of panic disorder. Louise admitted that she usually interpreted the first signs of a panic attack as an indication that she was going to have a stroke because she knew that strokes were sometimes a complication of high blood pressure.

Behavioral Assessment

Self-Monitoring

Louise was instructed in how to keep a daily diary of her activities (Figure 4.2) and generalized anxiety and panic (Figure 4.1) during the first session. These records were to be kept throughout the course of treatment.

Two weeks' worth of baseline data were collected, and during this time the diagnostic interview was completed. The daily diary of activity for the first two weeks is reproduced in Figure 8.1. Louise left the house on six out of seven days during that first week. The average length of time out of the house was 2.25 hours. She was always accompanied on her trips by her husband or a close friend. Routine activities such as attending twice weekly group counseling sessions and Sunday mass made up the bulk of her excursions. Trips to and from the family camp also occurred during this week. Her records for week 2 indicate less outside-the-home activity. Louise left the home on only three out of seven days for an average of 1.5 hours per day. Again, routine trips made up the bulk of the excursions.

The daily activity diaries suggest that Louise has developed a couple of "safe" places to which she can travel. They also provide support for her description that most of her excursions from home are in the company of one of two "safe" people.

The generalized anxiety and panic diary indicates that Louise experienced two panic attacks during the two-week baseline period. The first occurred at the family camp when she thought that her husband had left her alone. The second was experienced in the bathtub. Figure 8.2 provides an example of a completed panic diary. Louise's ratings of generalized anxiety indicate that anxiety is reliably associated with trips she takes away from the home.

Behavioral Test

Two forms of behavioral tests were used to evaluate Louise's range of mobility. The first was a standardized, eight-item test that is carried out from our clinic. The test involves four tasks that the client is asked to complete, first accompanied by her therapist and then alone. The test is not designed hierarchically. Rather, it samples four situations that are representative of the types of situations agoraphobic clients typically find difficult. The four steps are riding from the third to the first floor in the elevator, walking through the university library,

FIGURE 8.1   Louise's daily diary of activity during two-week baseline assessment.

Daily Diary

Date	Activity	Time Out	Time In	Alone	Anxiety Rating Trip	Anxiety Rating Day
11/5	went to counseling session	11:30 a.m.	2:30 p.m.	with friend	6	4
11/6						6
11/7	went to doctor with husband	3:15 p.m.	5:30 p.m.	with husband	6	4
11/8	went to camp with husband	10:30 a.m.	12:30 p.m.	with husband	4	7
11/9	went to mass	8:45 a.m.	10:00 a.m.	with husband	0	4
11/10	came back home from camp	6:45 a.m.	9:00 a.m.	with husband	2	4
11/10	went to counseling session	12:00 p.m.	1:30 p.m.	with friend	2	4
11/11	went to opening of new bridge with husband	9:30 a.m.	1:00 p.m.	with husband	4	4
11/12	went to counseling session	11:45 a.m.	1:30 p.m.	with friend	2	3
11/13						6
11/14						2
11/15	went to mass, did not feel good but stayed	3:45 p.m.	5:00 p.m.	with husband	6	4
11/16	went to see husband's aunt, she is not feeling well at all	1:15 p.m.	3:30 p.m.	with husband	2	2
11/17						4
11/18						2

0 = No anxiety
2 = Mild anxiety
4 = Definite anxiety
6 = Severe anxiety
8 = As anxious as I have ever been (panic)

FIGURE 8.2 Louise's daily rating of general anxiety and panic.

Client #   Today's date ____*11/13*____

Daily self-rating   Day of the week ____*Thursday*____

General anxiety (0 = no anxiety, 8 = extreme anxiety):

Morning	0	1	(2)	3	4	5	6	7	8
Afternoon	0	1	2	3	(4)	5	6	7	8
Evening	0	1	2	3	4	5	6	7	(8)
Bedtime	0	1	2	3	4	5	(6)	7	8

Panic attacks:

Each time you have an anxiety episode or attack when you would rate the level of anxiety at 4 or above on the 0–8 scale, please write down the following:

	Time It Started	Time It Ended	Highest Level (0–8)	Where You Were	What You Were Thinking About
Episode #1:	7:15	8:00	8	bathtub	nothing
Episode #2:					

Any other comments about your anxiety today:

Took a bath and had a panic attack while I was in the tub. This happens quite often.

walking through the university bookstore, and walking through the university field house (this task includes a walk down a thirty-yard "tunnel" that leads out of the building). Louise completed six of the eight items on the test. Significantly, the two items she did not complete (taking the elevator by herself, walking through the university field house by herself) both involved her being alone in places where there was either no one else or very few people around. Her own rating during the test indicated marked anxiety throughout, with increases to near-panic level when she completed tasks alone. Louise reported to her therapist that she felt great relief when she saw him at the end of the two steps that she did complete by herself. She stated, "I knew you'd know what to do if there was a problem."

The second type of behavioral test involved a hierarchy of items that was constructed by Louise and her therapist during their third session together. The criteria for including an item in the hierarchy were that it must be something she could feasibly do during the week between sessions and that was meaningful to her (that is, something she would like to be able to do but either could not do or could do only with great difficulty). Louise produced the hierarchy that is reprinted in Table 8.1. She was asked to complete as many items as she could during the week prior to their next session.

Although we did not realize it at the time, our individualized behavioral test was confounded. Lack of assertiveness and marital discord conspired against Louise's completing items during the week. Four of the items clearly involved some level of assertiveness (for example, asking a friend to accompany her to the doctor's office or on the bus, visiting a neighbor uninvited). Louise's husband might have accompanied her on some of the excursions, but she was afraid to ask him because their relationship had been strained recently. Not surprisingly, Louise completed no hierarchy items during the week. These problems were discussed during the fourth therapy session, and a reasonable solution was worked out. It was decided that Louise would ask a friend from the agoraphobia support group to which she belonged to accompany her on her excursions. This particular woman had made significant advances in dealing with her problem through participation in a self-help program. During the session, the therapist role-played with Louise assertive ways of asking her friend for help. Working through this problem and recruiting the other support group member turned out to have unexpectedly positive benefits later during treatment.

In the week between the fourth and fifth sessions, Louise completed two of the hierarchy items with the help of her friend from the agoraphobia support group. The two women went to her doctor's office and rode the elevator together. They also took a bus together (items

TABLE 8.1 Hierarchy of Items for Louise's Home-Based Behavioral Test

1. Walk to the end of the street and back home alone.
2. Walk to a neighbor's house for a visit.
3. Take the elevator in the doctor's office with someone else.
4. Take a bus downtown with someone.
5. Go to Sunday mass alone.
6. Cross the Memorial Bridge with someone.
7. Take the elevator in the doctor's office alone.
8. Take a bus downtown alone.

3 and 4). She rated her anxiety level as she completed each task as 6 on the 0–8 scale. Louise described her friend as a headstrong woman who was determined to help Louise by taking her under her wing. In discussing the behavioral test with her therapist, Louise admitted that she completed the hierarchy items that she did because those were the only ones with which she had asked her friend to help her. She reported that she was afraid to tell her friend about item number 6 (driving over the Memorial Bridge with someone) because she was sure that she would not be able to back out if she changed her mind and decided not to do it.

Questionnaire Measures

Louise completed a small battery of paper-and-pencil questionnaires at the conclusion of her third therapy session. Her responses on the Fear Questionnaire (for example, Agoraphobia Subscale—22), the Agoraphobic Cognitions Questionnaire (27), and the Body Sensations Questionnaire (29) were in the range expected of agoraphobic clients prior to treatment. Perhaps of greater interest were her scores on some of the adjunct measures. Her score on the Beck Depression Inventory (BDI) was 28, which clearly placed her in the depressed range. Weekly monitoring of her level of depression was initiated in order to assess changes in depression associated with treatment progress. Louise's scores on the Adult Self-Expression Scale (70) confirmed our view of her as a generally unassertive individual (more than 95 percent of the people tested in the Gay et al., 1975, study scored as more assertive). Her responses indicated that refusing unreasonable requests and expressing negative feelings were particularly difficult for her. Finally, Louise completed the Maudsley Marital Questionnaire, which indicated that she did not feel supported by her husband.

Treatment: Louise

The treatment plan for Louise was developed during the fifth therapy session. She stated as her primary goal for treatment to increase her freedom of movement. She reported that she wanted to be able to travel from home by herself and feel comfortable using the public transportation system. Given our assessment findings, we felt that it would be important to incorporate her husband into treatment. Her lack of assertiveness and the strain she described in her marriage suggested the possibility that he might interfere with her progress unless he was made an active member of the treatment team. We asked Louise to discuss with her husband the possibility of his participating in therapy. She was reluctant to do this because she was sure that he would refuse and she feared that her request might anger him. Once again, we modeled an assertive approach to making the request and role-played this with her in the session.

Louise arrived at the sixth session alone. She reported that, as she had expected, her husband had refused to participate in therapy. He cited an extremely busy work schedule as his reason for refusing. She reported, however, that she was surprised at the way in which he responded to her request. He did not become angry, nor did he ridicule her. The issue of her husband's involvement in treatment was dropped for the time being. The rest of session 6 was devoted to describing the rationale for in vivo exposure therapy (see Chapter 6) and beginning the work of exposure. Louise had few questions about the conditioning model. Her only concern was over how quickly she would be expected to tackle the most difficult items. We assured Louise that we would proceed at a pace that was comfortable to her and that she would determine how quickly we advanced. In the last part of the session, we began the actual work of in vivo exposure therapy. We picked as a convenient starting point riding in an elevator, because this was a meaningful item for Louise and it was available (there is an elevator in the building).

In vivo exposure in that session consisted of five rides in the elevator from the third to the first floor or vice versa. The therapist accompanied Louise on each of these exposure trials. Louise's anxiety ratings for the five trips were on the 0–8 scale, 6, 6, 4, 3, and 2. After the fifth exposure trial, we discussed the gradual decline in her anxiety across trials and emphasized this as an example of how the process of in vivo exposure works.

During the seventh session, increasingly difficult challenges involving riding the elevator were practiced. Considerable preparation was required before this session. Signs indicating that the elevator was out of order were made, and permission to hang them on each floor was obtained from the building maintenance supervisor. The session was held after hours to minimize further the risk of interference and to protect Louise's confidentiality. The task of riding the elevator alone was broken down into the following steps: riding the elevator with the therapist, allowing the elevator doors to close but not riding between floors alone; riding alone for one floor (for example, third to second) with the therapist taking the stairs to meet her when the elevator arrived; taking the elevator one floor and then back to the floor where the therapist waited; taking the elevator two floors with the therapist taking the stairs to meet the elevator; taking the elevator two floors and then back to where the therapist was waiting. Louise's progress through these steps was steady. She required two to four trials at each step before her anxiety level dropped to 3 or less. The trial that presented the most difficulty was the first one in which she rode the elevator alone. Having the therapist meet her when the elevator arrived at the next floor mitigated some of her concerns. Although an athletic challenge for the therapist, this proved to be an important intermediate step, which facilitated her progress.

During the last part of session 7, the therapist introduced the idea of in vivo homework assignments and Louise was encouraged to practice exposure at home. Item 1 from the behavioral test hierarchy was the first target for homework assignments. The task was broken down into progressive steps, and Louise was instructed to use the same criteria for progress as we used in the sessions. Louise and her therapist spent some time planning specific times each day when she would practice self-exposure at home.

Sessions 8 through 12 followed a similar pattern. The first part of the session was spent following up on the previous week's homework assignment. The daily diary of activity was utilized to monitor homework compliance. The largest portion of each session was devoted to in vivo exposure focused on problem situations that were difficult for Louise to try at home. For example, the therapist drove the client across a series of progressively longer bridges until she was finally able to cross the Memorial Bridge that was an item on her behavioral test. The last part of each session was spent designing that week's homework assignment. Louise's friend from the agoraphobia support group proved to be a valuable ally in assuring compliance with homework assignments. She was willing to accompany Louise on various excursions, such as riding a bus downtown and shopping at the local mall.

Louise's progress during these weeks was steady. Her daily diaries of activity indicated that she was spending much more time out of the house, although almost all excursions continued to be accompanied by her husband or her friend, with the exception of the planned homework assignments. The clinic-based standard behavioral test was readministered during session 12, and the results also confirmed that progress was being made. Louise completed all eight items on the test, and her anxity ratings were low, ranging from 0 to 3. Daily diaries of panic and anxiety indicated a decrease in panic attacks as well. She experienced her last panic during week 8. Her BDI scores showed a gradual decline but still suggested mild to moderate depression (for example, scores during weeks 8 through 12 averaged 16.5).

On the basis of our assessment of Louise's progress thus far, we decided to focus our intervention on increasing her mobility while alone during the next few sessions. The target of sessions 13 through 15 was riding the bus alone. Although she had made progress on riding the bus with her friend through homework assignments, she still avoided public transportation when alone. Louise was still concerned with feeling trapped on the bus if she were alone. She also worried that if she were incapacitated by a panic attack, no one would be available to help her. This problem was addressed during session 13 by having Louise get on the bus at a location near our clinic. Her therapist followed behind the bus in a car. Louise was instructed to stay on the bus until it reached its last dropoff point downtown, a trip of about 35 minutes. She was encouraged to resist the temptation to get off the bus at an earlier stop should she feel overwhelmed by panic. She knew, of course, that this was an option and that her therapist would be there if she did disembark. Louise was successful in making the entire trip without getting off the bus. She was very pleased with her progress but attributed her success to knowing that the therapist was behind the bus and would be available to help her. During session 14, the same procedure was repeated, but this time the therapist traveled the same route as the bus except that he was 10 minutes behind. Louise was again successful in making the trip and reported that she felt more confident. In session 15, Louise made the trip downtown on the bus and was met by the therapist when she got there.

The therapist made a point of intermittently inquiring about Louise's husband's response to her progress. She reported that in some ways he appeared to be very pleased. He ridiculed her less often and commented on her improved mood. He was also very pleased that he no longer had to accompany her to the grocery store, a chore that Louise and her friend now did together. On the other hand, he had occasionally become quite angry with her when the family routine was disrupted because she was not at home. This most frequently occurred when he returned home and his evening meal was not ready. Louise admitted to feeling guilty on these occasions because she saw meal preparation as her responsibility. According to Louise, she was most bothered by what she referred to as "smart comments" that her husband made to her. She explained that by this she meant that when she expressed her opinion, he usually responded with a sarcastic remark. She reportedly felt belittled when this happened. Her distress over these types of interactions with her husband appeared to be exacerbated by discussions with her friend, who frequently encouraged Louise to assert herself more strongly with her husband. For example, Louise related that her friend had encouraged her to buy TV dinners that her husband could serve himself if she was not available to make dinner. Louise reported, "I felt like I had to buy them or she would have been mad at me." She admitted that she threw the dinners away when she got home.

Louise's descriptions of situations like those described here suggested that some of her depression and perhaps some of her anxiety were due to, or at least exacerbated by, her poor skills at asserting herself with her husband and her friend. Our observations and the recommendation that assertiveness training might help her to be more effective in difficult interpersonal situations were discussed with Louise at the end of session 15. She agreed with our formulation and was interested in pursuing assertiveness training.

Sessions 15 through 20 were devoted to assertiveness training, with some time set aside each week to review home-based self-exposure. These sessions followed a general format in which Louise would describe situations that had occurred during the past week in which she was not comfortable with her own actions. Discussion of the situations would center on helping Louise to identify what she wished she had said or done in the situation. An appropriately assertive response would be modeled, and then Louise would practice the assertive response herself. The therapist provided feedback on her performance with respect to content as well as nonverbal behavior (for example, speech fluency, eye contact, body posture). Louise demonstrated assertive skills quite easily and required little constructive feedback. Finally, irrational beliefs and negative self-statements and their role in interfering with an assertive response were discussed. Sampling of thoughts that occurred during the role play was sometimes helpful. However, it proved necessary to use imaginal techniques to identify irrational beliefs that interfered with assertion.

Once an assertive response was identified, modeled, and rehearsed, Louise was asked to close her eyes and imagine the situation. Usually these visualizations involved negative interactions with her husband or her friend. As she imagined these encounters, in which she behaved in an assertive fashion, she was encouraged to say aloud any negative statements that came to mind. Once the negative cognitions were identified, the therapist used cognitive techniques to help Louise dispute them.

Louise maintained the progress she had made in decreasing her agoraphobic avoidance. She was now traveling by bus, which afforded her a significant increase in freedom and consequently decreased her dependence on her husband and her friend. Louise reported that she still worried about having a stroke, but that this occurred less frequently, a fact she attributed to a dropoff in panic attacks. Based on her self-report and her performance in therapy sessions, Louise's assertiveness improved, and by session 20 she felt that she was handling interpersonal conflicts more effectively. Further, her level of depression had dropped (BDI = 9 during session 20). A decision to terminate weekly therapy sessions was made during that session.

Three- and six-month follow-up interviews with Louise indicated that she had maintained the progress she made in therapy. She had continued to travel by bus alone, but admitted that she had what she referred to as "my routes" and that these were the only ones she used. She reported that marital conflict continued to be a problem in her life but that she felt she handled things much more effectively. In her words, "I don't take everything to heart so much anymore like I used to. If me and my husband fight or something, I get mad and say what I want, but I try not to let it bother me all day."

Comments on Louise

Exposure therapy with some attention to assertiveness issues proved to be helpful in increasing Louise's mobility, reducing depression, and essentially eliminating panic attacks. The reduction, and in some cases elimination, of panic attacks without directly targeting this problem in treatment occurs in some but not all agoraphobic clients treated with in vivo exposure methods (Barlow, 1988). Although the exact mechanism underlying this treatment effect is not known at this time, it may be that in vivo exposure precipitates the onset of panic-like feelings, which would be a form of exposure to panic cues. The client is provided with noncatastrophic information about panic attacks by the therapist's presence and demeanor as well as her own experience. This experiential learning may be more powerful than the verbal learning that takes place in cognitive therapy.

Marital conflict was apparent in this case and may have played a significant role in maintaining Louise's agoraphobic avoidance. The therapist's attempts at involving her husband in treatment were not fruitful. The therapist decided not to push this issue for fear that pressure on the husband to participate might exacerbate the marital conflict and result in Louise's dropping out of treatment. Although the informal data we collected at follow-up suggested that marital conflict was still present, Louise appeared to have developed the assertiveness skills she needed to deal with this conflict.

The ordering of therapeutic interventions was another clinical decision presented to the therapist. Assertiveness training might have preceded exposure therapy, given that assertiveness deficits were identified early in therapy. The decision to address the client's limited mobility first was based primarily on information presented by the client, who was clearly most impaired by the limited range of activities in which she was able to engage. Assertiveness issues were addressed only to the extent to which the client requested help with this problem and the therapist could see that assertiveness deficits interfered with the primary goals of treatment.

CLINICAL MANAGEMENT OF PANIC DISORDER: BARBARA

Barbara presented several interesting characteristics when she originally came to our clinic. First, she made a clear distinction between physical disorders and panic attacks. In her own words, "When it happens I worry, am I having a panic attack or is there really something wrong with me?" Despite the evidence to the contrary that was made available to her each time she had a panic attack, Barbara continued to worry that the attacks were indicative of some physical catastrophe. She described fearing that she would "lose consciousness and not wake up" when she had a panic attack, or that as a result of having the attack, "I am afraid I will become a vegetable or something."

A second interesting feature of Barbara's presentation was the connection she made between her use of illicit drugs, panic attacks, and her nagging fear that she suffered from some terrible physical problem. Barbara reported that she was sure that she had caused herself some permanent physical damage by using illicit substances. Since she never admitted to her doctors that she had used these drugs, she was never provided with evidence that contradicted her permanent brain damage theory. Her logic here went something like this: I can't tell the doctors that I used drugs; since they don't know that I used drugs, they can't detect what is really wrong with me; when they tell me that there is nothing physically wrong with me, I can't be sure that they are right, since they don't know that I used drugs; I am having panic attacks; there must really be something physically wrong with me.

The third interesting feature of Barbara's case is the role that family factors appeared to play in the maintenance of the disorder. Barbara's description of her relationship with her mother suggested that identifying the "true" cause of Barbara's physical problems was a central issue around which most of their conversations centered. This may have served to focus Barbara's attention onto bodily sensations, particularly those that might appear to be abnormal. This attention to physical anomalies is one of the essential characteristics of the panic disorder client, according to Beck (1988; see Chapter 3). Furthermore, given Barbara's brother's health problems and the family's concern that her sister might have a seizure disorder, it seemed likely that there would be a strong relationship between physical complaints and parental attention. In operant terms, Barbara's attention to physical sensations, her catastrophic interpretation of these, and her verbal complaints might all be reinforced by her mother's attention.

A final interesting feature of Barbara's presentation was her description of checking her pulse and the relationship between this behavior and the onset of a panic. Barbara reported that when she noticed any odd physical sensation such as mild dizziness or shortness of breath, she immediately checked her pulse. If she found that her pulse was in the normal range, she would feel some relief. If, on the other hand, she found that her heart rate was high (80 beats per minute or higher), she would begin to worry that some physical catastrophe such as a stroke was about to occur. This led to repeated checking, with her anxiety increasing along with her pulse rate. Barbara reported that during a significant subset of her panic attacks, she checked her pulse early in the onset of the attack.

Medication

Barbara had been taking alprazolam for about six months prior to coming to our clinic. Her prescription was for one pill (0.5 mg) twice a day, with the possibility of a third pill each day if she felt the need. This is a low dose (Ballenger et al., 1988). She reported on intake that she took the third pill almost every day but that she never took more than three in a day for fear of some adverse side effects.

Diagnosis: Barbara

The ADIS-R was completed with Barbara during her second session at our clinic. The results clearly supported the diagnosis of panic disorder. Barbara appeared to be most impaired by the disorder about a year prior to coming to our clinic. The frequency of panic attacks decreased coincident with the initiation of pharmacological treatment with alprazolam. No other anxiety disorders were revealed through the structured interview. However, Barbara did also meet diagnostic criteria for hypochondriasis, a disorder marked by a preoccupation with the fear that one has some serious disease. As in Barbara's case, hypochondriacal clients repeatedly seek reassurance from doctors, but their fear of having a physical disease persists despite medical evidence to the contrary.

Behavioral Assessment

Self-Monitoring

Barbara's self-monitoring during the first two weeks indicated mild to moderate generalized anxiety, with panic attacks occurring about three times a week. The panic attacks were not intense. Her anxiety level never rose beyond a 6 on the 0–8 scale. A similar pattern was noted on each day that she had a panic attack. She would notice some physical sensation, such as a headache or feeling warm. Her anxiety level would quickly rise. She would cope with the feelings by taking a pill (alprazolam), which usually resulted in a gradual decrease in anxiety. When we discussed her panic attacks during the treatment session, it became clear that these experiences would not meet criteria for a full panic attack but would be more accurately described as limited-symptom panic attacks. Barbara reported that she had not had a panic that reached a level higher than 6 in over a year.

Questionnaire Measures

Our assessment of Barbara was augmented by four questionnaire measures. The Fear Questionnaire was administered to check on avoidance tendencies that might not have been revealed during interviewing. Barbara's score on the Agoraphobia subscale (11) did not indicate that avoidance was an important component of her problem. Similarly, the Social Phobia and Blood–Injury subscales suggested no problems in these areas. The Beck Depression Inventory was administered to examine recent depressive symptoms. Her score (17) suggested mild to moderate depression. Barbara's scores on the Agoraphobic Cognitions Questionnaire (40) and the Body Sensations Questionnaire (54) were quite high. Her responses provide an excellent example of the catastrophic thinking and fear of body sensations that are central to the cognitive model of panic. She indicated that the thought that she would have a stroke always occurred when she was anxious. Thoughts that she had a brain tumor or would have a heart attack also usually occurred when she was frightened. On the Body Sensations Questionnaire, she reported that she was very frightened by a variety of physical sensations that occurred when she was anxious, such as heart palpitations, a feeling of pressure on her chest, or a lump in her throat. Her responses indicated that she was frightened by most of the body sensations that are normally associated with anxiety.

Treatment: Barbara

A treatment plan was reviewed with Barbara during her fourth session at our clinic. Because her generalized anxiety level was not particularly high, and because her self-report and responses on the Agoraphobic Cognitions Questionnaire indicated the central role catastrophic cognitions were playing in the problem, we decided to initiate treatment with cognitive therapy. This session was devoted to describing the cognitive model of panic disorder and providing the rationale for cognitive therapy (see Chapter 5). Barbara's response to the rationale was originally negative. Following is an excerpt from this session.

> **Barbara:** So, basically what you're saying is that it's all in my head.
>
> **Therapist:** Well, if by saying that it's all in your head you mean we think it's not real, then no, that is not what we are saying. We know that the panic attack is a real experience. When people panic, their heart rate does go up, they do have a difficult time breathing, and many people feel dizzy or nauseated. So we are not saying that these physical sensations and your fear are not real. What we are saying is that how you think influences how frightened you feel and can exacerbate all of the physical sensations associated with panic.

As the session progressed, it became clear that Barbara continued to cling to the idea that she suffered from some terrible physical condition; she did not believe that the way she thought about things was really related to the problem. Despite these reservations, Barbara agreed to participate in treatment. Rather than arguing with her, the therapist challenged Barbara to think of her belief that a life-threatening physical condition caused her to panic as one hypothesis. A second hypothesis would be that her panic attacks resulted from a cycle of catastrophic thoughts and physical sensations, as described in the cognitive model.

> **Therapist:** In therapy we will look as objectively as we can at the evidence for and against each hypothesis. We will also examine the implications of accepting each hypothesis as fact. By that I mean we will look at the consequences, in terms of what you do and how you feel, of accepting each view.

In session 5 the therapist continued with an overview of the cognitive model. Starting very broadly, the therapist explained the cognitive model of emotions. Here Ellis's A-B-C outline was utilized. Types of common cognitive distortion such as overgeneralizing and catastrophizing were also described. Next, the therapist reviewed the cognitive view of a panic attack. Finally, he gave a hypothetical example of how the cognitive model of panic would account for one of Barbara's panic attacks. Here the therapist used information gathered during the interview and from the Agoraphobic Cognitions Questionnaire and the Body Sensations Questionnaire. He pointed out, for example, that when she feels frightened Barbara nearly always thinks that she is having a stroke.

Barbara's participation in this session was not significant. She listened to the therapist's descriptions and responded to his questions in a manner that indicated that she followed what was going on. Her demeanor, however, suggested that she was skeptical. She was given the homework assignment of recording her thoughts immediately before and during any panic attacks she might have during the week. She was instructed to do this on the back of the daily diary of panic and generalized anxiety. The rationale for this homework assignment was that we wanted to gather data we could use to test the hypothesis that panic attacks were caused by catastrophic misinterpretation of normal physical sensations.

Barbara came to session 6 with her completed homework assignments. She had had two panic attacks during the week, one while she was alone in her bedroom reading before going to sleep and the second while at work. On the back of the daily diaries she had filled in only her thoughts during the panic attacks. She reported that she could not remember what she was thinking before the attacks came on. Barbara recorded the following thoughts after the first panic attack: "Thinking it's possible that I have a brain tumor or blood clot." She recalled the following thoughts after the second panic attack: "While I was having the attack, I thought I would probably have a stroke or 'something.' " These records were used to illustrate the role of cognitions in panic attacks. First, Barbara was asked to describe the type of cognitive distortion each of these thoughts represented. With some coaching, she was able to see these as examples of catastrophizing. Next, the therapist had Barbara explain how the panic attack might have developed using her own catastrophic thoughts and Figure 3.1. Finally, Barbara was introduced to the idea of challenging her thoughts. The therapist first demonstrated thought challenging by asking Barbara to describe the evidence she used to conclude that she had a brain tumor or blood clot. Barbara could offer as evidence only the physical feelings that she was having, which in this case consisted of a slight headache and mildly blurred vision. He then challenged Barbara to come up with an alternative explanation for these feelings. She could not, so the therapist offered the following:

> **Therapist:** Is it possible that you had a headache and your vision was mildly blurred because it was late and you were tired? I know sometimes if I am sleepy while reading, the words blur together.

This session ended with the therapist instructing Barbara to continue to keep a record of her thoughts during a panic attack but also to record how she challenged these thoughts. On the back of one of the daily panic diaries the therapist made three columns with the following three headings: *"Thoughts before/during a Panic Attack," "Evidence," "Alternative Interpretations."* Barbara was instructed to fill in each column when she had a panic attack.

Barbara came to session 7 and reported that she had had one panic attack during the week but that she had forgotten her diaries. The therapist spent some time emphasizing the importance of keeping accurate records and of working on the problem between therapy sessions. Barbara described the panic attack she had had during the week and the thoughts she had had during the attack.

> **Barbara:** I was at work at my desk and it just came on out of the blue. I checked my pulse and it was about 92. I thought, "Oh my God, I'm having a stroke."
>
> **Therapist:** What time of day did this happen?
>
> **Barbara:** It was in the afternoon.
>
> **Therapist:** What had your day been like before the panic attack?

Barbara: There was nothing special going on at work. But I did have a headache all day.

Therapist: You had a headache. What did you think caused it?

Barbara: I don't know [*pause*]. I guess I did think about maybe I had a blood clot.

Therapist: You were concerned that you might have a blood clot. What about during the attack? What were you thinking then?

Barbara: I just thought I was having a stroke or something. I mean maybe the blood clot had burst open or something.

Therapist: What evidence did you use to conclude that you had a blood clot?

Barbara: I had a headache and I thought that maybe that is what was causing it.

Therapist: How can you challenge that thought?

Barbara: Well, I had a CAT scan and the doctors didn't find any brain tumors. If I did have a brain tumor, there's nothing I could do at the moment anyhow. But then I think, maybe they will be able to save me.

Therapist: I'm not sure what you mean. Who will save you and from what?

Barbara: The doctors, if I have a brain tumor.

Therapist: Wait a minute. Let's go back. At what point did we conclude that you had a brain tumor? We know that you had a headache. But so far that's the only evidence I've heard for a brain tumor. People get headaches for all kinds of reasons. They're tired. Their sinuses are clogged. They're tense or stressed. In fact, most headaches are caused by these types of factors. What is the probability that you have a brain tumor?

Barbara: What do you mean?

Therapist: I mean what are the chances that you have a brain tumor, given your age and the fact that you have had a full physical exam?

Barbara: I guess it's not real likely. But what if I did?

During the rest of this session, the therapist helped Barbara to examine the consequences of accepting an event with very low probability as a fact. He pointed out that it was not surprising that she felt frightened. Most people would feel some fear if they believed they were about to die. The problem arose because Barbara accepted uncritically the thought that she had a brain impairment. The physical sensations associated with her fear were seen as further evidence of the catastrophic misinterpretations.

Barbara's involvement in therapy appeared to increase during sessions 8 and 9. She brought in her completed homework assignments each week. She had three minor or limited-symptom panic attacks during those two weeks. Her skill at identifying the catastrophic thoughts and finding alternatives increased. She continued, however, to doubt the alternative explanations she generated. She was continually bothered by the thought "but what if it really is" a brain tumor, heart attack, stroke, and so on. Barbara's mother provided her with an apparently endless supply of catastrophic interpretations for her physical feelings. She had suggested to Barbara, for example, that she might have Epstein-Barr virus, a rare blood disease she had read about. Without the therapist's knowledge, Barbara went to her family doctor and asked to be tested for the virus.

Exposure to panic cues was introduced during the tenth therapy session. As is our usual practice, we had secured the client's physician's approval before embarking on this phase of treatment. Barbara was reluctant but agreed to induce some symptoms of a panic attack by voluntarily hyperventilating. The therapist explained the basic physiology of hyperventilation and agreed to do the exercise with Barbara. Two exposure trials using the hyperventilation technique as described in Chapter 5 were completed. After overbreathing for two minutes, Barbara sat back in her chair and immediately checked her pulse. After about 30 seconds of focusing her attention on her physical sensations, Barbara opened her eyes and reported to the therapist that she was beginning to feel panicky. The therapist tried to get her to describe the thoughts that were going through her mind, but Barbara could say only that she felt nauseated and scared. In an effort to help normalize her feelings, the therapist proceeded to describe his own physical sensations after the two minutes of hyperventilation. He described feeling short of breath, mildly dizzy, and sweaty. He also described how he could feel his heart pounding. Barbara was given several minutes to recover before the therapist suggested a second trial of hyperventilation. At first, Barbara refused, stating that she was not feeling well enough to go through the procedure again. The therapist encouraged her to participate in one more trial.

Therapist: I understand that you don't feel well right now. Hyperventilation does lead to some unpleasant sensations. The important thing here, though, is that while these sensations are unpleasant, they are not dangerous. I think it's important that you expose yourself to the sensations of a panic again in today's session. By not avoiding these sensations, you are learning through direct experience that they are not dangerous.

Barbara then agreed to a second trial of hyperventiliation.

As it turned out, coaxing Barbara into a second dose of hyperventilation had a surprisingly positive therapeutic effect. As she concentrated on her physical sensations after two minutes of hyperventilation, she had what might be called an "aha experience."

Barbara: As I was thinking about my physical feelings, I noticed that my heart was pounding and that I was having trouble breathing. All of a sudden the thought popped into my mind, "I can't breathe." It just happened real fast. I don't think I would have noticed it if I was not paying attention. I got scared for a second but then I thought, "Wait a minute, that's the kind of thought we've been talking about."

Barbara went on to describe how this was the first time she had been aware of a catastrophic thought before she panicked. She knew that she thought about catastrophic things while she panicked, but she had understood this as a response to, rather than a cause of, the panic. Realizing that she had these types of thoughts *before* she panicked helped her to accept the notion that these thoughts could play a role in creating the panic.

During the next therapy session, Barbara was taught the respiratory control technique described in Chapter 5. Two more trials of exposure to panic cues via hyperventilation were conducted during this treatment session, but this time Barbara was instructed to use the respiratory control technique to bring her breathing under control.

Sessions 12 through 14 were devoted to experimenting with alternative exposure methods. Each session followed a similar pattern. Panic sensations were induced by running in place or some similar technique. Barbara would concentrate on the physical sensations she experienced and report any automatic negative thoughts she had. The therapist and Barbara would then work together to dispute these thoughts with rational evidence. Usually this involved Barbara simply reminding herself that the physical feelings she was experiencing were caused by the exposure procedure and were not indicative of some physical problem.

During sessions 12 and 13 Barbara's pulse-checking behavior was targeted for intervention. First the therapist and Barbara explored how checking her pulse might actually increase the chance that she would have a panic attack. The therapist also explained to Barbara a little bit about normal pulse rate fluctuation. Finally, an exposure with response prevention procedure was utilized. After panic sensations were induced, Barbara agreed to refrain from checking her pulse. By session 14, Barbara reported that she was able to catch herself whenever she got the urge to check her pulse and refrain from doing so without much difficulty.

Barbara's daily record indicated no panic attacks during those weeks. There were some incidents of increased anxiety, but these never reached the level of even a mild panic attack. Barbara reported during session 13 that she had stopped taking the extra alprazolam during the day. She now took two pills a day, one in the morning and one in the evening. Questionnaire measures were readministered at the end of session 14 to evaluate Barbara's progress. Her score on the Beck Depression Inventory (9) was in the nondepressed range, and her responses on the Agoraphobic Cognitions Questionnaire and the Body Sensations Questionnaire (total scores of 28 and 36, respectively) indicated a marked decrease in the frequency of catastrophic thoughts and fear of body sensations compared to her pretreatment responses.

Barbara reported during session 15 that she had enrolled in an aerobic exercise class at the local YMCA. Although she was very excited by the thought of restarting a fitness routine, she was concerned by her mother's response to the news.

> **Barbara:** My mother is worried that I'll have some kind of relapse if I take the aerobics class. She says stuff like, "I hope you know what you are doing." Sometimes I think she doesn't want me to get better.
>
> **Therapist:** What do you mean?
>
> **Barbara:** I don't know. It just seems like all we ever used to talk about was my health. If I am not sick, we don't have anything to talk about.

The therapist allowed Barbara some time to describe the insights she was gaining into her relationship with her mother. The therapist challenged Barbara to think about how she could use these new insights to help herself dispute irrational thoughts about illness. Barbara saw that when her mother suggested that she might be ill, this comment might not be based on any evidence indicating illness. Rather, her mother might make such comments out of habit or possibly out of some fear that her daughter would not need her anymore if Barbara were healthy.

Barbara had made significant progress in the first 15 weeks. She was no longer experiencing panic attacks and appeared to have gained significant skills at applying cognitive techniques to manage anxious feelings. The only problem remaining was that she wanted to get off of her medication but was afraid that she might begin to experience panic attacks again. Session 16 was devoted to developing a plan for removing her from the alprazolam. Barbara agreed to make an appointment to see her physician to discuss withdrawal of medication. The therapist talked to Barbara about the possible side effects of medication withdrawal. The therapist emphasized that certain physical sensations, such as mild dysphoria and insomnia, are sometimes associated with discontinuing the medication. It would be important that Barbara recognize these as symptoms of medication withdrawal and not as signs of relapse into panic disorder. Barbara's doctor assured her that he thought it unlikely that she would experience any significant side effects given the very low dose of medication she was taking.

Barbara was seen for three further sessions over a six-week period. During that time she had consulted her physician and gradually reduced her medication until she was medication-free. With the exception of a few nights of mild insomnia, Barbara had no difficulties with medication withdrawal.

Comments on Barbara

In many respects, Barbara's treatment proceeded without any significant complications. It seemed to the therapist that Barbara was doubtful about the value of therapy until the introduction of exposure to panic cues. It was during a session in which voluntary hyperventilation was used that Barbara first identified catastrophic thoughts preceding the onset of panicky feelings. This seemed to give Barbara the proof she needed to accept the cognitive model of panic that had been presented.

Barbara's mother appeared to be a key figure in Barbara's life and may have inadvertently contributed to the maintenance of panic disorder. In her mother, Barbara had a consistent support for her catastrophic interpretations of physical sensations. Her mother also supported Barbara's doubts about her physician's reassurances. The mother could almost always be counted on to come up with a rare disease that might be causing Barbara to feel as she did. The therapist used the least intrusive procedure possible to address the problems Barbara's mother presented. Rather than intervening directly with the mother, the therapist chose first to see whether or not Barbara could recognize how her mother might be undercutting the gains she was making in therapy. Barbara was then able to reframe her mother's expression of concern.

CLINICAL MANAGEMENT OF SEVERE PANIC DISORDER WITH AGORAPHOBIA: MARGARET

Margaret was referred to us by a friend who had been treated in a clinical research project. She was 38 years old when she first contacted our clinic, and she had not left the confines of her home for over seven years. She requested help for "anxiety attacks," which were the cause of her home-bound status. She was seen at her home for the initial evaluation and eventually for treatment.

Margaret had experienced her first panic attack about 10 years earlier. At that time she was living in California with her husband, who was stationed there with the U.S. Navy. Margaret's husband was frequently away from home, and she was left to care for their two children, whose ages were then 7 and 3. Margaret's marriage was very strained when she experienced her first attack. She and her husband had been reunited for only a few months before he was transferred to California, following a one-year trial separation during which she lived with her parents. Knowing that they would divorce if she did not accompany her husband to California, Margaret felt compelled to give the marriage another try. She suspected that her husband had been involved with another woman during the separation, a charge he steadfastly denied.

Margaret's first panic attack occurred while she was waiting in the checkout line at a grocery store. In her own words, "I felt like things were closing in on me. My heart started to race and I was sure that I was going to pass out. I remember thinking, 'Oh my God, what's going to happen to the kids if I pass out?' I managed to go through the checkout but I don't know how." Margaret reported that she felt better when she left the store, but she began to worry that she would have another attack. She consulted a physician on the naval base, who told her that he suspected she had an inner ear infection and prescribed antibiotic medication.

After the first attack, Margaret worried about being alone with her children. She was afraid that if she panicked and fainted, the children would be unprotected. She worried that they would be kidnapped or hit by a car while she was unconscious. Margaret began to place greater demands on her husband to be home more of the time and to let her know where he could be reached "if something happened." When Margaret had to go somewhere with her children, she would carry a note in her pocket on which she had written her husband's name and a phone number where he could be reached, as well as a message that he should be called if she was incapacitated. Margaret described how she planned to pull the note from her pocket if she began to feel herself pass out. During this period, Margaret began to experience panic attacks approximately two to three times a week.

Margaret's husband was scheduled to spend a year overseas before retiring from the Navy. This presented a crisis for Margaret, who felt she could not function on her own. It was decided that she would move back to New England and live with her parents while her husband was overseas. The family drove across the country, which proved to be very difficult for Margaret. She did not leave the car except to go to the bathroom or to their hotel room during the entire journey. She made her husband pull up close to the door before she would run from the car to the bathroom or hotel room.

In the year that Margaret lived with her parents, her panic attacks subsided in frequency. Nonetheless, she rarely left her parents' home unless accompanied by one of them. When her husband retired from the Navy, they bought a home near her parents and he opened a small pizza restaurant. During the next few years, marital conflicts reappeared and her agoraphobia worsened. She complained about the long hours he worked at the restaurant, and he complained that she was not supportive. Margaret's panic attacks increased in frequency, and she was afraid to leave her home. Margaret's parents worried about their daughter and tried to help by shopping for her and driving the children to school.

In the five years prior to contacting our clinic for treatment, Margaret experienced a succession of tragedies. Her father died suddenly of a heart attack, and her mother died approximately two years later of cancer. During this time period her husband's behavior became increasingly erratic. He began to drink heavily and would not return home until the early morning hours. His business began to fail, and the family experienced financial difficulties. About two years prior to her contacting us, Margaret's husband died in an automobile accident. He was intoxicated at the time.

Although Margaret was understandably shaken by this series of tragedies, her panic attacks and agoraphobia remained surprisingly constant. She continued to experience panic attacks approximately three to five times a week, and she steadfastly refused to leave her home. She did not attend the funeral of her mother, father, or husband. Financially, Margaret was fairly secure. A mortgage insurance policy covered the cost of the home after her husband's death, and she received social security benefits for the children. She had also received life insurance money after the death of her parents and husband. Margaret's younger sister and her oldest child, a daughter, did the shopping. Margaret supplemented her income by selling crafts, such as decorative pillows, which she made at home. These were sold for her at craft shows by her neighbor.

Diagnosis: Margaret

Margaret clearly met diagnostic criteria for panic disorder with agoraphobia. She provided a thoroughly detailed description of her panic attacks, which almost always started with a feeling of sickness in her stomach that appeared suddenly, followed by a rush of warm feelings that she described as emanating from her stomach and rushing up over her head. Her heart would begin to pound, and she would feel dizzy and unstable on her feet. In most instances, the first thought that would come to her mind was that she was about to pass out. She would typically lean against a wall or a piece of furniture to steady her balance. She felt that any movement would be enough to knock her off her feet. These attacks usually lasted about ten minutes, during which time Margaret would continually hold onto whatever she had found to steady herself. During the attack, she would worry that she was losing her mind. She was sure that any given attack was "the one" that would result in insanity. After an attack subsided, she would typically lie down for about an hour to compose herself. Margaret had read several self-help books about agoraphobia and had kept a log of her panic attacks, from which she had learned that the frequency of panic attacks was associated with her menstrual cycle. She panicked more frequently in the week prior to menstruation.

There were no other anxiety disorders revealed during the structured interview, nor were there any signs of significant depression or other forms of psychopathology. The clinician's impression at the time of the interview was that, with the exception of her panic attacks, Margaret continued to function quite well in her environment.

Behavioral Assessment

Self-Monitoring

Margaret was given daily panic and generalized anxiety diaries (Figure 4.2) to complete. She was very interested in the diaries and consistently completed them. During a week of baseline assessment, her generalized anxiety ratings remained generally low (most ratings were 1 or 2). She experienced two panic attacks, during which her anxiety levels reached a peak of 6. Margaret was also given a daily diary of activities (Figure 4.1) which proved not to be necessary at the time because she never left the house.

No formalized behavioral tests were carried out, given the long-standing and consistent nature of her avoidance behavior.

Questionnaire Measures

Margaret was given five questionnaires to complete—the Fear Questionnaire, the Mobility Inventory, the Agoraphobic Cognitions Questionnaire, the Body Sensations Questionnaire, and the Beck Depression Inventory. She scored at a near-maximum level on the Agoraphobia subscale of the Fear Questionnaire (38) and on the Mobility Inventory (108). On the latter questionnaire, the only items she did not rate as "Always Avoid" were open spaces (inside), high places, staying at home alone, and parties or social gatherings. She penciled in a note next to the last item which read "only if it's at my house." Her score on the Beck Depression Inventory (6) suggested that depression was not a current problem.

Treatment: Margaret

Treatment goals were developed in the third session with Margaret. She reported that although her eventual goal was to be able to leave her house, she was most disturbed by the panic attacks. She did not want to address any avoidance problems until she felt "safe" from panic attacks. Given her goals, it was decided that the first phase of treatment would focus on reducing the frequency and intensity of panic attacks. During the fourth and fifth therapy sessions, Margaret was introduced to the cognitive model of panic. She was provided with a copy of Figure 3.1, and the panic cycle was discussed at length. Margaret was instructed to record on her panic diaries any thoughts or images that came to mind when she experienced a panic attack. Relaxation training was not used in Margaret's treatment because high levels of generalized anxiety were not evident.

Margaret experienced two panic attacks between the fifth and sixth sessions. She noted in her panic diaries that during each attack she recalled having "thoughts about my children." She explained that during the attack she would think about what would happen to her children if she died or was hospitalized. She had already asked her younger sister to take care of the children for her. Because they were now adolescents, Margaret worried that her sister would not be able to care for the children adequately. During the attack, images came to her mind of her daughter arguing with her sister and threatening to run away from home. The therapist diagrammed Margaret's train of thought on a piece of paper to make sure he could follow her logic. The sequence of thoughts went as follows: The physical sensations mean I am having an attack; this attack will be "the one"; I will lose my mind and have to be hospitalized; my children will be left in the care of my sister; my sister won't be able to handle them; my daughter will run away from home. Several points were drawn from this example. First, Margaret assumed that the physical sensations were indicative of a panic attack. Second, she assumed that catastrophic consequences would result from the attack. Third, it made sense for her to feel as frightened as she did because she accepted the first two assumptions as facts.

The therapist devoted the rest of the session to helping Margaret challenge each of these assumptions. Three basic questions were presented repeatedly:

1. What is the evidence?
2. What is another way to look at this?
3. So what if it happens?

For example, for the first assumption Margaret was asked what evidence she used to conclude that she was about to have a panic attack. Margaret responded that the physical feelings as well as her past experience led her to conclude that she was about to have an attack. The therapist used the notion of a self-fulfilling prophecy to help

Margaret see that predicting she would have an attack on the basis of her past experience made an attack more likely. He then challenged her to generate alternative explanations for the physical sensations she felt. He used the fact that Margaret had noted a relationship between her menstrual cycle and panic attacks to make this point. The uncomfortable physical sensations that many women feel in the week prior to menstruation might be misinterpreted as signs of an impending panic attack. Finally, the therapist challenged Margaret's catastrophic expectations about the consequences of a panic attack by pointing out that she had experienced hundreds of attacks in the past and had always survived.

Sessions 7 and 8 followed a similar format. Margaret discussed the panic attacks she had had during the previous week, and these were analyzed following the cognitive model. The therapist began to do less direct challenging, but prompted Margaret to dispute her own catastrophic thoughts. Also during these sessions, Margaret and the therapist began to distinguish panic attacks from what they called "panicky feelings," brief episodes of fearful feelings that did not develop into a full-blown panic attack. The therapist helped Margaret to reframe these panicky feelings from mild negative experiences into positive experiences in which she had successfully prevented a panic attack. Panicky feelings were referred to as "successes."

Exposure to panic cues was introduced in the next session. Margaret was provided with a rationale like the one presented in Chapter 5, and voluntary hyperventilation was used to induce the sensations of a panic attack. Three exposure trials were completed in the session. Margaret did not like the exposure session and complained that she got a headache from hyperventilating. Nonetheless, she was surprised that she did not panic. She reported that she coped with the unpleasant feelings associated with the exercise by reminding herself that the therapist was with her and that he would know what to do if anything happened. She also reported that it was easier for her to deal with the feelings because she was sitting down throughout the exercise and did not have to worry about falling over and "hitting [her] head or something."

The tenth session of therapy was again focused on exposure to panic cues. The problem of Margaret's feeling unstable on her feet was targeted for intervention using an exposure with response prevention model. The therapist and Margaret first discussed her feeling unsteady on her feet when she had a panic attack. She reported that she knew that she would fall over if she could not find something to hold onto.

Therapist: How do you know that you will fall over?

Margaret: It's how I feel. I just feel real unsteady on my feet, like the least little thing will knock me over. I just have to hold onto something to steady myself.

Therapist: Have you ever fallen over during a panic attack?

Margaret: No. I always find something to grab onto or I just sit down.

Therapist: What would happen if you didn't grab onto something?

Margaret: I'd fall right over.

Therapist: So you would fall over. And you know that you would fall over because you always grab onto something. So each time you grab something it provides you with further evidence that you would fall over.

Margaret: Yeah . . . I guess.

Therapist: Do you see anything wrong with this logic?

Margaret: What do you mean?

Therapist: Well, it seems to me that you never give yourself the chance to prove yourself wrong. I mean, what if you didn't grab onto something and you didn't fall over? What would that mean?

Margaret: Huh? . . . I guess it would mean that I didn't have to hold onto something in the first place.

Therapist: Right. I want to test this idea out today. I wonder if we can see whether or not you really have to grab onto something.

The therapist arranged for Margaret to be exposed to some of the sensations of a panic attack and elicited from her a promise that she would not grab onto anything or sit down. The exercise was arranged as follows. Exposure would be initiated by two minutes of running in place, after which Margaret was instructed to remain standing with her eyes closed and concentrate on the physical sensations that she experienced for five minutes. In order to protect Margaret, the therapist stood on one side of her and assured her that he would support her if she seemed to be losing her balance. There was a couch on the other side of Margaret that would break her fall if she fell in that direction. The room was arranged so that she would not hit any furniture if she did in fact fall.

During the first exposure trial, Margaret ran in place and stood with her eyes closed for about a minute and a half before she sat down on the couch. She reported that she began to feel herself panic and had to sit down. The therapist asked what thoughts or images came to mind during the exercise. Margaret admitted that she had experienced a fleeting image of herself lying on the floor bleeding from the head. She then began to feel herself panic, and she opened her eyes and sat down.

> **Therapist:** Let's try to understand what happened here. The image came to mind of you lying on the floor and you are bleeding from the head. It seems to me that your reaction to that . . . I mean opening your eyes and sitting down . . . made sense if you believed that was about to happen. You took some reasonable steps to prevent it. But was that really going to happen? I mean, you didn't fall. And from what I could see, you didn't even seem to be unsteady on your feet. Is it possible that you responded to what you thought might happen as if it really were about to happen?

The exposure exercise was repeated, but this time Margaret was taught to interfere with whatever catastrophic image came to mind by thinking the word "Stop!" to herself. Margaret was able to complete two trials of exposure with response prevention without sitting down or holding onto anything for support.

The next therapy session was focused on reviewing goals for treatment. Margaret had not experienced any panic attacks in the past two weeks. She had a few instances of "panicky feelings," which she coped with effectively. The therapist introduced the idea of in vivo exposure exercises as the next logical step in treatment. Margaret could continue to work on managing panicky feelings, but these feelings would be precipitated by in vivo exposure exercises. The idea of increasing mobility was agreeable to Margaret, and some short-term goals were established. Margaret's immediate goals were to be able to leave her home and feel free to walk about in the neighborhood.

The next three sessions were devoted to in vivo exposure exercises. The therapist accompanied Margaret on walks of increasing length away from her house. This proved to be surprisingly easy. Margaret admitted that she felt more comfortable because the therapist was with her. During the thirteenth and fourteenth sessions, the therapist phased himself out of the exposure exercise. Margaret walked to designated spots at increasing distances from her home without the therapist. The therapist would first wait outside where he could see Margaret, but eventually he waited inside, out of sight. During the fourteenth session, Margaret agreed to a set of exposure homework exercises. She agreed to take a designated walk every day in the following week.

At the next session, Margaret admitted that she had not complied with the homework instructions. She claimed that she did not avoid the walks out of fear but, rather, because she was too busy. There was a craft fair coming up in a few weeks, and she stated that she had been too busy to take the walks. The therapist emphasized the need to practice the exercises on her own, and Margaret was instructed to take the walk while the therapist waited at her home. At the end of the session, Margaret suggested that she needed a "break from therapy." She was very pleased with the progress she had made but believed that she was "too busy" to continue with therapy at this time. The next session was arranged for one month later.

After the one-month hiatus from therapy, Margaret reported that she had generally maintained the gains she had made. She had experienced one panic attack during that time. A large part of the session was spent discussing this panic attack. At first Margaret maintained that the attack had hit her out of the blue, and it was difficult for her to recall any catastrophic thoughts she had during the attack. The therapist asked how things were going for her in general, and Margaret admitted that there had been some "family problems." Reluctantly, she disclosed to the therapist that her 17-year-old daughter was pregnant. The therapist devoted the rest of the session to listening empathically to Margaret and supporting her. Margaret was embarrassed by her daughter's pregnancy and blamed herself; she saw herself as an inadequate mother.

The next several sessions were divided between in vivo exposure exercises and supportive therapy focused on helping Margaret think through the difficult times that she and her daughter were experiencing. Margaret appeared to look forward to having the therapist come to her home. She admitted that he was the only person with whom she could discuss her feelings concerning her daughter's pregnancy. Progress toward increasing her mobility, however, seemed to have reached a plateau. With the therapist, or in response to the therapist's instructions, Margaret could travel freely around her neighborhood, but she continued to resist homework assignments. Each week she had a new set of excuses as to why she had not practiced exposure on her own. These excuses centered primarily around being busy with things in the home which interfered with her completing the exposure exercises.

The therapist developed a novel approach to helping Margaret practice in vivo exercises during the week. Margaret agreed to keep a diary of the activities she engaged in each day at home. These records indicated that besides the tasks necessary to maintain a household, Margaret spent a great deal of her time working on her crafts and talking to her sister on the telephone. The therapist elicited a promise from Margaret that she would not engage in these activities until she had practiced in vivo homework. She was free to talk to her sister on the telephone or work on her crafts only after she had completed her daily in vivo practice. A meeting was arranged with Margaret, her sister, her neighbor, and the therapist. The goal of this meeting was to elicit the support of these women in helping Margaret to spend more time outside of the home. Margaret's sister agreed that she would not talk to her sister on the telephone for longer than two minutes at a time. If the women wanted to talk, Margaret had to walk to her sister's home—a distance of about three blocks—or they had to meet elsewhere, outside of Margaret's home. Margaret's neighbor agreed to keep Margaret's craft materials at her home. Margaret was free to work on the crafts, but only after doing an exposure exercise and walking to the neighbor's house to get the material. The therapist drew up a contract among the women, and they agreed to adhere to it for a period of two weeks. Margaret kept a daily activity diary of the amount of time she spent outside of her home.

This strategy proved to be instrumental in increasing the frequency of Margaret's outside-the-home activities. Over the two-week period, Margaret left the home during 10 of the 14 days. She experienced panicky feelings, but no panic attacks, during several of her excursions.

At this point in treatment, the therapist began to withdraw from active participation in exposure therapy. Margaret's sister began to take on some of the responsibility for arranging for exposure experiences. During a meeting with the sister and Margaret, the therapist listened as Margaret explained the rationale behind in vivo exposure exercises. The therapist then helped the women design treatment targets for the following week. Therapy sessions were reduced to a once-a-month basis. During these sessions, the therapist followed up on Margaret's progress in increasing her mobility. Margaret spent much more time outside of the home but seemed to limit herself to two safe places—her sister's and her neighbor's homes. She still did not do her own grocery shopping, which was taken care of by her daughter and sister. Margaret was pleased with the progress she had made and resisted the therapist's suggestion that some of the more difficult problems, such as taking public transportation or traveling to the supermarket, might be targeted for treatment. During the last contact,

Margaret reported that she was busily working on preparing her home for the birth of her grandchild. Her daughter had decided to have the child and live at home with her mother. Margaret would take care of the child while her daughter attended classes at a local community college.

Comments on Margaret

Margaret was a severely limited agoraphobic client who made significant progress but continued to be disabled after several months of therapy. Her case illustrates several interesting issues. First, the therapist decided to target panic attacks before implementing in vivo exposure therapy. This matched the client's goals for treatment. At this point, there are no research findings indicating whether or not utilizing the newer psychological approaches to treating panic attacks prior to in vivo exposure therapy yields superior results when compared to in vivo exposure alone, or whether treatment of panic leads to greater mobility by itself. In Margaret's case, it seemed that structured in vivo exercises were necessary to break a long-standing pattern of extreme avoidance behavior.

A second interesting feature of this case was the therapist's incorporation of the client's sister and neighbor into the treatment plan. By making pleasurable activities contingent on in vivo practice, the client was motivated to expose herself to previously avoided situations in order to have access to these pleasurable activities.

Finally, in this case treatment was terminated despite the fact that the client continued to be disabled by her condition. The decision to discontinue treatment was reached only after extensive discussions with Margaret about options for continued intervention. Margaret was very pleased with the progress she had made. The goals of getting her to the point where she could use public transportation, shop at the supermarket, or eventually regain her driver's license came primarily from the therapist. These goals did not appear to be important to Margaret at this juncture in her life.

CONCLUDING REMARKS

Our purpose in writing this book was to provide clinicians with a set of guidelines for evaluating and treating panic disorder and agoraphobic clients. As the cases discussed in this chapter illustrate, however, cognitive-behavioral therapy involves more than applying a certain set of therapy techniques with any client who happens to meet diagnostic criteria for a given disorder. Successful treatment requires individualized assessment of the factors contributing to the maintenance of the anxiety disorder and interventions designed to change those factors. Theory and empirical findings provide the foundation on which the clinician must build a treatment plan that can meet the needs of the individual client.

The essential features of treatment appear to be exposure to avoided situations, emotions, and physical sensations, along with anxiety management strategies such as relaxation training and cognitive therapy. Panic disorder and agoraphobia are not separate problems. Rather, clients with panic disorder seem to vary on the dimension of avoidance. The case of Margaret represents one end of the continuum, where avoidance is at an extreme. Barbara was freer to engage in a wider variety of activities but would not allow herself to experience many normal physical and emotional feelings. Despite these differences, structured exposure experiences were at the heart of the treatment plan for each woman.

There are many treatment decisions that the clinician will face when working with panic disorder clients for which adequate guidelines are not yet available in the clinical research literature. The ordering of interventions is one example. Teaching clients panic management strategies prior to exposure exercises is intuitively appealing but has not been demonstrated to be a more effective treatment strategy. Another example is that of deciding when to consider alternative treatment approaches for the client who has failed to benefit from cognitive-behavioral therapy. The potential value of combining psychological and pharmacological treatments and issues surrounding the best method of implementing combined treatment strategies are questions that await further research. Despite these deficiencies in our knowledge base, the available evidence indicates that most panic disorder clients can be helped with the strategies described in this book.

Medical Conditions Associated with Anxiety and Panic

HYPERTHYROIDISM

Hyperthyroidism is one of the most common endocrine disorders that can produce symptoms of anxiety. The disorder is about eight times more common in women than in men (MacLeod, 1981) and has a prevalence of approximately 20 per 1,000 women (Hoffenberg, 1981). The clinical manifestations of hyperthyroidism include irritability, restlessness, overactivity, emotional lability, and distractibility. The somatic symptoms include many of the same ones used when making the diagnosis of panic disorder. For example, palpitations, dyspnea, and sweating are symptoms of both panic attacks and hyperthyroidism. Somatic symptoms of hyperthyroidism not necessarily seen in panic disorder include tiredness, weight loss, and muscle weakness. Protruding eyes (exophthalmos) and drooping eyelids are also frequently seen in hyperthyroid patients but not in panic disorder clients. The diagnosis of hyperthyroidism requires a thyroid function test using blood samples.

CUSHING'S SYNDROME

The condition known as Cushing's syndrome usually develops as a side effect of high doses of corticosteroids used in treating some inflammatory diseases. When the disorder develops in this way, it is sometimes called iatrogenic Cushing's syndrome. Spontaneous Cushing's syndrome can develop from tumors on the adrenal cortex or pituitary gland, but this is much rarer. The symptoms of Cushing's syndrome result from increased circulating levels of cortisol. Depression is the most common psychiatric side effect of the syndrome, but acute anxiety and hyperactivity are sometimes seen. There are some physical features of Cushing's syndrome that make it relatively easy to identify. These are rounding of the face, obesity, an accumulation of fat at the lower part of the back of the neck (sometimes called "buffalo hump"), easy bruising, and hirsutism (McCue & McCue, 1984).

HYPOPARATHYROIDISM

This syndrome usually develops following surgical removal of the parathyroid glands in the treatment of primary thyroid disorders. Sometimes the disorder can develop when there is damage to the parathyroid during neck surgery for unrelated problems, and sometimes the cause is unknown. The disturbance of parathyroid function can produce jumpiness, restlessness, and depression. When the disturbance in thyroid function is severe, or if it goes unchecked, an extreme anxiety state can result.

PHEOCHROMOCYTOMA

Pheochromocytoma refers to tumors, usually benign, that form on the adrenal glands and cause an excess secretion of catecholamines. The clinical picture closely resembles that of a panic attack. Palpitations, headache, dizziness, sweatiness, chest pain, dyspnea, subjective experience of fear, and an increase in blood pressure are all symptoms of the catecholamine excess. The diagnosis of pheochromocytoma requires a demonstration of increased levels of catecholamines or their metabolites in the urine (McCue & McCue, 1984). Because of the infrequency of the problem, routine testing for pheochromocytoma in panic clients does not seem necessary. Physical symptoms that might suggest the presence of this disorder include headache as a central complaint, profuse sweating, and persistent hypertension (Stein, 1986).

HYPOGLYCEMIA

Low blood sugar level, or hypoglycemia, can cause some of the same physical symptoms commonly seen in panic disorder. Weakness, sweating, palpitations, tremor, faintness, dizziness, and headache are often reported during hypoglycemic episodes. There are a variety of causes for hypoglycemia, including fasting and insulin overdose. The problem can develop as a side effect of certain medications or after stomach surgery. Identification of hypoglycemia requires measurement of blood sugar levels at the time of an attack. A hypoglycemic episode does not necessarily result in a panic attack. When panic disorder clients have been made hypoglycemic in the laboratory, they usually report "nervousness" but not panic (Schweizer, Winokur, & Rickels, 1986).

CAFFEINE INTOXICATION

Caffeine is a central nervous system stimulant that is present in many common drinks such as coffee, tea, cola, and cocoa. In moderate doses, caffeine can help reduce fatigue and produce a transient increase in mental efficiency. Higher doses, however, can produce nervousness, irritability, insomnia, and palpitations. Caffeine has been used in the laboratory to induce panic attacks in panic disorder clients. Many people with panic disorder learn to avoid caffeine because it exacerbates panic symptoms (Roulenger, Uhde, Wolff, & Post, 1984). A recent case in our clinic illustrates the role caffeine can play in producing panic-like symptoms. An undergraduate student was referred to our clinic from the campus counseling center for treatment of "math phobia." The client reported panic-like attacks each time she attempted to complete an assignment for her calculus course. In the course of the diagnostic interview, it became apparent that the client used an excessive amount of caffeine. She reported that she would drink an average of 10 to 12 cups of coffee a day. She also reported that she was intimidated by calculus and so, in order to "psych up" to do her homework assignments, she would consume an additional 4 to 6 cups of coffee in the evening the hour before she planned to work on her calculus. The first step in treatment of this client was, of course, to help her reduce her caffeine intake, in this case by gradually replacing her usual brew with decaffeinated coffee. Once she had reduced her caffeine intake, we were able to proceed with treatment of what'turned out to be a relatively mild case of math anxiety.

Caution needs to be exercised when working with a client who abuses caffeine given that withdrawal from the substance is usually accompanied by a set of physical and psychological symptoms, including headache, lethargy, restlessness, and a decrease in mental efficiency (Greden, 1974). It is usually a good idea to obtain medical consultation when helping a client reduce caffeine consumption.

MITRAL VALVE PROLAPSE

The relationship between mitral valve prolapse and panic disorder received a great deal of attention when it was reported that an unusually large number of panic disorder clients also presented with mitral valve prolapse (Gorman, Fyer, Gliklich, King, & Klein, 1981; Grunhaus, Gloger, Rein, & Lewis, 1982; Kantor, Zitrin, & Zeldis, 1980). The condition results from a defect in the mitral valve, which separates the left atrium from the left ventricle of the heart. In this condition, each time the heart contracts, tissue in the mitral valve billows (or prolapses) into the left atrium (McCue & McCue, 1984). The condition is relatively common, occurring in approximately 5 percent of the general population (Barritt, 1981; Beton, Brear, Edwards, & Leonard, 1983). Accurate identification of the disorder requires careful cardiological examination, including electrocardiogram. In some cases of mitral valve prolapse, the client experiences chest pain, palpitations, headache, and dyspnea.

The early findings of a relationship between panic disorder and mitral valve prolapse led to speculation that the condition might be a biological marker for panic. Newer and more sophisticated studies, however, suggest that the speculation was not well founded. Recent studies, reviewed by Barlow (1988), yielded the following findings:

1. The prevalence of mitral valve prolapse in samples of patients with panic disorder is actually no higher than in the normal population.
2. There is no difference in the incidence of panic disorder in mitral valve prolapse samples when compared with controls.
3. The reliability of the diagnosis of mitral valve prolapse is poor.
4. There is no difference in response to pharmacological treatment between panic disorder clients with and without mitral valve prolapse.

APPENDIX B ——————————————————————————————

Drug Therapy and
Panic Disorder

Pharmacological intervention may be the most common form of treatment panic disorder clients receive. Clients who present themselves at our clinic for treatment of anxiety and who are not on any form of anxiolytic medication have become the exception. Drug therapy is readily accessible to most clients. Medications tend to work rapidly and may prevent some of the very real negative outcomes that can be associated with panic disorder, including loss of employment or inability to carry out family responsibilities. Despite their easy accessibility and the positive effects that drug treatments can bring, the general public and agoraphobic clients tend to rate drug therapy as less desirable and likely less effective than other forms of treatment (Norton, Allen, & Hilton, 1983; Norton, Allen, & Walker, 1985).

The two types of pharmacological agents that have received the most attention in the treatment of anxiety and panic are antidepressant medications and the benzodiazepines and related tranquilizers. Research into the effectiveness of these drugs has been prolific in the past decade and has steadily improved in quality. We will briefly review the findings of the major studies on drug intervention and discuss the treatment implications of medication for the nonmedical therapist.

ANTIDEPRESSANTS

The antidepressant medication that has been most extensively investigated in treatment studies of panic disorder is the tricyclic anti-

229

depressant imipramine. Most studies of the effects of imipramine in the treatment of anxiety disorders have examined the drug in combination with some form of psychological treatment. These treatments have often included in vivo exposure therapy. In general, these studies have found an advantage for combined imipramine and exposure therapy in the treatment of panic disorder with agoraphobia (see Telch, 1988, and Telch, Tearnan, & Taylor, 1983, for reviews). Comparison studies typically find an advantage for combined imipramine plus exposure therapy over imipramine plus a placebo drug on global measures of clinical improvement (for example, Mavissakalian & Michelson, 1986a, 1986b; Zitrin, Klein, & Woerner, 1980; Zitrin, Klein, Woerner, & Ross, 1983). Inconsistent findings have been reported, however (Marks et al., 1983).

Although it is generally agreed that combining imipramine and exposure therapy is effective in treating agoraphobic clients, there is little agreement about the mechanism of action that underlies this enhancement of behavioral therapy. Donald Klein (1981) has argued from a biological perspective that imipramine has its beneficial effects by suppressing "spontaneous" panic attacks. Klein and Fink (1962) were the first to report that imipramine blocked spontaneous panic but had little impact on anticipatory anxiety. Klein's argument is weakened by findings that imipramine treatment with no accompanying exposure practice had little impact on phobic anxiety, avoidance, or panic in a group of agoraphobic clients (Telch, Agras, Taylor, Roth, & Gallen, 1985). Isaac Marks (1983) has taken the position that imipramine is helpful in the treatment of agoraphobia because of its antidepressant qualities. He supports this argument with findings that imipramine did not add to exposure therapy when agoraphobic clients were not depressed (Marks et al., 1983). David Barlow (1988) takes a different view. He argues that imipramine reduces generalized anxiety and that this reduction has secondary positive effects on phobic anxiety, avoidance, and panic. Finally, Michael Telch and his colleagues have proposed the dysphoria efficacy hypothesis to account for the improvement seen in agoraphobic clients treated with exposure therapy and tricyclic antidepressants (Telch et al., 1985). The alleviation of dysphoric mood may increase the chances that an agoraphobic will engage in self-directed exposure. In addition, the improved mood state may lead the agoraphobic client to evaluate her progress more objectively than she would if she were in a depressed state. A discussion of the relative merits of the different theoretical views is beyond the scope of this appendix. The interested reader might see Barlow (1988) or Telch (1988) for detailed discussions.

Imipramine therapy in combination with cognitive-behavioral treatment is not without its risks. Some of the potential issues presented when combining psychological and pharmacological treatments are discussed later in this appendix. Imipramine has certain side effects that most clients find distressing. Dry mouth, constipation, and agitation are common. These side effects can be so disturbing that they may lead clients to drop out of therapy. In trials of antidepressant drug treatment of agoraphobia, dropout rates have averaged between 25 percent and 40 percent (Telch, 1988), much higher than dropout rates in studies of nondrug treatments (Barlow & Mavissakalian, 1981). But perhaps the biggest disadvantage of using antidepressant medication in treating panic disorder clients is the high relapse rate associated with cessation of the drug. Relapse rates have ranged from 27 percent to 50 percent in studies of combined pharmacological and behavioral treatment of agoraphobia (Telch et al., 1983).

BENZODIAZEPINES AND RELATED TRANQUILIZERS

Benzodiazepine drugs such as Valium (diazepam) became enormously popular in the 1970s in treating various forms of situational and generalized anxiety. These drugs were considered relatively safe and nonaddictive by many people in the lay community and by some professionals. Experience, however, together with many well-controlled and well-executed studies, have shown that this benign view was not well founded. In addition to their anxiolytic effects, benzodiazepines are known to cause cognitive impairment and sedation. Furthermore, frequent users of these medications can become psychologically dependent and physically addicted. In addition to the risks associated with benzodiazepines, research findings indicate that their anxiety-reducing effects are only slightly larger than those seen with placebo medication and tend to disappear with continued use (Barlow, 1988).

Diazepam and the other milder benzodiazepines have been considered ineffective in treating panic attacks, despite the fact that until recently very little research has directly examined their panic-reducing qualities (for example, Noyes et al., 1984). A new class of benzodiazepine medications (triazolobenzodiazepines), however, have been shown to possess panic-reducing qualities. Alprazolam (Xanax) is the most thoroughly studied of these drugs, thanks to a large-scale multicenter research effort supported by the drug's manufacturer,

Upjohn Corporation (Ballenger et al., 1988). The multicenter trials included over 500 carefully diagnosed clients with panic disorder and panic disorder with agoraphobia and featured double-blind assignment of clients to either alprazolam or placebo conditions. The results indicated that alprazolam can eliminate panic attacks very quickly in a significant proportion of patients. Sixty percent of the alprazolam patients were panic-free after three weeks of treatment, as compared to 30 percent of clients receiving placebo medication. By the end of the first month of treatment, 84 percent of the alprazolam clients were rated as at least moderately improved, as compared to 43 percent of the placebo group.

Despite these encouraging findings, alprazolam treatment of panic disorder is not without its problems, the most serious of which appears to be the difficulty of removing the clients from the medication. Relapse rates across studies approach 100 percent (Fyer et al., 1987; Pecknold, Swinson, Kuch, & Lewis, 1988). Furthermore, some clients report experiencing panic attacks, after withdrawal from alprazolam, that are worse than those before treatment. These severe panic attacks have been called "rebound panics" and appear to occur in around a quarter of clients who are taken off the drug (Fyer et al., 1987). When withdrawal from alprazolam is very slow, rebound panics, but not relapse, can be avoided (Fontaine, Chouinard, & Annable, 1984).

Negative side effects of alprazolam have also been observed (Noyes et al., 1988). Sedation, coordination difficulties, fatigue, slurred speech, and memory difficulties have all been reported by a significant subsection of clients. These side effects appear to be more frequent in the first week of treatment. As with any drug, a small percentage of clients experience dangerously adverse reactions to the medication. Fortunately, with alprazolam this percentage is very low. Acute intoxication, mania, and hepatitis have been observed, however, in a very small subset of people taking alprazolam.

PHARMACOLOGICAL VERSUS PSYCHOLOGICAL TREATMENT OF PANIC

With the advent of effective psychological and pharmacological treatments of panic, it seems only natural to ask the direct question: Which approach works best? Unfortunately, because the emergence of the new generation of pharmacological and psychological treatments is relatively recent, there is not a wealth of empirical research findings relevant to this question. One comparison study, however, has appeared recently (Klosko, Barlow, Tassinari, & Cerny, 1988). These investigators examined panic clients before and after 15 weeks of either alprazolam therapy, cognitive-behavioral therapy (a treatment package that utilized procedures similar to those described in Chapter 5), placebo medication, or no treatment (clients were told that they were on a waiting list for treatment). On a global rating of clinical status, only the alprazolam and cognitive-behavioral therapy conditions were rated as higher than the waiting-list control group at the end of treatment. Eighty-seven percent of the clients treated with cognitive-behavioral therapy were panic-free, as compared to 50 percent of the alprazolam clients (this difference is not statistically significant). A significantly larger percentage of clients were panic-free after 15 weeks of cognitive-behavioral therapy compared with the placebo and waiting-list conditions.

The results of the one available study comparing cognitive-behavioral therapy with alprazolam shows some advantages for each intervention. Alprazolam may work more quickly, but the psychological treatment resulted in a greater percentage of panic-free clients. Obviously, much more research needs to be done before any firm conclusions about the superiority of one approach over another can be drawn. The results of this study are encouraging, however, in light of the survey data reported earlier showing that there is a preference in the general population for nondrug treatment of emotional problems. Cognitive-behavioral treatment appears to be a viable alternative to pharmacological therapy of panic disorder.

COMBINED PHARMACOLOGICAL AND PSYCHOLOGICAL TREATMENT OF PANIC: IF EACH IS GOOD, ARE BOTH BETTER?

There appear to be at least two types of intervention that are helpful in reducing, and in many cases eliminating, panic attacks: alprazolam and cognitive-behavioral therapy. If both are effective, would a treatment package that combines the two be even better, or would psychological and pharmacological interventions interact in such a way as to cancel each other out? Concerns about negative pharmacotherapy–psychotherapy interactions may be raised on theoretical grounds. Clients may attribute therapeutic gains to the medication rather than crediting themselves with having learned skills to cope with anxiety

(Telch, 1988). The risk of relapse would be higher if, for example, an agoraphobic who has made significant progress through a combination of drugs and in vivo exposure expects to lose the therapeutic gains once the drug has been withdrawn (Zitrin, 1981). The problem seems even more salient when one thinks about combining drugs with the cognitive-behavioral treatment of panic attacks described in Chapter 5. Exposure to panic cues and application of relaxation and cognitive techniques to manage anxious feelings may be moot if the client believes he is protected from having a panic attack by the medication.

The question of whether drugs and cognitive-behavioral therapy will interact adversely or synergistically is one that is certain to draw the attention of clinical researchers in the near future. To date, however, there is little in the way of empirical findings to guide the nonmedical clinician faced with a panic disorder client who is on alprazolam, antidepressants, or other antipanic medications. Based on the information available on side effects, withdrawal problems, and rebound panic, as well as our own experience, we can offer the following recommendations.

The first step for the nonmedical therapist is to contact the physician who has prescribed the medication so that treatment efforts can be coordinated. In many cases this will be the person who referred the client for psychological treatment. We ask the physician to keep us informed about any changes in medication or the client's general health status. We also explain the basics of the cognitive-behavioral intervention and ask if there are any medical contraindications to this kind of treatment. We are particularly careful in describing the exposure procedures that might be utilized. Respiratory problems such as asthma may eliminate the use of voluntary hyperventilation, for example. In our experience, most physicians are happy to coordinate treatment efforts.

As a second step, assessment of the client's compliance with the medical regimen as prescribed is very important. We have our clients record their intake of medication every day on the panic diary. Many clients deviate from the recommended doses and schedules of medication depending on how they are feeling. Given the problems with rebound panics and relapse associated with rapid withdrawal of benzodiazepines, therapists should warn clients against unsupervised efforts to reduce or eliminate medication. Overuse of medication can also be a problem, of course, and may be potentially life-threatening. When deviations in medication use are observed, we recommend consultation with the physician who originally prescribed the medication. Reevaluation and stabilization of pharmacological treatment is sometimes necessary prior to initiating a cognitive-behavioral intervention.

We discuss with the client his goals regarding continued use of medication early in therapy. Although some clients are so pleased with the benefits of medication that they plan to continue using the drug indefinitely, this is not typically the case. Clients who seek nonpharmacological therapy are typically either not benefiting from their medication or, though satisfied with the results, would prefer a nonpharmacological approach to the problem. When cessation of drug treatment is the goal, we recommend to our clients that they maintain their current doses of medication until withdrawal can be carefully planned with their physician. Establishing a target date to begin withdrawal from medication can be helpful in motivating some clients for cognitive-behavioral therapy.

Therapy for panic disorder follows the procedures described in Chapter 5. We do not recommend special modifications for clients who are on medication other than periodically checking the sort of attributions the client is making regarding progress. Withdrawal of medication should begin after the client has demonstrated some skills in coping with panic cues. This seems important because withdrawal of medication is often associated with an increase in anxiety and some panicky feelings. A schedule for gradual reduction and eventual withdrawal from medication needs to be coordinated between the physician, the client, and the cognitive-behavioral therapist. In preparing a client to initiate medication withdrawal, we usually spend some time educating him about the typical side effects of medication cessation. The goal here is to anticipate the client's attribution of withdrawal side effects to the return of panic. When panic attacks do occur during medication withdrawal, the therapist can try to help the client make sense of them in terms of the cognitive model of panic (see Chapter 3). In addition, the therapist should challenge the client to view the panic as a temporary setback and an opportunity to hone anxiety management techniques rather than as a relapse into panic disorder.

_____

Treatment of Nonpanic, Nonagoraphobic Anxiety Disorders

The pioneers of behavior therapy for anxiety in the 1950s focused on problems like phobias and obsessive-compulsive behavior that seem to be linked to specific situations. Generalized anxiety problems received much less attention. The chief reasons for this may be that the situational disorders are amenable to interpretation in learning terms and can be treated relatively easily by behavioral methods. If simple phobias and compulsive rituals represent conditioned responses and reinforced operants, then they can be treated by means of procedures based on extinction. With the cooperation of the client, the therapist can usually produce situations that will evoke the problem so that it can be dealt with conveniently by means of such procedures. A number of well-controlled clinical experiments indicate that therapeutic, systematic exposure to feared stimuli, while the client refrains from making the escape response (avoiding or ritualizing), is an extremely helpful procedure for treating phobic and obsessive-compulsive syndromes (Barlow, 1988; Marks, 1981b, 1987).

Initially, generalized anxiety was dealt with as if it really represented phobic anxiety linked to an undetermined stimulus. Wolpe suggested that clients with generalized anxiety really fear something specific, but that it is a pervasive stimulus—for example, patterns of light and shade contrasts. This view is problematic because we would assume extinction to occur with all that prolonged exposure to the relevant stimuli! Early treatments for generalized anxiety consisted largely of relaxation training, but more recently cognitive restructuring methods have been used together with relaxation.

SIMPLE PHOBIA

A variety of treatment techniques are still in common use for simple phobias. Systematic desensitization, which has been all but discredited in application to agoraphobia or obsessive-compulsive disorder, remains a viable treatment for simple phobias, particularly those that are too abstract or too rarely encountered to allow in vivo techniques. Imaginal flooding can be highly effective, but clients may suffer short-term side effects of dysphoric mood or bad dreams; clients and therapists alike generally dislike the procedure (Thorpe & Burns, 1983). Real-life exposure, confrontive or graduated, is overall the most helpful approach, given the client's approval. However, many clients understandably refuse to contemplate a treatment plan that involves bringing them rapidly into contact with phobic stimuli. Studies by Agras, Leitenberg, and their colleagues in the late 1960s confirmed the therapeutic value of real-life exposure to phobic stimuli. Specific feedback of therapeutic progress was associated with rapid improvement in a claustrophobic woman whose therapy consisted of self-paced confinement in a small room. Gradual exposure to phobic stimuli was also effective in treating a client with a phobia of sharp knives, but the therapists were unable to show that praise contingent upon progress added any therapeutic benefit (Leitenberg, Agras, Thompson, & Wright, 1968). With phobic and obsessive-compulsive clients, the general recommendation to confront, rather than avoid, feared situations has received consistent and extensive support (Greist, Marks, Berlin, Gournay, and Noshirvani (1980). Participant modeling, in which the therapist demonstrates appropriate behavior in the client's phobic situation and then guides the client toward effective coping, has received strong empirical support in analogue studies. Finally, the cognitive restructuring techniques, including rational-emotive therapy and stress inoculation training, have proved to be a helpful adjunct to graded practice in some studies (Thorpe, Hecker, Cavallaro, & Kulberg, 1987). Nevertheless, it must be remembered that, taken by themselves, cognitive restructuring methods are inferior to graded practice in the treatment of some representative simple phobias (Biran & Wilson, 1981). A typical progression in phobia treatment is from imaginal methods, such as systematic desensitization, to graded practice in vivo, possibly abetted by stress inoculation training during clinic therapy sessions.

SOCIAL PHOBIA

The whole range of techniques applicable to simple phobias are potentially applicable to social phobia as well, but, in contrast with the findings on simple phobia, the cognitive restructuring methods have been shown to be particularly helpful in treating social phobia. Such findings were perhaps foreshadowed by an early study of Meichenbaum's, in which, prompted by the work of Paul (1966), he sought to investigate further the treatment of public speaking anxiety. In the study, Meichenbaum, Gilmore, and Fedoravicius (1971) had shown not only that an experimental form of a cognitive restructuring therapy was effective, but also that it was potentially more general in its effects—that participants with more widespread difficulties with social anxiety responded particularly well to the cognitive treatment procedure. More recently, Emmelkamp and his colleagues have shown that college students form an unusually relevant population from which to draw subjects for social phobia research, possibly because the typical age at onset for this disorder is in the adolescent years, and accordingly, unlike most other anxiety disorders, social phobia is well represented among students. Consistent results from college and general community samples indicate that cognitive restructuring is a helpful treatment for social phobia, producing results comparable with those from real-life practice programs (Emmelkamp, Mersch, & Vissia, 1985; Emmelkamp, Mersch, Vissia, & van der Helm, 1985).

OBSESSIVE-COMPULSIVE DISORDER

Procedures applicable to phobias seem appropriate for obsessive-compulsive disorder (OCD) because, like phobias, it has situational aspects—the client is troubled by a particular set of ideas and may ritualize in certain specific surroundings, for example. However, research studies have supported the use of only some of the possible techniques. Systematic desensitization has not been the subject of extensive research on OCD treatment, practically all of the reports on its use being case studies (Thorpe & Olson, 1990). Like agoraphobia, OCD has not responded very well to treatment via systematic desensitization.

Among the psychological therapies, the treatment of choice for OCD is exposure with response prevention. Drawn from laboratory studies of the extinction of conditioned avoidance behavior, exposure with response prevention entails asking the client to come into contact with ritual-evoking stimuli and then to refrain from ritualizing while confronting those stimuli (Marks, 1981b). In this way the client confronts feared stimuli without avoiding them, analogous to the exposure treatment recommended for agoraphobics. The technique permits the operation of extinction processes in that the client is confronting what may be conditioned stimuli for a fear response. A two-factor theory account of OCD posits the compulsive ritual as an escape response in the same way that running from a shopping mall could be an escape response for an agoraphobic.

For example, consider the male administrator with OCD introduced in Chapter 2. His treatment plan included exposure with response prevention aimed at his obsessions with contamination and his compulsive cleansing rituals. The therapist would urge him to touch the door handle of an entrance to a large public building, a performance that would usually elicit prolonged hand-washing. After he touched the door handle, the client and therapist would return to the office and talk for an hour while the client endured the distressing feelings produced by the "contamination." By failing to wash his hands, the client was not using his escape response and was therefore confronted by anxiety-producing stimuli. Gradual reductions in his subjective distress were reported both within and across sessions; whether the therapeutic process involved is extinction, habituation, or something else is open to question (Marks, 1981b).

In clients whose OCD does not involve obvious rituals, the therapist is in the same position as when dealing with generalized, rather than situational, anxiety. It is difficult to know which response to prevent and which stimuli to persuade the client to confront. In an ingenious demonstration, Salkovskis (1983) designed an effective treatment plan for a client whose rituals were themselves, like the triggering obsessions, covert thoughts. The client felt compelled to repeat certain thoughts to himself a fixed number of times whenever those thoughts entered his head. Salkovskis treated him by repeatedly playing back a tape recording of the client giving voice to his obsessional thoughts. The client was unable to "neutralize" each thought as it arose and, accordingly, confronted the obsessional stimuli without being able to make the escape response by ritualizing!

GENERALIZED ANXIETY DISORDER

Formerly known as free-floating anxiety or anxiety neurosis, generalized anxiety disorder presents a challenge for behaviorally oriented therapists because there is no obvious evoking stimulus for the client's pervasive anxiety. Research in the 1980s has confirmed clinicians' earlier impressions that relaxation training and cognitive restructuring were suitable treatments for this disorder. Both techniques can be deployed as general coping strategies and can be implemented without presenting specific stimuli in an extinction paradigm. Woodward and Jones (1980), for example, showed that neither systematic desensitization nor cognitive restructuring was particularly helpful for generalized anxiety, but that the combination of both techniques produced clinical improvement. It is possible that the relaxation training element of systematic desensitization was the vital aspect. Similar results were found by Barlow, Cohen, Waddell, Vermilyea, Klosko, Blanchard, and DiNardo (1984), for whom the combination of relaxation and cognitive restructuring was distinctly more helpful than no treatment in a sample of generalized anxiety disorder clients.

Relaxation training and cognitive restructuring were also recommended by Deffenbacher and Suinn (1987) as a result of their review of treatments for generalized anxiety, but they identified two more approaches as well: flooding and exposure methods, and stimulus control. In recommending flooding and exposure methods, Deffenbacher and Suinn are suggesting that methods applicable to other anxiety disorders can be used, where appropriate, in generalized anxiety disorder. Although there are practically no guidelines in the literature as yet, exposure methods can be used when the client identifies distinct themes for his or her worry and pervasive anxiety. This is potentially quite practical, because the DSM-III-R characterization of generalized anxiety disorder includes the idea that the client is troubled by continued worry over two or more life circumstance issues, such as finances, the health of the children, the prospect of unemployment, and so on. In such cases, the client could confront imagery of loss or threat for prolonged periods in the same way that a phobic client could be exposed to imaginal flooding with phobic theme material.

"Stimulus control" capitalizes on the phenomenon that behavior tends to be situation-specific and that, reinforcement factors being equal, people tend to repeat what they last did in a given situation. The term derives from laboratory studies on the tendency of discriminative stimuli to pull strongly for the behavior that is usually reinforced in their presence. To use stimulus control to help a client with generalized anxiety, the therapist would urge the client to set aside a particular place in which to do his or her worrying. This could mean that the client would immediately go to the particular location (for example, a backyard shed or a chair in the attic) whenever he or she is aware of increased anxiety or worrying. Successfully doing so would result in the worrying thoughts and anxiety becoming attached to that location and detached from all others; the client is effectively associating the problem behavior with a particular stimulus situation. After a while, the chosen location sets the occasion for anxiety, but no other environment will do so. Similar reasoning applies when the client is asked to postpone the worrying until a given half-hour period later in the day, whereupon he or she is to worry in earnest (Borkovec, Wilkinson, Folensbee, & Lerman, 1983).

POSTTRAUMATIC STRESS DISORDER

As we have indicated in Chapter 2, posttraumatic stress disorder (PTSD) differs from the other anxiety disorders in that it has its origins in a genuinely distressing event, beyond the bounds of typical human experience. The only aspect of PTSD that can be seen as disordered or irrational is the persistence of unnecessary anxiety in the months or years after the traumatic experience. Treatment focuses, therefore, on the client's current distress and impairment, which includes by definition a certain degree of diminished involvement with the outside world, involuntary reexperiencing of stress-related stimuli, and a variety of symptoms of general tension, stress, or anxiety. In practice, identifying treatment targets is made easier or more difficult by the nature of the original trauma. In the case of combat veterans of the Vietnam War whose PTSD is related to memories of the battlefield, it can be acceptable to follow an imaginal flooding procedure in which the stimuli presented are frightening scenes from combat. Because the client is unlikely to encounter wartime conditions again, and because the anxiety disorder is so obviously linked to images and memories of combat, it has been acceptable to clients, therapists, and the wider community to make aversive reactions to war experiences the target of psychotherapy. It is not unimportant, of course, that such therapy can be quite successful and bring relief to people who have suffered significant and chronic distress (Fairbank & Keane, 1982).

Similar points can be made about the victims of civilian disasters or automobile accidents who develop PTSD in the aftermath of their traumatic experiences. Therapeutic exposure to anxiety-evoking theme material has brought benefit, and the prospects for future successes with such methods seem encouraging (Foy, Donahoe, Carroll, Gallers, & Reno, 1987; McCaffrey & Fairbank, 1985).

When a client develops PTSD after victimization by sexual assault or other abuse of this kind, the selection of treatment targets is a more controversial matter. Take the example of the client mentioned in Chapter 2, whose PTSD was precipitated by chronic sexual abuse in childhood. Is it appropriate to desensitize her to sex offense perpetrators, or to scenes of rape? Such a treatment plan would be inappropriate because it would seek to treat reasonable fears and concerns as if they were unreasonable ones. It is possible to use imaginal flooding to remembered scenes of abuse, but clinicians must use careful judgment in deciding with the client on suitable targets and methods (Kilpatrick & Best, 1984; Rychtarik, Silverman, van Landingham, & Prue, 1984). Simply to avoid helping the client come to terms with traumatic memories is not a good solution, because dealing in some suitable fashion with such stimuli can facilitate trauma processing, which has been accepted as a desirable therapeutic activity (Foy et al., 1987).

One solution to the problems of treatment target selection is to recognize that reducing emotional arousal to feared stimuli is not the only avenue to successful therapy for PTSD; another approach is to help the client learn general coping skills. In this way, he or she can deploy the skills learned in therapy to deal with episodes of anxiety when they arise, whether or not the original traumatic material has been addressed specifically in therapy. The techniques used in coping skills training include relaxation, anger management procedures, and stress inoculation training (Fairbank & Brown, 1987).

CONCLUDING REMARKS

Some of the treatments available for panic and agoraphobic syndromes are applicable to the other anxiety disorders, particularly exposure in vivo and cognitive restructuring. In the anxiety disorders characterized by distress and avoidance evoked by particular stimuli, methods akin to extinction procedures have generally been successful, although it is not known whether extinction mechanisms are, in fact, the vital ones. In posttraumatic stress disorder it can be inappropriate to present stimuli drawn from memories of trauma as if those stimuli are innocuous and as if the client's fears are altogether irrational. In generalized anxiety disorder and in PTSD, it can be helpful to teach the client general coping skills, which include relaxation training, some forms of cognitive restructuring, and stimulus control techniques. In phobic and obsessive-compulsive patterns, the best outcomes have been associated with exposure in vivo and related procedures, although in the particular case of social phobia, cognitive restructuring can be as helpful as the performance-based in vivo methods.

References

Adler, C. M., Craske, M. G., & Barlow, D. H. (1987). Relaxation-induced panic (RIP): When resting isn't peaceful. *Journal of Integrative Psychiatry, 5,* 94–112.

Agras, W. S., Leitenberg, H., & Barlow, D. H. (1968). Social reinforcement in the modification of agoraphobia. *Archives of General Psychiatry, 19,* 423–427.

Agras, W. S., Sylvester, D., & Oliveau, D. C. (1969). The epidemiology of common fears and phobias. *Comprehensive Psychiatry, 10,* 151–156.

American Psychiatric Association. (1968). *Diagnostic and statistical manual of mental disorders* (2nd ed.). Washington, DC: Author.

American Psychiatric Association. (1980). *Diagnostic and statistical manual of mental disorders* (3rd ed.). Washington, DC: Author.

American Psychiatric Association. (1987). *Diagnostic and statistical manual of mental disorders* (3rd ed., revised). Washington, DC: Author.

Appleby, I. L., Klein, D. F., Sachar, E. J., & Levitt, M. (1981). Biochemical indices of lactate-induced panic: A preliminary report. In D. F. Klein & K. Rabkin (Eds.), *Anxiety: New research and changing concepts* (pp. 411–423). New York: Raven.

Arkes, H. R. (1981). Impediments to accurate clinical judgment and possible ways to minimize their impact. *Journal of Consulting and Clinical Psychology, 49,* 323–330.

Arkes, H. R., & Harkness, A. R. (1980). The effect of making a diagnosis on subsequent recognition of symptoms. *Journal of Experimental Psychology: Human Learning and Memory, 6,* 568–575.

Arnow, B. A., Taylor, C. B., Agras, W. S., & Telch, M. J. (1985). Enhancing agoraphobia treatment outcome by changing couple communication patterns. *Behavior Therapy, 16,* 452–467.

Baer, J. (1976). *How to be an assertive (not aggressive) woman in life, in love and on the job: A total guide to self-assertiveness.* New York: Rawson.

Ballenger, J. C., Burrows, G. D., Dupont, R. L., Lesser, I. M., Noyes, R., Jr., Pecknold, J. C., Rifkin, A., & Swinson, R. P. (1988). Alprazolam in panic disorder and agoraphobia: Results from a multicenter trial. *Archives of General Psychiatry, 45,* 413–422.

Barlow, D. H. (1987). The classification of anxiety disorders. In G. L. Tischler (Ed.), *Diagnosis and classification in psychiatry: A critical appraisal of DSM-III.* Cambridge: Cambridge University Press.

Barlow, D. H. (1988). *Anxiety and its disorders.* New York: Guilford.

Barlow, D. H., & Cerny, J. A. (1988). *Psychological treatment of panic.* New York: Guilford.

Barlow, D. H., Cohen, A. S., Waddell, M. T., Vermilyea, B. B., Klosko, J. S., Blanchard, E. B., & DiNardo, P. A. (1984). Panic and generalized anxiety disorders: Nature and treatment. *Behavior Therapy, 15,* 431–449.

Barlow, D. H., Craske, M. G., Cerny, J. A., & Klosko, J. S. (1989). Behavioral treatment of panic disorder. *Behavior Therapy, 20,* 261–282.

Barlow, D. H., Mavissakalian, M., & Hay, L. R. (1981). Couples treatment of agoraphobia: Changes in marital satisfaction. *Behaviour Research and Therapy, 19,* 245–255.

Barlow, D. H., O'Brien, G. T., & Last, C. G. (1984). Couples treatment of agoraphobia. *Behavior Therapy, 15,* 41–58.

Barlow, D. H., Vermilyea, J., Blanchard, E. B., Vermilyea, B. B., DiNardo, P. A., & Cerny, J. A. (1985). The phenomenon of panic. *Journal of Abnormal Psychology, 94,* 320–328.

Barlow, D. H., & Wolfe, B. (1981). Behavioral approaches to anxiety disorders: A report of the NIMH–SUNY research conference. *Journal of Consulting and Clinical Psychology, 49,* 448–454.

Barlow, D. H., & Mavissakalian, M. (1981). Directions in the assessment and treatment of phobia: The next decade. In M. Mavissakalian & D. Barlow (Eds.), *Phobia: Psychological and pharmacological treatment.* New York: Guilford.

Barrett, D. W. (1981). Mitral valve prolapse. *Journal of the Royal College of Physicians of London, 15,* 193–196.

Barrios, B. A. (1988). On the changing nature of behavioral assessment. In A. S. Bellack & M. Hersen (Eds.), *Behavioral assessment: A practical handbook* (3rd ed.) (pp. 3–41). New York: Pergamon.

Baum, M. (1970). Extinction of avoidance responding through response prevention (flooding). *Psychological Bulletin, 74,* 276–284.

Beck, A. T. (1985). Generalized anxiety disorder and panic disorder. In A. T. Beck, G. Emery, & R. L. Greenberg, *Anxiety disorders and phobias: A cognitive perspective* (Chapter 6, pp. 82–114). New York: Basic Books.

Beck, A. T. (1988). Cognitive approaches to panic disorder: Theory and therapy. In S. Rachman & J. Maser (Eds.), *Panic: Psychological perspectives.* Hillsdale, NJ: Lawrence Erlbaum Associates.

Beck, A. T., & Emery, G. (1985). *Anxiety disorders and phobias: A cognitive perspective.* New York: Basic Books.

Beck, A. T., Rush, J. A., Shaw, B. F., & Emery, G. (1979). *Cognitive therapy of depression.* New York: Guilford.

Beck, A. T., Ward, C. H., Mendelson, M., Mock, J., & Erbaugh, J. (1961). An inventory for measuring depression. *Archives of General Psychiatry, 4,* 561–571.

Berg, I., Marks, I., McGuire, R., & Lipsedge, M. (1974). School phobia and agoraphobia. *Psychological Medicine, 4,* 428–434.

Bernstein, D., & Borkovec, T. (1973). *Progressive relaxation training: A manual for the helping professions.* Champaign, IL: Research.

Beton, D. C., Brear, S. G., Edwards, J. D., & Leonard, J. C. (1983). Mitral valve prolapse: An assessment of clinical features, associated conditions and prognosis. *Quarterly Journal of Medicine, New Series LII, 206,* 193–196.

Bibb, J. L., & Chambless, D. L. (1986). Alcohol use and abuse among diagnosed agoraphobics. *Behaviour Research and Therapy, 24,* 49–58.

Biran, M., & Wilson, G. T. (1981). Treatment of phobic disorders using cognitive and exposure methods: A self-efficacy analysis. *Journal of Consulting and Clinical Psychology, 49,* 886–899.

Bland, K., & Hallam, R. S. (1981). Relationship between response to graded exposure and marital satisfaction in agoraphobics. *Behaviour Research and Therapy, 19,* 335–338.

Borkovec, T., Wilkinson, L., Folensbee, R., & Lerman, C. (1983). Stimulus control applications to the treatment of worry. *Behaviour Research and Therapy, 21,* 247–251.

Boulenger, J. P., Uhde, T. W., Wolff, E. A., & Post, R. M. (1984). Increased sensitivity to caffeine in patients with panic disorder. *Archives of General Psychiatry, 41,* 1067–1071.

Bowen, R. C., Cipywnyk, D., D'Arcy, C., & Keegan, D. (1984). Alcoholism, anxiety disorders, and agoraphobia. *Alcoholism: Clinical and Experimental Research, 8,* 48–50.

Bowen, R. C., & Kahout, J. (1979). The relationship between agoraphobia and primary affective disorders. *Canadian Journal of Psychiatry, 24,* 317–322.

Boyd, J. H., Derr, K., Grossman, B., Lee, C., Sturgeon, S., Lacock, D. D., & Bruder, C. I. (1983). Different definitions of alcoholism: II. A pilot study of 10 definitions in a treatment setting. *American Journal of Psychiatry, 140,* 1314–1317.

Brehony, K. A., & Geller, E. S. (1981). Agoraphobia: Appraisal of research and a proposal for an integrative model. In M. Hersen, R. M. Eisler, & P. M. Miller (Eds.), *Progress in behavior modification* (Vol. 12.). New York: Academic.

Breier, A., Charney, D. S., & Henninger, G. R. (1984). Major depression in patients with agoraphobia and panic disorder. *Archives of General Psychiatry, 41,* 1129–1135.

Breuer, J., & Freud, S. (1974). Studies on hysteria. In J. Strachey & A. Strachey (Eds. and Trans.), *The pelican Freud library* (Vol. 3). Harmondsworth, UK: Penguin. (Original work published 1895.)

Brooks, R. B., Baltazar, P. L., & Munjack, D. J. (1989). Co-occurrence of personality disorders with panic disorder, social phobia, and generalized anxiety disorder: A review of the literature. *Journal of Anxiety Disorders, 3,* 259–285.

Bruner, J. S. & Tagiuri, R. (1954). The perception of people. In G. Lindsey (Ed.), *Handbook of social psychology.* Reading, MA: Addison-Wesley.

Buglass, D., Clarke, J., Henderson, A. S., Kreitman, N., & Presley, A. S. (1977). A study of agoraphobic housewives. *Psychological Medicine, 7,* 73–86.

Burns, L. E. (1977). *An investigation into the additive effects of behavioural techniques in the treatment of agoraphobia.* Unpublished doctoral dissertation, University of Leeds.

Burns, L. E., & Thorpe, G. L. (1977a). The epidemiology of fears and phobias (with particular reference to the National Survey of Agoraphobics). *Journal of International Medical Research, 5*(Supplement 5), 1–7.

Burns, L. E., & Thorpe, G. L. (1977b). Fears and clinical phobias: Epidemiological aspects and the National Survey of Agoraphobics. *Journal of International Medical Research, 5*(Supplement 1), 132–139.

Burns, L. E., Thorpe, G. L., & Cavallaro, L. A. (1986). Agoraphobia 8 years after behavioral treatment: A follow-up study with interview, self-report, and behavioral data. *Behavior Therapy, 17,* 580–591.

Carr, D. B., & Sheehan, D. V. (1984). Evidence that panic disorder has a metabolic cause. In J. C. Ballenger (Ed.), *Biology of agoraphobia.* Washington, DC: American Psychiatry Press.

Casat, C. D. (1988). Childhood anxiety disorders: A review of the possible relationship to adult panic disorder and agoraphobia. *Journal of Anxiety Disorders, 2,* 51–60.

Cavallaro, L. A. (1987). *Cognitive-behavioral assertiveness training with agoraphobics.* Unpublished doctoral dissertation, University of Maine.

Chambless, D. L. (1988, November). *Spacing of exposure sessions in the treatment of phobia.* Paper presented at the 22nd annual meeting of the Association for Advancement of Behavior Therapy, New York.

Chambless, D. L., Caputo, G. C., Bright, P., & Gallagher, R. (1984). Measurement of fear of fear in agoraphobics: The Body Sensations Questionnaire and the Agoraphobic Cognitions Questionnaire. *Journal of Consulting and Clinical Psychology, 52,* 1090–1097.

Chambless, D. L., Caputo, G. C., Jasin, S. E., Gracely, E. J., & Williams, C. (1985). The mobility inventory for agoraphobia. *Behaviour Research and Therapy, 23,* 35–44.

Chambless, D. L., Cherney, J., Caputo, G. C., & Rheinstein, B. J. G. (1987). Anxiety disorders and alcoholism: A study of inpatient alcoholics. *Journal of Anxiety Disorders, 1,* 29–40.

Chambless, D. L., Foa, E. B., Groves, G. A., & Goldstein, A. J. (1982). Exposure and communications training in the treatment of agoraphobia. *Behaviour Research and Therapy, 20,* 219–231.

Chambless, D. L., Hunter, K., & Jackson, A. (1982). Social anxiety and assertiveness: A comparison of the correlations in phobic and college student samples. *Behaviour Research and Therapy, 20,* 403–404.

Chambless, D. L., & Mason, J. (1986). Sex, sex-role stereotyping, and agoraphobia. *Behaviour Research and Therapy, 24,* 231–235.

Chambless, D. L., & Renneberg, B. (1988, September). *Personality disorders of agoraphobics.* Paper presented at the World Congress on Behaviour Therapy, Edinburgh, Scotland.

Charney, D. S., Heninger, G. R., & Breier, A. (1984). Noradrenergic function in panic anxiety, effects of yohimbine in healthy subjects and patients with agoraphobia and panic disorder. *Archives of General Psychiatry, 41,* 751–763.

Clark, D. M. (1986). A cognitive approach to panic. *Behaviour Research and Therapy, 24,* 461–470.

Clark, D. M. (1988). A cognitive model of panic attacks. In S. Rachman & J. Maser (Eds.), *Panic: Cognitive views.* Hillsdale, NJ: Lawrence Erlbaum Associates.

Clark, D. M., & Beck, A. T. (1988). Cognitive approaches. In C. Last & M. Hersen (Eds.), *Handbook of anxiety disorders.* New York: Pergamon.

Clark, D. M., Salkovskis, P. M., & Chalkley, A. J. (1985). Respiratory control as a treatment for panic attacks. *Journal of Behavior Therapy and Experimental Psychiatry, 16,* 23–30.

Clark, L. A. (1989). The anxiety and depressive disorders: Descriptive psychopathology and differential diagnosis. In P. C. Kendall & D. Watson (Eds.), *Anxiety and depression: Distinctive and overlapping features* (pp. 83–129). New York: Academic.

Clarke, J. C., & Wardman, W. (1985). *Agoraphobia: A clinical and personal account.* Sydney: Pergamon.

Cloninger, C. R., Martin, R. L., Clayton, P., & Guze, S. B. (1981). A blind follow-up and family study of anxiety neurosis: Preliminary analysis of the St. Louis 500. In D. F. Klein & J. G. Rabkin (Eds.), *Anxiety: New research and changing concepts* (pp. 137–154). New York: Raven.

Cobb, J. P., Mathews, A. M., Childs-Clarke, A., & Blowers, M. (1984). The spouse as co-therapist in the treatment of agoraphobia. *British Journal of Psychiatry, 144,* 282–287.

Cohen, A. S., Barlow, D. H., & Blanchard, E. B. (1985). Psychophysiology of relaxation-induced panic attacks. *Journal of Abnormal Psychology, 94,* 96–101.

Cook, E. W., Melamed, B. G., Cuthbert, B. N., McNeil, D. W., & Lang, P. J. (1988). Emotional imagery and the differential diagnosis of anxiety. *Journal of Consulting and Clinical Psychology, 56,* 734–740.

Cooper, J. E., Gelder, M. G., & Marks, I. M. (1965). The results of behaviour therapy in 77 psychiatric patients. *British Medical Journal, 1,* 1222–1225.

Coryell, W., Noyes, R., & Clancy, J. (1982). Excess mortality in panic disorder: A comparison with unipolar depression. *Archives of General Psychiatry, 39,* 701–703.

Cox, B. J., Norton, G. R., Dorward, J., Fergusson, P. A. (1989). The relationship between panic attacks and chemical dependencies. *Addictive Behaviors, 14,* 53–60.

Craske, G., Rachman, S. J., Tallman, K. (1986). Mobility, cognition, and panic. *Journal of Psychopathology and Behavioral Assessment, 8,* 199–209.

Crowe, M. J. (1978). Conjoint marital therapy: A controlled outcome study. *Psychological Medicine, 9,* 623–636.

Crowe, R. R., Noyes, R., Pauls, D. L., & Slymen, D. (1983). A family study of panic disorder. *Archives of General Psychiatry, 40,* 1065–1069.

Deffenbacher, J. L., & Suinn, R. M. (1987). Generalized anxiety syndrome. In L. Michelson & L. M. Ascher (Eds.), *Anxiety and stress disorders: Cognitive-behavioral assessment and treatment* (pp. 332–360). New York: Guilford.

deSilva, P., & Rachman, S. J. (1981). Is exposure a necessary condition for fear reduction? *Behaviour Research and Therapy, 19,* 227–231.

DiNardo, P. A., Barlow, D. H., Cerny, J., Vermilyea, B. B., Vermilyea, J. A., Himaldi, W., & Waddell, M. (1985). *Anxiety Disorders Interview Schedule—Revised (ADIS-R).* Albany: Phobia and Anxiety Disorders Clinic, State University of New York at Albany.

Ellis, A. (1962). *Reason and emotion in psychotherapy.* New York: Lyle Stuart.

Ellis, A. (1979). A note on the treatment of agoraphobics with cognitive modification versus prolonged exposure in vivo. *Behaviour Research and Therapy, 17,* 162–164.

Emmelkamp, P. M. G. (1980). Agoraphobics' interpersonal problems: Their role in the effects of exposure in vivo therapy. *Archives of General Psychiatry, 37,* 1303–1306.

Emmelkamp, P. M. G. (1982a). *In vivo* treatment of agoraphobia. In D. L. Chambless & A. J. Goldstein (Eds.), *Agoraphobia: Multiple perspectives on theory and treatment* (pp. 43–75). New York: Wiley.

Emmelkamp, P. M. G. (1982b). *Phobic and obsessive-compulsive disorders: Theory, research, and practice.* New York: Plenum.

Emmelkamp, P. M. G., Kuipers, A. C., & Eggeraat, J. B. (1978). Cognitive modification versus prolonged exposure in vivo: A comparison with agoraphobics as subjects. *Behaviour Research and Therapy, 16,* 33–41.

Emmelkamp, P. M. G., & Mersch, P. P. (1982). Cognition and exposure in vivo in the treatment of agoraphobia: Short-term and delayed effects. *Cognitive Therapy and Research, 6,* 77–90.

Emmelkamp, P. M. G., Mersch, P. P., & Vissia, E. (1985). The external validity of analogue outcome research: Evaluation of cognitive and behavioral interventions. *Behaviour Research and Therapy, 23,* 83–86.

Emmelkamp, P. M. G., Mersch, P. P., Vissia, E., & van der Helm, M. (1985). Social phobia: A comparative evaluation of cognitive and behavioral interventions. *Behaviour Research and Therapy, 23,* 365–369.

Emmelkamp, P. M. G., van der Hout, A., & de Vries, K. (1983). Assertive training for agoraphobics. *Behaviour Research and Therapy, 21,* 63–68.

Emmelkamp, P. M. G., & Wessels, H. (1975). Flooding in imagination vs.

flooding in vivo: A comparison with agoraphobics. *Behaviour Research and Therapy, 13*, 7–15.

Epstein, W. S. (1982). *Fear of anxiety: Development and validation of an assessment scale.* Unpublished doctoral dissertation. University of Illinois at Chicago.

Evans, I. M. (1972). A conditioning model of a common neurotic pattern: Fear of fear. *Psychotherapy: Theory, research, and practice, 9*, 238–241.

Everaerd, W. T., Rijken, H. M., & Emmelkamp, P. M. G. (1973). A comparison of "flooding" and "successive approximation" in the treatment of agoraphobia. *Behaviour Research and Therapy, 11*, 105–117.

Fairbank, J. A., & Brown, T. A. (1987). Current behavioral approaches to the treatment of posttraumatic stress disorder. *The Behavior Therapist, 10*, 57–64.

Fairbank, J. A., & Keane, T. M. (1982). Flooding for combat-related stress disorders: Assessment of anxiety-reduction across traumatic memories. *Behavior Therapy, 13*, 499–510.

Fisher, L. M., & Wilson, G. T. (1985). A study of the psychology of agoraphobia. *Behaviour Research and Therapy, 23*, 97–107.

Fishman, S. (1980). *Agoraphobia: Multiform behavioral treatment.* New York: BMA Audiocassette Publications.

Foa, E. B., Jameson, J. S., Turner, R. M., & Payne, L. L. (1980). Massed vs. spaced exposure sessions in the treatment of agoraphobia. *Behaviour Research and Therapy, 18*, 333–338.

Fodor, I. G. (1978). *Phobias in women: Therapeutic approaches.* New York: BMA Audiocassette Publications.

Fontaine, R., Chouinard, G., & Annable, L. (1984). Rebound anxiety in anxious patients after abrupt withdrawal of benzodiazapine treatment. *American Journal of Psychiatry, 141*, 848–852.

Foy, D. W., Donahoe, C. P., Carroll, E. M., Gallers, J., & Reno, R. (1987). Posttraumatic stress disorder. In L. Michelson & L. M. Ascher (Eds.)., *Anxiety and stress disorders: Cognitive-behavioral assessment and treatment* (pp. 361–378). New York: Guilford.

Franks, C. M., & Wilson, G. T. (Eds.). (1978). *Annual review of behavior therapy: Theory and practice* (Vol. 5). New York: Brunner/Mazel.

Freeman, A., & Leaf, R. C. (1989). Cognitive therapy applied to personality disorders. In A. Freeman, K. M. Simon, L. E. Beutler, & H. Arkowitz (Eds.), *Comprehensive handbook of cognitive therapy* (pp. 403–433). New York: Plenum.

Freud, S. (1955). Analysis of a phobia in a five-year-old boy. In J. Strachey (Ed. and Trans.), *The standard edition of the complete psychological works of Sigmund Freud* (Vol. 10, pp. 5–149). London: Hogarth. (Original work published 1909.)

Fyer, A. J., Liebowitz, M. R., Gorman, J. M., Campeas, R., Levin, A., Davies, S. O., Goetz, D., & Klein, D. F. (1987). Discontinuation of alprazolam in panic patients. *Archives of General Psychiatry, 144*, 303–308.

Galassi, M. D., & Galassi, J. P. (1977). *Assert yourself!* New York: Human Services Press.

Galassi, J. P., Galassi, M. D., & Fulkerson, K. (1984). Assertion training in theory and practice: An update. In C. M. Franks (Ed.), *New developments in behavior therapy: From research to clinical application* (pp. 319–376). New York: Haworth.

Gay, M. L., Hollandsworth, J. G., & Galassi, J. P. (1975). An assertiveness inventory for adults. *Journal of Counseling Psychology, 22,* 340–344.

Gelder, M. G., Bancroft, J. H. J., Gath, D. H., Johnston, D. W., Mathews, A. M., & Shaw, P. M. (1973). Specific and nonspecific factors in behaviour therapy. *British Journal of Psychiatry, 123,* 445–462.

Gelder, M. G., & Marks, I. M. (1966). Severe agoraphobia: A controlled prospective trial of behaviour therapy. *British Journal of Psychiatry, 112,* 309–319.

Gelder, M. G., Marks, I. M., & Wolff, H. (1967). Desensitization and psychotherapy in the treatment of phobic states. *British Journal of Psychiatry, 113,* 53–73.

Ghosh, A., & Marks, I. M. (1987). Self-treatment of agoraphobia by exposure. *Behavior Therapy, 18,* 3–16.

Gitlin, B., Martin, M., Shear, K., Frances, A., Ball, G., & Josephson, S. (1985). Behavior therapy for panic disorder. *Journal of Nervous and Mental Disease, 173,* 506–508.

Goldfried, M. R. (1971). Systematic desensitization as training in self-control. *Journal of Consulting and Clinical Psychology, 37,* 228–234.

Goldstein, A. J. (1970). Case conference: Some aspects of agoraphobia. *Journal of Behavior Therapy and Experimental Psychiatry, 1,* 305–313.

Goldstein, A. J., & Chambless, D. L. (1978). A reanalysis of agoraphobia. *Behavior Therapy, 9,* 47–59.

Gorman, J. M., Fyer, A. F., Gliklich, J., King, D., & Klein, D. F. (1981). Effects of imipramine on prolapsed mitral valves of patients with panic disorder. *American Journal of Psychiatry, 138,* 977–978.

Gottman, J. M. (1979). *Marital interaction: Experimental investigations.* New York: Academic.

Greden, J. F. (1974). Anxiety or caffeinism: A diagnostic dilemma. *American Journal of Psychiatry, 131,* 1089–1092.

Greist, J. H., Marks, I. M., Berlin, F., Gournay, K., & Noshirvani, H. (1980). Avoidance versus confrontation of fear. *Behavior Therapy, 11,* 1–14.

Griez, E., & van den Hout, M. A. (1986). CO_2 inhalation in the treatment of panic attacks. *Behaviour Research and Therapy, 24,* 145–150.

Grunhaus, L., Gloger, S., Rein, A., & Lewis, B. S. (1982). Mitral valve prolapse and panic attacks. *Israel Journal of Medical Sciences, 18,* 221–223.

Gurman, I. S. (1980). Behavioral marital therapy in the 1980s: The challenge of integration. *American Journal of Family Therapy, 8,* 86–96.

Hafner, R. J. (1977). The husbands of agoraphobic women and their influence on treatment outcome. *British Journal of Psychiatry, 131,* 289–294.

Hafner, R. J. (1979). Agoraphobic women married to abnormally jealous men. *British Journal of Medical Psychology, 52,* 99–104.

Hafner, R. J. (1982). The marital context of the agoraphobic syndrome. In D. L. Chambless & A. J. Goldstein (Eds.), *Agoraphobia: Multiple perspectives on theory and treatment* (pp. 77–117). New York: Wiley.

Hafner, J., & Marks, I. M. (1976). Exposure in vivo of agoraphobics: The contribution of diazepam, group exposure and anxiety evocation. *Psychological Medicine, 6,* 71–88.

Hallam, R. S., & Rachman, S. J. (1976). Current status of aversion therapy. In M. Hersen, R. Eisler, & P. Miller (Eds.), *Progress in behavior modification.* (Vol. 21). New York: Academic.

Hamilton, S. A. (1982). Symptoms and assessment of depression. In E. S. Paykel (Ed.), *Handbook of affective disorders.* Boston: Little, Brown.

Hand, I., & Lamontagne, Y. (1976). The exacerbation of interpersonal problems after rapid phobia-removal. *Psychotherapy: Theory, Research, and Practice, 13,* 405–411.

Hand, I., Lamontagne, Y., & Marks, I. M. (1974). Group exposure (flooding) in vivo for agoraphobics. *British Journal of Psychiatry, 124,* 588–602.

Hecker, J. E., & Thorpe, G. L. (1987). Fear reduction processes in imaginal and in vivo flooding: A comment on James' review. *Behavioural Psychotherapy, 15,* 215–223.

Heide, F. J., & Borkovec, T. D. (1983). Relaxation-induced anxiety: Paradoxical anxiety enhancement due to relaxation training. *Journal of Consulting and Clinical Psychology, 51,* 171–182.

Heide, F. J., & Borkovec, T. D. (1984). Relaxation-induced anxiety: Mechanisms and theoretical implications. *Behaviour Research and Therapy, 22,* 1–12.

Hibbert, G. A. (1984). Ideational components of anxiety: Their origin and content. *British Journal of Psychiatry, 144,* 618–624.

Hillenberg, J., & Collins, J. (1982). A procedural analysis and review of relaxation training research. *Behaviour Research and Therapy, 30,* 251–260.

Himaldi, W. G., Cerny, J. A., Barlow, D. H., Cohen, S., & O'Brien, G. T. (1986). The relationship of marital adjustment to agoraphobia treatment outcome. *Behaviour Research and Therapy, 24,* 107–115.

Hoffenberg, R. (1981). Hyperthyroidism, hypothyroidism and thyroid function testing. *Medicine International* (U.K. edition), *1,* 256–266.

Holden, A. E., & Barlow, D. H. (1986). Heart rate and heart rate variability recorded in vivo in agoraphobics and nonphobics. *Behavior Therapy, 14,* 545–556.

Holden, A. E., O'Brien, G. T., Barlow, D. H., Stetson, D., & Infantino, A. (1983). Self-help manual for agoraphobia: A preliminary report of effectiveness. *Behavior Therapy, 14,* 545–556.

Hollon, S. D. (1981). Cognitive-behavioral treatment of drug-induced pansituational anxiety states. In G. Emery, S. D. Hollon, & R. C. Bedrosian

(Eds.), *New directions in cognitive therapy: A casebook.* New York: Guilford.

Hope, D. A., Rapee, R. M., Heimberg, R. G., & Dombeck, M. J. (1990). Representation of the self in social phobia: Vulnerability to social threat. *Cognitive Therapy and Research, 14,* 177–189.

Jacob, R. G., & Rapport, M. D. (1984). Panic disorder: Medical and psychological parameters. In S. M. Turner (Ed.), *Behavioral theories and treatment of anxiety* (pp. 187–237). New York: Plenum.

Jacobson, E. (1938). *Progressive relaxation* (rev. ed.). Chicago: University of Chicago Press.

James, J. E. (1986). Review of the relative efficacy of imaginal and *in vivo* flooding in the treatment of clinical fear. *Behavioural Psychotherapy, 14,* 183–191.

Jansson, L., & Ost, L. G. (1982). Behavioral treatments for agoraphobia: An evaluative review. *Clinical Psychology Review, 2,* 311–336.

Kantor, J. S., Zitrin, C. M., & Zeldis, S. M. (1980). Mitral valve prolapse in agoraphobia patients. *American Journal of Psychiatry, 137,* 467–469.

Kelley, H. H., & Thibaut, J. W. (1978). *Interpersonal relations: A theory of interdependence.* New York: Wiley.

Kilpatrick, D. G., & Best, C. L. (1984). Some cautionary remarks on treating sexual assault victims with implosion. *Behavior Therapy, 15,* 421–423.

Klein, D. F. (1981). Anxiety reconceptualized. In D. F. Klein & J. Rabkin (Eds.), *Anxiety: New research and changing concepts.* New York: Raven.

Klein, D. F., & Fink, M. (1962). Psychiatric reaction patterns to imipramine. *American Journal of Psychiatry, 119,* 438.

Klein, D. F., Zitrin, C. M., & Woerner, M. G. (1977). Imipramine and phobia. *Psychopharmacological Bulletin, 13,* 24–27.

Klosko, J. S., Barlow, D. H., Tassinari, R. B., & Cerny, J. A. (1988). Comparison of alprazolam and cognitive behavior therapy in the treatment of panic disorder: A preliminary report. In I. Hand & H.-U. Wittchen (Eds.), *Treatments of panic and phobias: Modes of application and variables affecting outcome.* Berlin: Springer-Verlag.

Klosko, J. S., Rotunda, R., & Barlow, D. H. (1987, November). *A descriptive study of first panic attacks of patients diagnosed with agoraphobia with panic attacks or panic disorder.* Paper presented at the meeting of the Association for the Advancement of Behavior Therapy, Boston.

Knapp, T. J. (1988). The beginnings of agoraphobia. In T. J. Knapp (Ed.) & M. T. Schumacher (Trans.), *Westphal's "Die Agoraphobie"* (pp. 1–57). Lanham, MD: University Press of America.

Kraepelin, E. (1914). *Lectures on clinical psychiatry* (2nd ed.) (T. Johnstone, Ed., 3rd English ed.). New York: William Wood and Co. (Original work published 1901.)

Lader, M. (1991). The biology of panic disorder: A long-term view and critique. In J. Walker, G. Norton, & C. Ross (Eds.), *Panic disorder and agoraphobia: A guide for the practitioner* (pp. 150–174). Pacific Grove, CA: Brooks/Cole.

Lang, P. J. (1979). A bio-informational theory of emotional imagery. *Psychophysiology, 16,* 495–512.

Lang, P. J., Levin, D. N., Miller, G. A., & Kozak, M. J. (1983). Fear behavior, fear imagery, and the psychophysiology of emotion. *Journal of Abnormal Psychology, 92,* 276–306.

Lapouse, R., & Monk, M. A. (1959). Fears and worries in a representative sample of children. *American Journal of Orthopsychiatry, 29,* 803–818.

Leitenberg, H., Agras, W. S., Thompson, L. E., & Wright, D. E. (1968). Feedback in behavior modification: An experimental analysis in two phobic cases. *Journal of Applied Behavior Analysis, 1,* 131–137.

Levin, D. N., Cook, E. W., & Lang, P. J. (1982). Fear imagery and fear behavior: Psychophysiological analysis of clients receiving treatment for anxiety disorders (Abstract). *Psychophysiology, 19,* 571–572.

Lewinsohn, P. M. (1974). A behavioral approach to depression. In R. J. Friedman & M. M. Katz (Eds.), *The psychology of depression: Contemporary theory and research.* New York: Wiley.

Lewis, J. A., Dana, R. Q., & Blevins, G. A. (1988). *Substance abuse counseling: An individualized approach.* Pacific Grove, CA: Brooks/Cole.

Ley, R. (1985). Agoraphobia, the panic attack, and the hyperventilation syndrome. *Behaviour Research and Therapy, 23,* 79–81.

Liebowitz, M. R., Gorman, J. M., Fyer, A., Dillon, D., Levitt, M., & Klein, D. F. (1986). Possible mechanisms for lactate's induction of panic. *American Journal of Psychiatry, 143,* 499–502.

Liebowitz, M. R., Gorman, J. M., Fyer, A. J., Levitt, M., Dillon, D., Levy, G., Appleby, I. L., Anderson, P. M., Davies, S. O., & Klein, D. F. (1985). Lactate provocation of panic attacks: II. Biochemical and physiological findings. *Archives of General Psychiatry, 42,* 709–722.

Linehan, M. M. (1987). Dialectical behavior therapy: A cognitive-behavioral approach to parasuicide. *Journal of Personality Disorders, 1,* 328–333.

Lipschitz, A. (1988). Diagnosis and classification of anxiety disorders. In C. G. Last & M. Hersen (Eds.), *Handbook of anxiety disorders* (pp. 41–65). New York: Pergamon.

Lum, L. C. (1976). The syndrome of habitual chronic hyperventilation. In O. W. Hill (Ed.), *Modern trends in psychosomatic medicine* (Vol. 3). London: Butterworths.

MacLeod, J. (1981). *Davidson's principles and practice of medicine.* Edinburgh: Churchill Livingstone.

Maisto, S. A. (1985). Behavioral formulation of cases involving alcohol abuse. In I. D. Turkat (Ed.), *Behavioral case formulation.* New York: Plenum.

Margraf, J., Ehlers, A., & Roth, W. T. (1986). Biological models of panic disorder and agoraphobia—A review. *Behaviour Research and Therapy, 24,* 553–567.

Marks, I. M. (1969). *Fears and phobias.* London: Heinemann Medical.

Marks, I. M. (1971). Phobic disorders four years after treatment: A prospective follow-up. *British Journal of Psychiatry, 118,* 683–688.

Marks, I. M. (1972). Perspective on flooding. *Seminars in Psychiatry, 4,* 129–138.

Marks, I. M. (1978). *Living with fear: Understanding and coping with anxiety.* New York: McGraw-Hill.

Marks, I. M. (1981a). Behavioural concepts and treatments of neuroses. *Behavioural Psychotherapy, 9,* 137–154.

Marks, I. M. (1981b). *Cure and care of neuroses.* New York: Wiley.

Marks, I. M. (1983). Comparative studies of benodiazepines and psychotherapies. *L'Encephale, 9,* 23–30.

Marks, I. M. (1987). *Fears, phobias, and rituals: Panic, anxiety, and their disorders.* New York: Oxford University Press.

Marks, I. M., Boulougouris, J., & Marset, P. (1971). Flooding vs. desensitization for phobic patients: A crossover study. *British Journal of Psychiatry, 119,* 353–375.

Marks, I. M., & Gelder, M. G. (1965). A controlled retrospective study of behaviour therapy in phobic patients. *British Journal of Psychiatry, 111,* 571–573.

Marks, I. M., Grey, S., Cohen, S. D., Hill, R., Mawson, D., Ramm, E. M., & Stern, R. S. (1983). Imipramine and brief therapist-aided exposure in agoraphobics having self-exposure homework: A controlled trial. *Archives of General Psychiatry, 40,* 153–162.

Marks, I. M., & Mathews, A. M. (1979). Brief standard self-rating for phobic patients. *Behaviour Research and Therapy, 17,* 263–267.

Marshall, W. L., Gauthier, J., & Gordon, A. (1979). The current status of flooding therapy. In M. Hersen, R. M. Eisler, and P. M. Miller (Eds.), *Progress in behavior modification* (pp. 205–275). New York: Academic.

Masserman, J. H. (1943). *Behavior and neurosis.* Chicago: University of Chicago Press.

Mathews, A. M., Gelder, M. G., & Johnston, D. W. (1981). *Agoraphobia: Nature and treatment.* New York: Guilford.

Mathews, A. M., Johnston, D. W., Lancashire, M., Munby, M., Shaw, P. M., & Gelder, M. G. (1976). Imaginal flooding and exposure to real phobic situations: Treatment outcome with agoraphobic patients. *British Journal of Psychiatry, 129,* 362–371.

Mathews, A. M., Teasdale, J., Munby, M., Johnston, D., & Shaw, P. (1977). A home-based treatment program for agoraphobia. *Behavior Therapy, 8,* 915–924.

Mavissakalian, M. (1986a). Clinically significant improvement in agoraphobia research. *Behaviour Research and Therapy, 24,* 369–370.

Mavissakalian, M. (1986b). The Fear Questionnaire: A validity study. *Behaviour Research and Therapy, 24,* 83–85.

Mavissakalian, M., & Barlow, D. M. (1981). Phobia: An overview. In M. Mavissakalian & D. Barlow (Eds.), *Phobia* (pp. 1–33). New York: Guilford.

Mavissakalian, M., & Michelson, L. (1986a). Agoraphobia: Relative and combined effectiveness of therapist-assisted in vivo exposure and imipramine. *Journal of Clinical Psychiatry, 47,* 117–122.

Mavissakalian, M., & Michelson, L. (1986b). Two-year follow-up of exposure and imipramine treatment of agoraphobia. *American Journal of Psychiatry, 143,* 1106–1112.

McCaffrey, R. J., & Fairbank, J. A. (1985). Behavioral assessment and treatment of accident-related posttraumatic stress disorder: Two case studies. *Behavior Therapy, 16,* 406–416.

McCue, E. C., & McCue, P. A. (1984). Organic and hyperventilatory causes of anxiety-type symptoms. *Behavioural Psychotherapy, 12,* 308–317.

McNally, R. J. (1990). Psychological approaches to panic disorder: A review. *Psychological Bulletin, 108,* 403–419.

McNally, R. J., & Steketee, G. S. (1985). The etiology and maintenance of severe animal phobias. *Behaviour Research and Therapy, 23,* 431–435.

McPherson, F. M., Brougham, L., & McLaren, S. (1980). Maintenance of improvement in agoraphobic patients treated by behavioral methods—Four-year follow-up. *Behaviour Research and Therapy, 18,* 150–152.

Meichenbaum, D. (1977). *Cognitive-behavior modification: An integrative approach.* New York: Plenum.

Meichenbaum, D. H., Gilmore, J. B., & Fedoravicius, A. (1971). Group insight versus group desensitization in treating speech anxiety. *Journal of Consulting and Clinical Psychology, 36,* 410–421.

Meyer, R. G. (1989). *The clinician's handbook: The psychopathology of adulthood and adolescence.* Needham Heights, MA: Allyn and Bacon.

Meyer, V. (1957). The treatment of two phobic patients on the basis of learning principles. *Journal of Abnormal and Social Psychology, 55,* 261–266.

Meyer, V., & Gelder, M. G. (1963). Behaviour therapy and phobic disorders. *British Journal of Psychiatry, 109,* 19–28.

Michelson, L. (1987). Cognitive-behavioral assessment and treatment of agoraphobia. In L. Michelson & L. M. Ascher (Eds.), *Anxiety and stress disorders: Cognitive-behavioral assessment treatment* (pp. 213–279). New York: Guilford.

Michelson, L., & Marchione, K. (1989, November). Cognitive-behavioral treatments of panic disorder with agoraphobia: A comparative outcome investigation. In L. Michelson (Chair), *Emerging issues in assessment and treatment of anxiety disorders.* Symposium conducted at the annual meeting of the Association for Advancement of Behavior Therapy, Washington, DC.

Miller, W. R. (1977). Behavioral self-control training in the treatment of problem drinkers. In R. B. Stuart (Ed.), *Behavioral self-management: Strategies, techniques, and outcomes.* New York: Brunner/Mazel.

Miller, W. R. (1980). Treating the problem drinker. In W. R. Miller (Ed.), *The addictive behaviors: Treatment of alcoholism, drug abuse, smoking, and obesity.* New York: Pergamon Press.

Miller, W. R., & Munoz, R. F. (1982). *How to control your drinking.* Albuquerque: University of New Mexico Press.

Milton, F., & Hafner, J. (1979). The outcome of behavior therapy for agoraphobia in relation to marital adjustment. *Archives of General Psychiatry, 36,* 807–811.

Mineka, S. (1985). Animal models of anxiety-based disorders: Their usefulness and limitations. In A. H. Tuma & J. D. Maser (Eds.), *Anxiety and the anxiety disorders* (pp. 199–244). Hillsdale, NJ: Lawrence Erlbaum Associates.

Mizes, J. S., & Crawford, J. (1986). Normative values on the Marks and Mathews Fear Questionnaire: A comparison as a function of age and sex. *Journal of Psychopathology and Behavioral Assessment, 8,* 253–262.

Modestin, J. (1989). Symptomatic panic disorder in borderline personality disorder. *European Journal of Psychiatry, 3,* 133–137.

Monk, M. (1987). Epidemiology of suicide. *Epidemiology Review, 9,* 51–69.

Moore, R. A. (1972). The diagnosis of alcoholism in a psychiatric hospital: A trial of the Michigan Alcohol Screening Test (MAST). *American Journal of Psychiatry, 128,* 115–119.

Mowrer, O. H. (1947). On the dual nature of learning as a reinterpretation of "conditioning" and "problem-solving." *Harvard Educational Review,* 102–148.

Mullaney, J. A., & Trippett, C. J. (1979). Alcohol dependence and phobias: Clinical description and relevance. *British Journal of Psychiatry, 135,* 565–573.

Munby, M., & Johnston, D. W. (1980). Agoraphobia: The long-term follow-up of behavioural treatment. *British Journal of Psychiatry, 137,* 418–427.

Munjack, D. J., & Moss, H. B. (1981). Affective disorders and alcoholism in families of agoraphobics. *Archives of General Psychiatry, 38,* 869–871.

Myers, J. K., Weissman, G. L., Tischler, G. L., Holzer, C. E., Leaf, P. J., Orvaschel, H., Anthony, J. C., Boyd, J. H., Burke, J. D., Kramer, M., & Stoltzman, R. (1984). Six-month prevalence of psychiatric disorders in three communities. *Archives of General Psychiatry, 41,* 959–967.

Nelson, R. O. (1983). Behavioral assessment: Past, present, and future. *Behavioral Assessment, 5,* 195–206.

Norton, G. R., Allen, G. E., & Hilton, J. (1983). The social validity of treatments for agoraphobia. *Behaviour Research and Therapy, 21,* 393–399.

Norton, G. R., Allen, G. E., & Walker, J. R. (1985). Predicting treatment preferences for agoraphobia. *Behaviour Research and Therapy, 23,* 699–701.

Norton, G. R., Dorward, J., & Cox, B. J. (1986). Factors associated with panic attacks in nonclinical subjects. *Behavior Therapy, 17,* 239–252.

Norton, G. R., Harrison, B., Hauch, J., & Rhodes, L. (1985). Characteristics of subjects experiencing relaxation and relaxation-induced anxiety. *Journal of Behavior Therapy and Experimental Psychiatry, 16,* 211–216.

Noyes, R., Jr., Anderson, D. J., Clancy, J., Croe, R. R., Slymen, D. J., Ghoneim, M. M., & Hinrichs, J. V. (1984). Diazepam and propranolol in panic disorder and agoraphobia. *Archives of General Psychiatry, 41,* 287–292.

Nunn, J. D., Stevenson, R. J., & Whalen, G. (1984). Selective memory effects in agoraphobic patients. *British Journal of Clinical Psychology, 23,* 195–201.

Ost, L. G. (1988). Applied relaxation in the treatment of panic disorder. *Behaviour Research and Therapy, 26,* 13–22.

Ottaviani, R., & Beck, A. T. (1987). Cognitive aspects of panic disorders. *Journal of Anxiety Disorders, 1,* 15–28.

Paul, G. L. (1966). *Insight versus desensitization in psychotherapy: An experiment in anxiety reduction.* Stanford, CA: Stanford University Press.

Pecknold, J. C., Swinson, R. P., Kuch, K., & Lewis, C. P. (1988). Alprazolam in panic disorder and agoraphobia: Results from a multicenter trial. *Archives of General Psychiatry, 45,* 429–436.

Peterson, R. A., & Heilbronner, R. L. (1987). The anxiety sensitivity index: Construct validity and factor analytic structure. *Journal of Anxiety Disorders, 1,* 117–121.

Pfohl, B., Stangl, D., & Zimmerman, M. (1984). The implications of DSM-III personality disorders for patients with major depression. *Journal of Affective Disorders, 7,* 309–318.

Rachman, S. J. (1978). *Fear and courage.* San Francisco: W. H. Freeman.

Rachman, S. J. (1983). The modification of agoraphobic avoidance behaviour: Some fresh possibilities. *Behaviour Research and Therapy, 21,* 567–574.

Rachman, S. J. (1984). Agoraphobia: A safety signal perspective. *Behaviour Research and Therapy, 22,* 59–70.

Rachman, S., Craske, M., Tallman, K., & Solyom, C. (1986). Does escape behavior strengthen agoraphobic avoidance? A replication. *Behavior Therapy, 17,* 366–384.

Rachman, S., & Wilson, G. T. (1980). *Effects of psychotherapy.* Oxford: Pergamon.

Rapee, R. M. (1985). Distinction between panic disorder and generalized anxiety disorder: Clinical presentation. *Australian and New Zealand Journal of Psychiatry, 19,* 227–232.

Reiss, S., Peterson, R. A., & Gursky, D. M. (1987). Anxiety sensitivity, injury sensitivity, and individual differences in fearfulness. *Behaviour Research and Therapy, 26,* 341–345.

Reiss, S., Peterson, R. A., Gursky, D. M., & McNally, R. J. (1986). Anxiety sensitivity, anxiety frequency, and the prediction of fearfulness. *Behaviour Research and Therapy, 24,* 1–8.

Rychtarik, R. G., Silverman, W. K., van Landingham, W. P., & Prue, D. M. (1984). Treatment of an incest victim with implosive therapy: A case study. *Behavior Therapy, 15,* 410–420.

Salkovskis, P. M. (1983). Treatment of an obsessional patient using habituation to audiotaped ruminations. *British Journal of Clinical Psychology, 22,* 311–313.

Salkovskis, P. M., Jones, D. R. O., & Clark, D. M. (1986). Respiratory control in the treatment of panic attacks: Replication and extension with concurrent measurement of behavior and pCO_2. *British Journal of Psychiatry, 148,* 526–532.

Salkovskis, P., Warwick, H., Clark, D., & Wessels, D. (1986). A demonstration of acute hyperventilation during naturally occurring panic attacks. *Behaviour Research and Therapy, 24,* 91–94.

Schuckit, M. S., Irwin, M., & Brown, S. A. (1990). The history of anxiety symptoms in 171 primary alcoholics. *Journal of Studies on Alcohol, 51,* 34–41.

Schwartz, R. M., & Gottman, J. M. (1976). Toward a task analysis of assertive behavior. *Journal of Consulting and Clinical Psychology, 44,* 910–920.

Schweizer, E. E., Winokur, A., & Rickels, K. (1986). Insulin-induced hypoglycemia and panic attacks. *American Journal of Psychiatry, 143,* 654–655.

Selzer, M. L. (1971). The Michigan Alcohol Screening Test: The quest for a new diagnostic instrument. *American Journal of Psychiatry, 39,* 1653–1658.

Sheehan, D. V. (1984). Strategies for diagnosis and treatment of anxiety disorders. In R. O. Pasnau (Ed.), *Diagnosis and treatment of anxiety disorders.* Washington DC: American Psychiatric Press.

Sheehan, D. V., & Sheehan, K. H. (1982). The classification of anxiety and hysterical states, Part 1: Historical review and empirical delineation. *Journal of Clinical Pharmacology, 2,* 235–244.

Smail, P., Stockwell, T., Canter, S., & Hodgson, R. (1984). Alcohol dependence and phobic anxiety states: I. A prevalence study. *British Journal of Psychiatry, 144,* 53–57.

Spanier, G. B. (1976). Measuring dyadic adjustment: New scales for assessing the quality of marriage and similar dyads. *Journal of Marriage and the Family, 38,* 15–28.

Spitzer, R. L., & Williams, J. B. (1984). *Structured clinical interview for the DSM-III.* New York: Biometric Research Department, New York Psychiatric Institute.

Stampler, F. M. (1982). Panic disorder: Description, conceptualization, and implications for treatment. *Clinical Psychology Review, 2,* 469–486.

Stein, M. B. (1986). Panic disorder and medical illness. *Psychosomatics, 27,* 833–838.

Stern, R., & Marks, I. (1973). Brief and prolonged flooding: A comparison in agoraphobic patients. *Archives of General Psychiatry, 28,* 270–276.

Stuart, R. B. (1980). *Helping couples change: A social learning approach to marital therapy.* New York: Guilford.

Teasdale, J. D., Walsh, P. A., Lancashire, M., & Mathews, A. M. (1977). Group exposure for agoraphobics: A replication study. *British Journal of Psychiatry, 130,* 186–193.

Telch, M. J. (1988). Combined pharmacological and psychological treatments for panic sufferers. In S. Rachman & J. D. Maser (Eds.), *Panic: Psychological perspectives* (pp. 167–188). Hillsdale, NJ: Lawrence Erlbaum Associates.

Telch, M. J., Agras, W. S., Taylor, C. B., Roth, W. T., & Gallen, C. C. (1985). Combined pharmacological and behavioral treatment for agoraphobia. *Behaviour Research and Therapy, 23,* 325–335.

Telch, M. J., Tearnan, B. H., & Taylor, C. B. (1983). Antidepressant medication in the treatment of agoraphobia: A critical review. *Behaviour Research and Therapy, 21,* 505–527.

Thibaut, J. W., & Kelley, H. H. (1959). *The social psychology of groups.* New York: Wiley.

Thorpe, G. L. (1975). Desensitization, behavior rehearsal, self-instructional training and placebo effects on assertive-refusal behavior. *European Journal of Behavioural Analysis and Modification, 1,* 30–44.

Thorpe, G. L., & Burns, L. E. (1983). *The agoraphobic syndrome: Behavioural approaches to evaluation and treatment.* Chichester, UK: Wiley.

Thorpe, G. L., Burns, L. E., Smith, P. J., & Blier, M. J. (1984). Agoraphobia: Research developments and clinical implications. In C. M. Franks (Ed.), *New developments in behavior therapy* (pp. 281–317). New York: Haworth.

Thorpe, G. L., Freedman, E. G., & Lazar, J. D. (1985). Assertiveness training and exposure in vivo for agoraphobics. *Behavioural Psychotherapy, 13,* 132–141.

Thorpe, G. L., & Hecker, J. E. (1991). Psychosocial aspects of panic disorder. In J. R. Walker, G. R. Norton, & C. A. Ross (Eds.), *Panic disorder and agoraphobia: A guide for the practitioner* (pp. 175–207). Pacific Grove, CA: Brooks/Cole.

Thorpe, G. L., Hecker, J. E., Cavallaro, L. A., & Kulberg, G. E. (1987). Insight versus rehearsal in cognitive-behavior therapy: A crossover study with sixteen phobics. *Behavioural Psychotherapy, 15,* 319–336.

Thorpe, G. L., & Olson, S. L. (1990). *Behaviour therapy: Concepts, procedures, and applications.* Boston: Allyn and Bacon.

Thyer, B. A., & Curtis, G. C. (1984). The effects of ethanol intoxication on phobic anxiety. *Behaviour Research and Therapy, 22,* 559–610.

Thyer, B. A., & Himle, J. (1985). Temporal relationship between panic attack onset and phobic avoidance in agoraphobia. *Behaviour Research and Therapy, 23,* 607–608.

Thyer, B. A., Nesse, R. M., Cameron, O. G., & Curtis, G. C. (1985). Agoraphobia: A test of the separation anxiety hypothesis. *Behaviour Research and Therapy, 23,* 75–78.

Thyer, B. A., Nesse, R. M., Curtis, G. C., & Cameron, O. G. (1986). Panic disorder: A test of the separation anxiety hypothesis. *Behaviour Research and Therapy, 24,* 209–211.

Thyer, B. A., Parrish, R. T., Curtis, G. C., Nesse, R. M., & Cameron, O. G. (1985). Ages of onset of DSM-III anxiety disorders. *Comprehensive Psychiatry, 26,* 113–122.

Turner, S. M., Beidel, D. C., & Jacob, R. G. (1988). Assessment of panic. In S. J. Rachman & J. D. Maser (Eds.), *Panic: Psychological perspectives.* Hillsdale, NJ: Lawrence Erlbaum Associates.

Uhde, T. W., Roy-Byrne, P. P., Vittone, B. J., Boulenger, J. P., & Post, R. M. (1985). Phenomenology and neurobiology of panic disorder. In A. H. Tuma & J. D. Maser (Eds.), *Anxiety and the anxiety disorders* (pp. 557–576). Hillsdale, NJ: Lawrence Erlbaum Associates.

van der Molen, G. M., van den Hout, M. A., Vroemen, J., Lousberg, H., &

Griez, E. (1986). Cognitive determinants of lactate-induced anxiety. *Behaviour Research and Therapy, 24,* 677–680.

Vermilyea, J. A., Boice, R., & Barlow, D. H. (1984). Rachman and Hodgson (1974) a decade later: How do desynchronous response systems relate to the treatment of agoraphobia? *Behaviour Research and Therapy, 22,* 615–621.

Waddell, M. T., Barlow, D. H., & O'Brien, G. T. (1984). A preliminary investigation of cognitive and relaxation treatment of panic disorder: Effects of intense anxiety vs. "background" anxiety. *Behaviour Research and Therapy, 22,* 393–402.

Watson, J. P., Mullett, G. E., & Pillay, H. (1973). The effects of prolonged exposure to phobic situations upon agoraphobic patients treated in groups. *Behaviour Research and Therapy, 11,* 531–545.

Weekes, C. (1968). *Hope and help for your nerves.* New York: Hawthorne.

Weiss, R. L. & Wieder, G. B. (1982). Marital distress. In A. S. Bellack, M. Hersen, & A. E. Kazdin (Eds.), *International handbook of behavior modification and therapy* (pp. 767–809). New York: Plenum.

Weissman, M. M. (1985). The epidemiology of anxiety disorders: Rates, risks, and familial patterns. In A. H. Tuma & J. D. Maser (Eds.), *Anxiety and the anxiety disorders* (pp. 275–296). Hillsdale, NJ: Lawrence Erlbaum Associates.

Weissman, M. M., Klerman, G. L., Markowiz, J. S., & Ouellette, R. (1989). Suicidal ideation and suicide attempts in panic disorder and attacks. *New England Journal of Medicine, 321,* 1209–1214.

Westphal, C. F. O. (1988). Agoraphobia: A neuropathic phenomenon. In T. J. Knapp (Ed.) & M. T. Schumacher (Trans.), *Westphal's "Die Agoraphobie"* (pp. 59–91). Lanham, MD: University Press of America. (Original work published 1871.)

Williams, J. M. G., Watts, F. M., MacLeod, C., & Mathews, A. (1988). *Cognitive psychology and emotional disorders.* Chichester, UK: Wiley.

Williams, K. E., & Chambless, D. L. (1990). The relationship between therapist characteristics and outcome of in vivo exposure treatment for agoraphobia. *Behavior Therapy, 21,* 111–116.

Wilson, G. T. (1982). Adult disorders. In G. T. Wilson & C. M. Franks (Eds.), *Contemporary behavior therapy: Conceptual and empirical foundations* (pp. 505–562). New York: Guilford.

Wolpe, J. (1958). *Psychotherapy by reciprocal inhibition.* Stanford, CA: Stanford University Press.

Wolpe, J. (1970). Identifying the antecedents of an agoraphobic reaction: A transcript. *Journal of Behavior Therapy and Experimental Psychiatry, 1,* 299–304.

Wolpe, J. (1973). *The practice of behavior therapy* (2nd ed.). New York: Pergamon.

Wolpe, J., & Lang, P. J. (1964). A fear survey schedule for use in behavior therapy. *Behaviour Research and Therapy, 2,* 27–30.

Wolpe, J. (1981). *Our useless fears.* Boston: Houghton Mifflin

Wolpe, J., & Lang, P. J. (1969). *Fear survey schedule.* San Diego, CA: Educational and Industrial Testing Service.

Woodruff Borden, J., Clum, G. A., & Broyles, S. E. (1989). MMPI correlates of panic disorder and panic attacks. *Journal of Anxiety Disorders, 3,* 107–116.

Woodward, R., & Jones, R. (1980). Cognitive restructuring treatment: A controlled trial with anxious patients. *Behaviour Research and Therapy, 18,* 401–407.

Zitrin, C. M. (1981). Combined pharmacological and psychological treatment of phobias. In M. Mavissakalian & D. H. Barlow (Eds.), *Phobia: Psychological and pharmacological treatment.* New York: Guilford.

Zitrin, C. M., Klein, D. F., & Woerner, M. G. (1980). Treatment of agoraphobia with group exposure in vivo and imipramine. *Archives of General Psychiatry, 37,* 63–72.

Zitrin, C. M., Klein, D. F., Woerner, M. G., & Ross, D. C. (1983). Treatment of phobias: I. Comparison of imipramine hydrochloride and placebo. *Archives of General Psychiatry, 40,* 125–138.

Name Index _____

Subject Index